The Antagonists

Recent Titles in
Contributions in Military History

American Sea Power in the Old World:
The United States Navy in European and Near Eastern Waters, 1865-1917
William N. Still, Jr.

A Hollow Threat: Strategic Air Power and Containment Before Korea
Harry R. Borowski

The Quest for Victory: The History of the Principles of War
John I. Alger

Men Wanted for the U.S. Army: America's Experience with an All-Volunteer Army
Between the World Wars
Robert K. Griffith, Jr.

Bullets and Bureaucrats: The Machine Gun and the United States Army, 1861-1916
David A. Armstrong

General John M. Palmer, Citizen Soldiers, and the Army of a Democracy
J.B. Holley, Jr.

History of the Art of War: Within the Framework of Political History, The Middle Ages
Hans Delbrück, translated by *Walter J. Renfore, Jr.*

"Dear Bart": Washington Views of World War II
Glen C. H. Perry

Fighting Power: German and U.S. Army Performance, 1939-1945
Martin van Creveld

Two If by Sea: The Development of American Coastal Defense Policy
Robert S. Browning III

Hitler's Luftwaffe in the Spanish Civil War
Raymond L. Proctor

The Antagonists

A Comparative
Combat Assessment
of the
Soviet and American Soldier

RICHARD A. GABRIEL

Foreword by Senator Sam Nunn

Contributions in Military History, Number 34

Greenwood Press
Westport, Connecticut • London, England

Library of Congress Cataloging in Publication Data

Gabriel, Richard A.
  The antagonists.

  (Contributions in military history, ISSN 0084-9251; no. 34)
  Bibliography: p.
  Includes index.
  1. Soldiers—Soviet Union. 2. Soldiers—United
States. 3. Soviet Union—Armed Forces. 4. United
States—Armed Forces. 5. Sociology, Military—Soviet
Union. 6. Sociology, Military—United States.
I. Title. II. Series.
UA770.G23 1983   355.3'0947   83-1645
ISBN 0-313-23127-3 (lib. bdg.)

Library of Congress Catalog Card Number: 83-1645
ISBN: 0-313-23127-3
ISSN: 0084-9251

First published in 1984

Greenwood Press
A division of Congressional Information Service, Inc.
88 Post Road West
Westport, Connecticut 06881

Printed in the United States of America

10 9 8 7 6 5 4 3 2 1

To Jim and Sybil Stockdale, Friends Who Have Given Much; Gunther Wassenberg, a magnificent anachronism; and to Adolfo Gabrielle, *resquiescat in pace*.

And through some mooned Valhalla there will pass
Battallions and battallions, scarred from hell;
The unreturning army that was youth,
The legions who have suffered and are dust

—Siegfried Sassoon
"The Troops"

Contents

Figures & Tables

Foreword

National defense and, more particularly, the military balance between the United States and the Soviet Union have become topics of intense public debate in recent years. This debate has generally focused on the most visible issues and programs: the overall size of the defense budget; the advent of new weapons systems, both nuclear and conventional; the number of divisions fielded by each side; and the deployment of each side's troops. These assessments are critical to any serious analysis of America's military capabilities. At the same time, however, even in this age of increasing reliance on sophisticated military technology, combat-effectiveness is still in large measure dependent on the performance of individual soldiers and individual units. Until now, the military balance at this most fundamental level, the level of the soldiers who could conceivably face each other in combat, has received inadequate attention. In *The Antagonists*, Richard A. Gabriel addresses some fundamental national security questions from precisely the perspective of these soldiers. In so doing, he provides a much needed additional point of view from which to consider our defense posture.

The Antagonists builds upon previous scholarship on American and Soviet military manpower, including Professor Gabriel's own works on the American Army and *The New Red Legions*, his pathbreaking two-volume study of the Soviet Army. *The Antagonists* is a comprehensive overview of the comparative combat capabilites of the American and Soviet armies based on a thorough analysis of the voluminous material available on the all-volunteer force and an innovative but judicious use of scarce unclassified Soviet sources. The result is a much clearer and more complete portrait comparing the two armies than has existed previously. Professor Gabriel analyzes the potential adversaries on each level, from the enlisted ranks to the NCOs and the officer corps, and considers the impact of such factors as morale, discipline, and unit cohesion on combat-effectiveness.

By making direct comparisons with the Soviet military, Professor Gabriel brings some of the basic difficulties that have plagued the all volunteer force since its inception into sharper focus. He argues that the army has undergone drastic structural changes in an attempt to compete with components of the civilian economy for manpower. In the process, the traditional institutional supports for military life have been weakened and, in some cases, eliminated entirely. According to Gabriel, many of the reforms designed to help "sell" the army as a career choice, such as significant pay raises, fewer demands on soldiers' time, and the greater latitude allowed military members in the area of living arrangements, have actually undermined the development of peer identification, unit cohesion, and discipline. The present army, Professor Gabriel finds, consists of unmotivated soldiers who feel little identification with their peers or units and are alienated from both mainstream American society and the military itself.

Previous studies of past conflicts have found that unit cohesion—the close bonds between members of military units—is a critically important factor in determining combat performance. From that perspective, *The Antagonists* paints a disquieting picture of the all volunteer force. It should be noted, however, that Army Chief of Staff, General Edward Meyer, has undertaken many leadership initiatives to improve unit cohesion and to decrease personnel turbulence, while at the same time improving the quality of new recruits and those who reenlist. These efforts are bound to pay large dividends in terms of addressing this serious problem. None of this is to suggest that the Soviets have no problems. Professor Gabriel's account clearly identifies deficiencies that could severely diminish the Red Army's proficiency in the field. For example, he judges the American NCO and officer corps to be generally, and often substantially, superior to their Soviet counterparts.

Professor Gabriel's evidence and conclusions deserve to be considered carefully by military leaders and the nation's policymakers so that appropriate corrective actions can be taken as needed. *The Antagonists* is another in a long series of major professional contributions to defense policy issues for which Professor Richard Gabriel has become well known and highly respected.

Senator Sam Nunn
Chairman
Senate Armed Services Committee

The Antagonists

Introduction

Armies are among the oldest anthropological structures devised by man. What evidence we have of early man suggests that the first form of integrated social action was not the family, the religious cult, the farming group, or anything else so benign. What anthropology suggests is that, when early man crawled from his cave, the first social structure he constructed was some form of rudimentary organized hunting or warrior group, first to protect the extended family or tribe, second to hunt collectively for food, and third to engage in warfare against his fellow men. Moreover, the historical evidence seems beyond doubt that no society since the dawn of man has been able to get along without some form of organized structure dedicated to collective violence. In a sense, no society has ever been without the need for an army.

Armies consume tremendous resources and are often further advanced organizationally and sociologically than the societies they serve. With regard to technology, they are often the stimulus to the development of new machines and techniques, and, in many instances, they are the originators of technology designed for war which, in prolonged periods of peace, finds other wider uses. Finally, they are the vehicle for the expression of man's most constant (and perhaps most fascinating) form of social action, organized warfare.

Armies are important in the modern world because they possess the technological means to destroy us all. The study of military forces used to be at best an academic curiosity. Perhaps that was because armies had the weaponry to destroy only some of us some of the time. With the advent of nuclear weapons, they now possess almost unimaginable destructive power. Decisions fostered by the military can directly or indirectly influence other decisions capable of exterminating entire civilizations, societies, cultures, and, indeed in some scenarios, even the entire planet. Accordingly, they are terribly interesting things to study and ought to have drawn the attention of scholars far sooner than they did.

More than armies themselves is the interest we should have in the people who serve in them whether as conscripts or professionals, enlisted men and women or officers. Such people are an appropriate subject for study, for military force requires the organization of large numbers of human beings to undertake the dastardly business of destroying other human beings. Indeed, that phenomenon alone, the ability of men to organize into groups in order to destroy other men, is a fascinating object of study.

Although armies are interesting in their own right, it would be appropriate to ask why this book has been written. The answer is partly personal and partly professional. From a personal perspective I have served in, worked for, and been in and about the U.S. military establishment for over seventeen years. In this time, I have spent ten years studying and analyzing the Soviet Army for the American Army and have patterned my academic career on the study of other armies for another eight years. Moreover, as time passes and as more and more Soviet and American treasure is poured into defense budgets, it seems to me that a comparative work on the Soviet and American soldier is both natural and logical. Although there are a number of works analyzing the American Army or the Soviet Army, we have only a handful of papers and monographs that purport to analyze and assess both armies as potential antagonists to one another. A comparative work of some depth on the Soviet and American soldier seems long overdue.

This book differs somewhat from other works on the subject in that it seeks to examine the two forces from the perspective of the soldiers who serve in them and who ultimately must die for them. While this book discusses and examines each army's organizational structure and hardware in some detail, its focus is on what the soldier in each army knows, thinks, and feels. This perspective has been taken because, although armies are remarkably complex human institutions, perhaps always far more complex than their host societies, they are ultimately comprised of individuals. These individuals have feelings, fears, hopes and dreams. More than that, the problems of an army's performance are only secondarily related to the type of equipment it has and the organization it brings to battle. Far more important to the ability of any army to perform under fire is the human dimension, the relationship of its soldiers to one another and to the institution in which they find themselves. Effective behavior on the battlefield is fundamentally a human condition, not an organizational one. Thus, an appropriate focus for a comparison of the Soviet and American armies would be on the men who will be asked to do the fighting, the killing, and ultimately the dying, namely, the soldiers themselves and the pictures that are in their heads.

Perhaps the key question is what makes men stay and fight when all the evidence of their senses, intellect, and instincts tells them that they ought to flee? What we know from history and psychology on the subject suggests that the answer is not very complex. The central problem of warfare is to motivate men to fight. More specifically, the problem is to get military units to cohere under the stress of the battlefield. History and social science combine to suggest that technology, systems, training, and even technical expertise count for little if fighting units are not reliable from the perspective of human group cohesion.

The problem is, therefore, essentially a problem of human psychology. All military organizations structure themselves around some conceptual model as to what must be done in order to motivate soldiers to effective combat behavior. These theoretical notions provide an army with basic assumptions about the way in which troops may be conditioned to remain together and fight under the stress of battle. Inevitably, these theories or doctrines specify in at least general terms the role of the soldier vis-à-vis his society, his peers, and his unit. These theories provide the foundation for an army's training doctrines and the techniques that are developed from them.

Social scientists have shown considerable attention to the human problems associated with warfare so that a considerable archive exists on the subject. Probably the most definitive, although not the earliest, work on the subject is the Shills and Janowitz study of the German Army in World War II.[1] They found that German combat units held together under severe combat stress largely because of loyalties generated and sustained by the primary groups within the units themselves. Soldiers of all ranks comprised a supporting web of strong personal attachments and relationships generated by the shared experience of combat itself. Soldiers came to feel a mutual responsibility for peers and superiors as well as an attachment to the unit as being above the individual. They also felt that their superiors truly cared for their welfare and were prepared to expose themselves to the same risks to which their men were exposed. In this process the primary group—usually no larger than the company and most commonly as small as the squad—was the generator and recipient of mutually supporting personal attachments. The group became more than the sum of its parts in the minds of those who served in it, and attachments to it were truly corporative and not purely instrumental in nature.[2] In these circumstances, attachments among soldiers and to the group were rooted in something stronger than either ideology or entrepreneurial utility.

The findings of the Shills and Janowitz study were anticipated by the earlier work of S.L.A. Marshall in his study of the American Army.[3] Samuel Stouffer's more comprehensive study of the American soldier produced the same findings.[4] More recently, John Keegan in *The Face of Battle* studied the behavior of soldiers in three battles: Agincourt, the Somme, and Waterloo. He found that in each case cohesion rested in a mutual hardship and suffering that all involved—officers, noncommissioned officers, and common soldiers alike—shared. The unit became the focus of intensely held, almost "priestlike" attachments that prompted units to fight well.[5] Allan Lloyd's study of British forces in World War I comes to the same conclusion, as do Samuel Rolbant and Reuven Gal in both their studies of the Israeli Army.[6] *Crisis in Command*, my own work and that of Paul Savage on the American Army in Vietnam, reinforces the same conclusions.[7]

What past research into the cohesion of military units suggests is that neither ideology nor entrepreneurial utility, elements central to Soviet and American doctrines of battle behavior, is a major factor in developing and maintaining unit cohesion on the field of battle. This observation seems valid cross-culturally in British, German, American, and Israeli armies, and it also appears to hold trans-historically regardless of the level of military technology or the killing power of weaponry. Cohesion appears to be a function of strong personal loyalties to small groups developed through and sustained by the perception that all partic-ipants of the group are united by similar hardship, risk, fear, and the under-standing, often unspoken, that all members, regardless of rank or position, will endure the same conditions and not expose other members to unnecessary risk. When these conditions are not present, then no amount of technical expertise, ideological indoctrination, or entrepreneurial utility seems likely to produce ef-fective and cohesive battle units. Hence one problem in evaluating the combat-effectiveness of the Soviet and American soldier is to discern and assess the degree to which these personal attachments develop within their units and to evaluate the extent to which organizational forces sustain these ties.

The focus of this book rests in the thoughts, feelings, and perceptions of the Soviet and American soldier insofar as they relate to his ability to perform his military role, which is to stand, to fight, to endure, to kill, and ultimately to die as a member of a military organization. The question is this: How good is the American and Soviet soldier given the tasks they are expected to perform in their respective armies? Their attitudes and feelings are relevant, too, insofar as they relate to questions affecting their military roles and insofar as they are relevant to leadership, discipline, morale, training, fighting ability, and a whole range of other perceptions that exist in the mind of the soldier about factors important to military effectiveness. That is what this book does: it examines the "pictures" inside the heads of Soviet and American soldiers in order to discern whether these perceptions are supportive of those habits, practices, values, and actions that have historically been associated with effective military forces.

Studying the two armies presents truly distinct problems. With regard to the American Army, information is readily available, for the United States is the most open society in the current world and perhaps, in history. As a consequence, far more information is available about all aspects of its government, including the military, than is available in most other countries. With the Vietnam War over for a decade, a considerable archive of official and unofficial information on the combat performance of the American Army has finally come to light. With the advent of the all volunteer force (AVF) in 1973, a great deal of information concerning the operation of the military also has been made available. This information is the result of a series of studies undertaken by the military itself as part of its attempt to restructure the army along the lines of the business corporation.[8] This restructuring logically required a range of "management" studies on the performance of the "business." Since 1973, the American Army has almost studied itself to death, producing substantial amounts of valuable information on its structure and performance in the process.

Equally important as a stimulus to the production of studies by the army is the recognized failure of the all volunteer force. This failure has touched off a frenzy of internal examinations to see what went wrong. Important, too, is the debate generated in Congress and in the academic community about the validity of the AVF. Fortunately, many of the available studies are in the form of survey research data, so that we have a good deal of attitudinal and perceptual information about how the American soldier and his officers perceive the state of affairs within the army itself. Thus, the analysis can move beyond often sterile considerations of organizational form and examine the human dimension of military force.

Many of the studies undertaken by the army remain either classified or ''internal working documents,'' a designation that puts the information beyond the reach of the Freedom of Information Act. In theory at least, the military can conceal information that might be unfavorable to it. Happily, through judicious changes in the law and the fact that internal working documents can often be obtained through unofficial sources, a substantial archive of this usually ''close hold'' information is available.

Thus, we have an adequate data base upon which to construct an analysis of the American soldiers' perceptions and behavior. Since this book is a comparison of the American and the Soviet soldier, the available studies noted above represent an important source of data for this study.

Analyzing the Soviet Army presents the a very different and difficult challenge. A totalitarian political order does not offer ready access to information. The problem is made even more complex when one attempts to investigate an institution that the regime regards as vital to its very existence and not only prohibits the gathering of the most elementary information, but also goes to great lengths to distort what information is available to conform to the regime's judgment of what it wants the observer to know. Consequently, most efforts to study the Soviet soldier have been blunted or distorted by a failure to circumvent these substantive obstacles to data collection.

Most studies of the Soviet Army concentrate upon the most easily measured aspects of the Soviet military. There has been strong emphasis upon those items of analysis and comparison that are most easily obtainable through official Soviet sources. The result is a number of studies that compare the Soviet Army with other military forces in terms of ''meaningful combat indicators,'' such as number of divisions, size of reserve forces, number of tanks, and artillery pieces. But there is a lack of studies concerning such human problems as cohesion, discipline, morale, societal support for conscription, and other elements addressing the attitudinal dimensions of the Soviet soldier.

Much of our knowledge of the Soviet Army from the perspective of its soldiers, its institutions, and the way it functions is quite limited once the researcher steps outside the confines of official data. We know very little, for example, about such important aspects as morale, the degree of cohesion that can be expected of Soviet units, the quality of life in these units, their ability to perform under combat stress, the extent to which the officers are seen as remote from their men, and the degree to which the NCO corps can carry out its tasks. That these elements are important in their own right is obvious. For an army is something more than a group of individuals arranged in a row decked out in uniforms. It is primarily a fighting force, and the ability to fight in groups is essentially a sociopsychological disposition that transcends the possession of the mere military means to do battle.

Perhaps no where is this point made more clearly than in an examination of the Russian victory over the German Army in World War II. In each of the four wars it fought between 1905 and 1940, the Russian Army suffered serious defeats. On all four occasions, large battle formations dissolved in the heat of battle, and staggering losses were suffered. Paradoxically, on the eve of World War II, most Western analysts judged the Soviet Army to be an able fighting force capable of at least defending its homeland. When the Nazi *blitzkrieg* struck, both the magnitude and rapidity of the collapse surprised everyone, including the attackers.

The reasons for the rapid Russian collapse are complex, but what seems to have failed the Russian Army in 1940 was its will to fight. The Soviet Army had hundreds of divisions, most of which were relatively well equipped. Its tanks were generally a technological match for the German vehicles, as were its aircraft and artillery. Indeed, by war's end Soviet technology had a clear battle-field advantage. The Russian Army collapsed because its soldiers, officers, and units lost the psychological disposition to cohere and fight.

The Soviet Army had institutionalized a range of practices which seemed almost guaranteed to destroy that psychological disposition among Soviet units. Soviet officers were terrorized by purges so that they no longer dared establish close ties to anyone—not each other, not their men, nor their units. They became remote and bureaucratic as a way of escaping Stalin's paranoia. The regime itself, stressing the secular nature of its purpose, undercut many of the traditional appeals—religion, ethnicity, and nationalism—that served as bonds of cohesion among soldiers. The stress on the Soviet state's international mission further weakened the soldiers' almost mystical attachment to the motherland. The ever-present secret police and the primacy of the political officer within military units made command effectiveness almost impossible, forcing officers and men to grow even further apart as their suspicions of anything official increased. When the blow fell in 1940, the famed Russian steamroller fell off the track and rolled over.

For two years, the Soviet Army suffered defeat after defeat, remaining intact only through luck and the German Army's inability to conquer such a large land mass as Russia. Yet, by 1943, the Soviet Army had rallied its troops and was on the offensive. How? Again the answers are complex, but the root cause seems to have been a rediscovery of the will to fight. While the exact mix of variables may never be known, it does seem clear that the Soviet Army turned around when it began to repudiate many of the practices that had eroded the confidence of men and officers in each other. The purges were stopped. Disgraced officers were released from prison and given commands. The dreaded secret police was brought to heel, if only temporarily, and the power of the political officer in military units was drastically reduced. At the same time, the Soviets abandoned their secular and internationalist appeals and moved strongly in the direction of emphasizing traditional ties of religion and ethnicity. Certainly, appealing to the Russian soldier as a Russian defending his motherland instead of as a proletarian internationalist projecting some vague international revolution had an incalculable effect. In the end, the Soviet Army fought hard, suffered greatly, and gained a much deserved victory.

The Russian Army's experiences from 1905 through World War II suggest that the will to fight is a far better predictor of that army's performance under fire than its means to fight. In each of its wars this century—in 1905 against the Japanese, in 1914 against the Axis powers, in 1922 against the Poles, and in 1938 against the Finns (and even at the beginning of World War II against the Nazis)—the Russian Army had the distinct numerical advantage in manpower and equipment. In the first four of those wars, it suffered clear defeats because it lacked the will to fight. The Russian Army seems to fight best when there is a clear threat or invasion to the Russian homeland and when traditional bonds of family, religion, ethnicity, and nationalism are allowed to come to the fore of the soldier's consciousness. Thus, it would seem that any analysis of the modern Soviet Army's ability to perform in battle would have to address itself to the psychological aspects of the soldier's motivation as well as to the material elements needed for successful combat.

Such an analysis would tend to demonstrate the Soviet soldier's almost continual tension between traditional values and the institutionalization of secular Communist practices within the military. The Soviet Army today seems to have institutionalized a number of values and practices which work directly counter to sustaining the soldier's will to fight. At the same time, in other areas it stresses—as in the oath of the soldier—traditional Russian values of motherland and family. It is the balance between the two, between traditional Russian values and modern Soviet secular values, that is in danger in the modern Soviet Army. Russian history has proven that when the balance moves too far from traditional values, the Russian soldier does not fight well. And it is this psychological disposition, this willingness to fight and endure, that remains a crucial element in any assessment of the Soviet Army.

Past researchers have not focused directly on the mind of the Soviet soldier because they have not been able to assemble the relevant data. For genuine insights in this area they have had to rely upon defectors or the occasional emigré. Until very recently, researchers have not been able to get to the Soviet soldier to find out what he thinks. Significant numbers of Soviet soldiers were interviewed in a systematic manner in my earlier work, *The New Red Legions*.[9] This book incorporates considerable data drawn from this earlier research.

The data dealing with the attitudes of the Soviet soldier are drawn from a systematic survey of 134 Russian emigrés, all former soldiers, undertaken over a three-month period in 1979. Interviews took place with former Soviet soldiers now resident in Canada, Italy, England, Israel, and the United States. While the data are admittedly narrow, they are no less so than those gathered by the well-accepted techniques used in the intelligence community of debriefing emigrés and defectors. Moreover, narrow data are by no means inaccurate or "dirty" data, and analysis of the sample's responses reveals that substantial confidence can be placed in them.[10] For example, the data are remarkably accurate in portraying age, date of service entry, number who served, branch, type of unit, rank, and social composition of the sample. The data suggest that when sample respondents are stratified along several "known" dimensions, their range of defining characteristics is close to what we would expect to find among any randomly selected group of conscripts in the Soviet Army.[11] The data gathered from the survey will, therefore, suffice until a more complete and larger study is feasible.

With regard to whether the sample accurately represents the Soviet soldier's experiences, here it is appropriate to raise a question central to the study. Since the bulk of the respondents are Jews, it could well be argued that the respondents are outside the mainstream of Soviet life and that, accordingly, their views of the military are biased. Moreover, it could be suggested that the fact that the respondents are emigrés in itself implies a high degree of social alienation that would also bias their perceptions. How valid is this argument? If the sample is biased, then an examination of the pages and pages of raw data should reveal the presence of statistical "lumps" among the response profiles. Such an examination must show that the data are biased *in the same direction* if the argument is to have merit. A thorough statistical examination of the data across 161 variables reveals no particularly extreme bulges. In any case, only one of two positions in such a critique is acceptable: one assumes that the data are biased in the direction of overly negative views of the Soviet Army or overly positive views. The only other alternatives are (1) that the data are unbiased and, therefore, valid or (2) that the data are randomly distributed, in which case no statistically valid relationships would appear. Since no significant skewing appears in the spread of the data, one is hard pressed from either position to explain both the very positive and negative things respondents say about the Soviet Army from the perspective of systematic sample bias. If it is assumed that the bias is negative, then positive perceptions cannot be logically explained, and the reverse is also true. In any case, an analysis of the data for statistical skewing does not reveal any meaningful statistical idiosyncrasies, and most certainly it does not reveal any kind of consistent statistical bias along any discernible dimensions. In the absence of any other studies that deal directly with the perceptions of the Soviet soldier based on actual interviews, the analyst must use what he has.

The data presented here are at least generally accurate and are the basis for the only truly empirical examination of the attitudes and perceptions of the Soviet soldier undertaken in the last four decades. Nonetheless, no claim is offered that this work is definitive or that the data are free from error or that the conclusions drawn from it are to be accepted without question. The only claim advanced for the existing data is that they are available, systematic, empirical, generally representative, largely reliable, and, above all, useful.

This study is organized into eight chapters, each of which deals with some aspect of the Soviet and American Army's performance of its combat role. The emphasis is on conventional weaponry and employment, and almost no attention is given to the comparative nuclear capabilities of each force. This approach was taken on the grounds that the most likely form of combat employed by either army in the future will be in the conventional mode.

In Chapter 1, The Armies, an attempt is made to analyze each force from the point of view of its organizational strengths and weaknesses, with an emphasis upon comparative weaponry, manpower, deployment, and mobilization capacity. This overview of each army serves as a backdrop against which the rest of the analysis unfolds. Chapter 2, The Soldiers, focuses upon what might be called the character of the soldier, his quality, background, and experiences. It analyzes the general quality of men which each army must produce in order to have effective combat forces. Chapters 3 and 4, respectively, The NCOs and The Officers, evaluate the quality of officer and NCO leadership available, especially within the combat environment. An analysis of the extent to which officers and NCOs are perceived as effective leaders by their superiors and their men is emphasized. Chapter 5, Morale and Discipline, deals with these two important characteristics in each army, focusing upon the degree to which indicators of morale and discipline might affect unit performance on the battlefield. Chapter 6, Unit Cohesion, analyzes Soviet and American training doctrines as they relate to producing cohesion and how each soldier perceives the level of cohesion of his units in each army. Chapter 7, Combat Ability, assesses the ability of each army and its soldiers to fight and to fight well relative to a range of factors dealing with training, leadership, and technical skills. Finally, Chapter 8, Conclusions, presents a graphic comparison of the soldiers of both armies across a range of sixty variables aimed at assessing the strengths and weaknesses of each army relative to its combat ability.

No book on such a complex subject is ever really complete, and the speed with which changing political and economic conditions in both the United States and Soviet Union can affect the quality of military force makes any conclusion open to debate, especially as time passes. Nonetheless, if this book merely succeeds in raising new questions or casting old ones in a new light so as to provoke further research and thought, then it will have accomplished its purpose.

Notes

1. Edward A. Shills and Morris Janowitz,"Cohesion and Disintegration in the German Wehrmacht in World War II," *Public Opinion Quarterly* 12 (1948):280-315.

2. For more information on the distinction between corporative and instrumental attachments in small military groups, see Richard A. Gabriel, "Modernism vs. Pre-Modernism:The Need to Rethink the Basis of Military Organizational Forms," in James

Brown and Michael Collins, eds., *Military Ethics and Professionalism* (Washington: National Defense University Press, 1981), pp. 55-74.

3. S.L.A. Marshall, *Men Against Fire* (New York: William Morrow, 1947).

4. Samuel Stouffer, *The American Soldier* (Princeton, N.J.: Princeton University Press, 1949).

5. John Keegan, *The Face of Battle* (New York: Viking Press, 1976).

6. Samuel Rolbant, *The Israeli Soldier* (London: T. Yoseloff, 1970); Reuven Gal, "Characteristics of Heroism," paper delivered at the Canadian Leadership Symposium, Royal Roads Military College, Victoria, British Columbia (June 5, 1981); Allan Lloyd, *War in the Trenches* (London: McKay, 1977).

7. Richard A. Gabriel and Paul L. Savage, *Crisis in Command: Mismanagement in the Army* (New York: Hill and Wang, 1978).

8. For more data on the linkage between the AVF and the army conceptualized as a business, see Gabriel and Savage, *Crisis in Command*, Chapter 1.

9. Richard A. Gabriel, *The New Red Legions: An Attitudinal Portrait of the Soviet Soldier* (Westport, Conn: Greenwood Press, 1980).

10. For a complete defense of the data used in this study as it relates to the survey of Russian soldiers, see Gabriel, *The New Red Legions*, Chapter 1.

11. Ibid.

1

The Armies

The Soviet Army

The Soviet Army is the largest standing army in the world and one of the best equipped. The term *army* as understood in the Soviet context implies a somewhat different type of military institution than in the West. The Soviet Army includes within it five separate components: strategic rocket forces, ground forces, airborne forces, air defense forces, and special troops. All components are operationally unified under a General Staff and are administered and commanded at the national level by a cabinet-level official, the minister of defense. The Soviet military system encompasses large numbers of additional component troops that could be made available in time of crisis but that in peacetime perform their own separate missions. Most of these component forces have their own chain of command and are not subordinated to the minister of defense. For example, border guard troops fall under the Committee for State Security (KGB), and internal security troops come under the Ministry of Interior (MVD). The personnel for all services, including KGB and MVD troops, are procured through the central conscription system and are trained by the same system that drafts and assigns conscripts throughout the ground forces.

There is nothing new in the fact that the Soviet Union maintains a very large ground army. Historically, Russia has maintained one of the largest standing military forces in Europe. The size of the Russian Army has consistently prompted critics to characterize it as the ''Russian Steamroller.'' Russian military thought has always been predicated upon the first principle of war, the principle of mass. Hence, the size of Russian ground forces today is more explicable in terms of tradition than in terms of the rise of Communism in the Soviet Union.

The Soviet Army is fundamentally a classic European army modeled after the armies characteristic of Europe around the turn of the century and persisting throughout World War II. This European army was based on relatively small and professional officer and NCO corps which were expected to provide central direction in the training, leadership, and maintenance of large conscript and reserve forces.

Traditional European armies were also mass armies which depended heavily upon universal conscription. The clearest examples of such armies are found in Bismarckian Germany and in Napoleonic France. A corollary to universal conscription was the practice of relying heavily upon the ability to mobilize reserves rapidly as a mechanism for mobilizing the total population for war. This practice, a durable remnant of the Napoleonic era, remained characteristic of European armies through World War II. Today the Soviet Army continually conducts reserve mobilization exercises in the classic tradition to demonstrate that it is capable at any time of mobilizing millions of trained reserves for war. As in other classic armies, military service in the Soviet Union is closely linked to the rights and privileges of citizenship. It is understood that every individual in Soviet society has a basic obligation as a condition of citizenship to serve in the military.

The modern Soviet Army remains very much cast in the traditional European mold and, as such, can be distinguished from the present-day armies of the Western powers. If one relates the social and economic structures of the West to stages of industrialization, it is clear that the West has entered what has been called the postindustrial era. As a consequence, the military structures of these states have undergone significant changes in organizational form and direction when compared to the traditional armies of World War I and World War II. These changes by and large have not taken place in the Soviet military.

There are other major points of difference between Western and Soviet military structures. First, the size of the standing armies in the West both absolutely and relatively is small compared with that of Soviet Army. This is true not only in terms of the number of men under arms but also in terms of the percentage of the gross national product (GNP) consumed by each. It is also true in terms of the importance of the military as a social institution within its host society. To the extent that the size of its standing military force is a function of the degree of socio-industrialization, the Soviet Army remains a very different structure from Western armies.

One characteristic that has accompanied the transformation of the military structures of the West is reduced reliance upon conscription as a means of filling military ranks. At least three of the major states of the North Atlantic Treaty Organization (NATO) alliance—Canada, Great Britain, and the United States—as well as most of the minor ones, rely upon volunteer armies rather than upon conscription. Even in those states that still rely upon conscription such as West Germany, political authorities are making more and more efforts to utilize voluntarism. As a consequence, the percentage of actual conscripts is declining. The Soviet Army, on the other hand, continues to rely almost exclusively upon conscription to furnish its military manpower. Even significant numbers of its officers started as conscripts, as did almost the entire noncommissioned officer corps. Perhaps as many as 95 percent of all serving noncommissioned officers at any time are still drawn directly from the conscript ranks.[1]

Yet another difference between Western armies and the Soviet Army is the tendency in the West to develop modern organizational forms and to utilize modern motivational techniques. As the West reduces the size of armies and eliminates conscription, the tendency is to use those organizational forms that have proven effective in the economic sphere of capitalist societies. The organizational and normative assumptions used so extensively by business organizations are being applied directly to the armies of the West. By contrast, the Soviets have adopted few modern organizational forms in the military and even fewer modern motivational techniques. One reason is that many organizational forms characteristic of Soviet society have been adopted from those found in traditional military organizations, thus reversing the process. Moreover, a totalitarian society, especially one that concentrates upon developing its industrial base, is prone to emphasize those mechanisms of control and organization that have already proven effective. In the Soviet case, this means the use of traditional bureaucratic methods of control. As a result, there is a noticeable lack of modern approaches to industrial organization within the larger society that could be transferred to the military. Rather, the opposite is often the case. When an experiment in the military proves effective, the civilian society often adopts it. Thus, Soviet military structures remain highly traditional rather than modern in organizational form and operation.

The same seems true with regard to motivational techniques. Given the Soviet penchant for control supported by a firm belief in ideology and a long history of using traditional forms to generally good effect, the Soviets have been reluctant to implement motivational techniques that deviate from proven methods. Thus, all the traditional forms of organization and motivation associated with classic European armies continue largely unchanged in the Soviet Army today, while in the West they have been greatly modified or totally replaced by more modern mechanisms.

The Soviet Army is different, then, from the armies of the West at least in terms of size, reliance upon conscription, and the continued use of traditional organizational and motivational forms. To a great extent, this is understandable in terms of the level of Russian industrialization as well as the ideological nature of the regime. The Soviet Union remains fundamentally in the developmental stages of modern industrialization. Consequently, it has not yet felt any need to use more modern forms of organization and motivation in either its society or its armed forces.

Another reason why the Soviet Army remains a traditional military organization has to do with the nature of the political system. With its emphasis on control and ideology, the Soviet regime must inevitably resist any movement toward postindustrialization. By definition, postindustrial societies maximize leisure and income as labor becomes less and less intensive, with machines and sophisticated technology being more intensely used. Inevitably, these conditions produce pressures within the society for a shift in the direction of consumerism and the desire for expanded political and civil liberties. The Soviet regime is acutely aware that such pressures necessarily require loosening its control. Consequently, the regime resists this movement and, corollarily, stifles the conditions that gave rise in the West to small standing armies, the elimination of conscription, and the adoption of modern organizational structures.

There are still other reasons why the Soviet Army remains a traditional army that go beyond considerations of political control and economic development. The Soviet Army serves wider functions as a social institution than do the armies of the democratic West. At least four additional functions can be identified that augment its function as a military force.[2] First is the role the army plays in nation-building. Nearly one-half of the Soviet population is comprised of nationality groups that are ethnically, linguistically, racially, and religiously distinct from the Slavic majority. Thus, the Soviet Union has a major problem in trying to build a national consciousness that transcends the strong subnational loyalties of its minorities. A primary mechanism for accomplishing this goal is universal military service. What Frederick the Great said of the German Army, that it was a "school of the nation," is also true of the Soviet Army. Accordingly, some of the Soviet Army's organizational forms and practices reflect its need to serve as a giant socialization mechanism for the disparate peoples who are to be integrated into the larger cultural and national milieu.

Another function of military service in the Soviet Union is education.[3] The party quite openly views the army as a giant educational mechanism, especially from the point of view of teaching nationality groups the Russian language. The Soviet Army makes no provision for issuing orders and commands in any language except Russian. As part of the larger socialization process, service in the Soviet military is designed to accelerate the process of linguistic assimilation, which the regime considers important to building a common sense of national identity.

Universal conscription also develops habits of obedience and acquiescence to authority that are important to maintaining social control in a totalitarian society. The Russians have wholeheartedly adopted the Bismarckian notion that universal conscription cultivates a respect for authority and established order among the citizenry. The view prevails that a two-year tour of military duty reinforces obedience to commands, lack of individual liberty, physical hardships, and ways of dealing with bureauacracy that are commonplace in a totalitarian social order.

A related task of the Soviet Army is to suppress and control the younger elements of Soviet society during adolescence. In any society, dissent and revolution are likely to be stimulated by the young who have little stake in the social order: they usually have not yet married, invested in careers, or given hostages to the future with their children. The young are at once the most pliable and potentially the most disruptive members of any society. By forcing this group into military service at the age of eighteen, the army can control and channel their normal degree of social discontent. The Soviet Army absorbs groups that are most likely to create social trouble and places them in an environment in which indiscipline and dissent can be expressed only at great risk. At the same time, it reinforces habits and practices that erode any propensity for social deviance. The circle of control is tightly closed. In order to understand the Soviet Army in its larger social context, it must be understood that its functions extend beyond those of military service. Its task is to serve the regime in a number of different ways not specifically connected with the application of military force.

A fourth function of the Soviet Army and a major point of contrast with the armies of the West is that, as the West has moved toward the development of modern organizational forms within its military institutions, it has tended to sever the crucial link between citizenship and the obligation of military service. The rise of volunteer armies centered around modern organizational forms and predicated upon economic motivational models has supposedly made such a linkage obsolete. By relying upon conscription, the Soviets have not only maintained this linkage but, because of the additional social functions military service performs, have also tried strongly to reinforce it. In this sense, the Soviet Army reflects its classical and traditional heritage. The linkage of military service to citizenship was a fundamental tenet of traditional European societies and formed the basis of the mass army beginning with Napoleon and ending with World War II. Herein lies a major difference between Western and Soviet military institutions. The basis of Soviet military institutions is closely linked to the traditional concept of citizenship and involves the participation of a much broader segment of the general population and other societal institutions than it does in Western societies. The Western linkage has been weakened where it has not been severed altogether, a natural consequence of the evolution to the contemporary volunteer army.

The American Army

The American Army is starkly different from the Soviet Army in its origins, traditions, practices, and even its very reason for being. Furthermore, the American Army can be seen as a unique result of a distinct cultural, economic, and historical heritage. It is even radically different in many ways from the armies of the other Western states. These differences, established as they are in our history, make themselves felt today in the way the American Army is raised, configured, and meant to be employed.

The very beginnings of the American Army were almost an afterthought. During the colonial period, most of our experience with organized armies was with foreign armies, usually British or French, which came to be viewed as armies of occupation. The use of military forces in the domestic realm was viewed with fear and suspicion. A basic fear of the Founding Fathers was the fear of executive power being unleashed upon a defenseless civilian population. Such apprehensions were justified inasmuch as the only extant model of executive power was monarchical, founded on the concept of divine right and sustained by military forces loyal to the monarch. A major strain of American political thought developed which came to see executive power even in a republic as not rooted directly in the will of the people and, as such, power with a great potential for abuse. From this perspective, a standing domestic army was seen as an instrument of executive power and, therefore, as potentially oppressive. Thus, through most of its early history the United States took very few measures to raise any kind of significant military force. The American view of standing ground armies somewhat paralleled that of the English who, as an insular nation, emphasized the role of its navy and sustained only marginal ground forces, most of which were deployed abroad. So, too, in the United States in the early days there was considerable support for naval forces and almost no support for ground forces on the grounds that naval forces could less easily be used to suppress domestic liberty.

By linking standing ground armies with the fear of executive power gone wild, from the beginning the very existence of the American Army has been subject to question. Even when armies were not associated with domestic oppression, they were linked with oppression in foreign countries and even became viewed as a cause of war per se. President Woodrow Wilson, for example, naively thought that large standing armies as well as autocratic forms of government were in themselves causes of war.

Corollarily, except in time of war, the American Army has never enjoyed either wide social support or prestige among the populace that national armies have in Europe. The military has usually been viewed as a place where the socially marginal go because they cannot succeed anywhere else. Historically, when the United States has not been at war, its ranks have been filled with immigrants and others located at the bottom of the social order. Such epithets as "the Irish make the best fighters" (Civil War) or "sailors and dogs keep off the grass" (World War I) or "NCO—no chance outside" (World War II) or the Vietnam-era classic, "LIFER—lousy inefficient fuck-off expecting retirement," seem to accurately describe what the American populace has thought of the peacetime soldier: a person who could do nothing else but join the army.

In addition, the lack of a feudal tradition which established the principle of having the rich and propertied classes serve made it very difficult for the American military to draw heavily on the upper social orders for its membership, even in the officer corps. Service in the officer corps has never been viewed as an acceptable occupation for the sons of the wealthy and powerful, as it has been in Europe. To be sure, men of property have served in the militia and National Guard throughout our history, but the regular forces have drawn only marginally from the upper classes, even for officers and even less so for common soldiers. In all its wars, beginning with the Civil War, the nation has provided large loopholes through which the rich and powerful could escape military service. The ability to hire a substitute, as in the Civil War, or to remain in graduate school, as during the Vietnam War, are examples.

Another reason why the American military has not occupied an important place in the social values of the country is that it played a very limited role in the foundation, expansion, growth, and, indeed, even the defense of the country right from the beginning. Unlike the Soviet Union which saw the use of military force as an instrument of national unification and continental expansion, American ground forces fought no major wars within the nation's borders. Even when the military was employed as a tool of domestic expansion, more often than not it was done in a very limited way. Those who would equate the role of the Russian Army in the expansion of Czarist Russia with the U.S. experience overlook the fact that the American effort was not official policy, involved far fewer actual engagements, caused far fewer casualities, and involved a much smaller force. In most instances, the U.S. Army was employed against the Indians, in reaction to specific and sporadic incidents, and not as a consistent policy of genocide or national expansion. Rather than having the flag follow the sabre as was the Russian experience, more often the call for the army post and health officer came *after* settlers and capital had already settled a section of the interior. The American military played no role like that of the German and French armies which directly helped shape their respective states, serving as instruments of national unification. In the Civil War, the American military helped save a nation already in existence, and did not create one through force of arms. Its small role in national unification was further limited by the fact that the United States was virtually created out of whole cloth in terms of constitutional power. In contrast, in Europe the state developed very gradually through a "normal" transition from feudalism to modern nation-state, requiring the constant application of military force to subdue competing parochial centers of power. Thus, the lack of support for standing ground forces in the United States reflects a long tradition in which ground forces have been viewed with suspicion, played a limited role in the expansion and growth of the country, and had virtually no role in its national unification.

Because the historical and economic conditions of the United States were so different even from other states of the West as well as the Soviet Union, its failure to develop a large military force is not surprising. At the same time, the nation realized that some type of military force was needed, and so it drew on the English tradition and established a local militia.[4] The American militia was established as a result of very specific historical factors. In the first place, the Founding Fathers thought the need for a military force to be only sporadic and limited rather than constant. Moreover, the militia tradition drew heavily upon the belief that a militia was likely to be far more controllable than a national force and thus less of a threat to domestic liberty. Even during the War of Independence, when national forces were authorized, they were basically made up of local militia appended to a very small national force. This tradition is still maintained today under the "total force concept" of the American military by which is meant that the reserve and National Guard forces, rather than a large standing army, become the primary means for filling out the standing force in times of trouble.

The link between social, economic, and political opportunities and military service was never as clear in the United States as it was in Germany, France, or even the Soviet Union. Historically, in the West, social and economic privileges and opportunities were frequently extended to segments of the populace as a consequence of their military service. (Britain was the clear exception.) This practice was utilized in Napoleonic France where military service was traded-off for social and economic opportunities; the same situation occurred in Bismarckian Germany where military service qualified a person for certain jobs and extended social benefit programs, a situation that continued until the German defeat in 1945. In Scandinavia, even political participation required military service. The right to vote in Sweden requires prior military service for all males. And, too, the Soviet Union's gradual expansion of conscription seemed generally to link the requirement to serve in the military with expanded economic or social privileges. Even today, soldiers who do well in the military are given any number of job preferences in the civilian economy over those with no or lesser military records. Soviet propaganda aimed at its domestic population continually stresses that military service and defense of the motherland is a consequence and duty of Soviet citizenship.

In the United States, however, citizenship and rights have their roots far more in economic and social activity than in military service. Utilization of a free enterprise society in which individuals achieve rights and privileges largely through economic activity, with their own resources and without the intervention of government, made the familiar European formula of trading rights for military service and universal conscription anathema to Americans. To be sure, this doctrine had limited use in the 1960s when pressure for black and other minority rights was linked to the fact that they had fought and borne equal burdens in World War II, Korea, and Vietnam. But the argument, although it had been made on behalf of blacks since the Revolution, ran contrary to the fact that the United States never associated political rights with either conscription or military service. Quite the contrary, the citizen's rights are seen to flow from the rule of law and his privileges essentially from his own abilities, exercised in a free enterprise economy with minimal government interference. In this sense, the contrast between the American and most Western armies is most marked.

There is yet another sense in which the American Army differs from the Soviet Army in its relationship to the civil order. In the United States, the military has never been seen as a socialization mechanism or even as a place to integrate disparate ethnic or racial populations. The American Army has traditionally been so small relative to the civilian population, and its isolation in mostly rural military posts buttressed by long tours of duty has been so complete that it could not act as a vehicle of upward mobility for any sizable segment of the population. In addition, until World War II few post-service benefits were granted to those who left, so that military service could not serve as a launching pad to upward mobility for any large number of people. As noted earlier, this is a fundamental task of the Soviet armed forces. The difference is understandable in terms of the different traditions that the Soviets and Americans bring to their armies, not the least of which is a free enterprise economic system. The theory behind this system either ignored the need for socialization or relegated it entirely to private institutions. While the complexities of America's ethnic group are certainly equal to those of the Soviet Union, national assimilation was not seen as a function of military service or, indeed, even as a proper function of the state at all. Rather, it was perceived to be a function of the educational process and economic opportunity. It was assumed that participation in the country's economic, social, and educational process would at some point create the "melting pot" for which America was to become famous.

As mentioned earlier, the American Army has generally relied upon a very small standing army, ostensibly to be augmented by reserves and mobilization in time of crisis. Even the ability to augment the national army by National Guard and reserve forces was not formalized until the National Defense Act of 1920.[5] There are many reasons for this reliance upon reserves, some of which have already been discussed. But the overriding reason is that the policy of maintaining a small standing army, supported by militia forces, worked very well for the United States right up to World War I. Until then, the American use of military force had generally been limited to sporadic forays into China, the Philippines, Cuba, and Central America. For all these occasions, volunteer forces seemed adequate to the task. In addition, no major wars have been fought on U.S. soil, so the enemy has never been close enough to justify the formation of a large standing national army. Our neighbor to the north, Canada, after dealing the United States two military defeats, has not been a problem for well over a century, while our neighbor to the south, Mexico, has never been a significant military force. Oceans on either side have provided strong barriers to invasion, given the state of technology, and since the Civil War there has been no domestic threat that would require the use of large military forces. Thus, the United States has maintained a small national army because its own history indicates that it has worked very well.

Unlike European forces which have traditionally relied on conscription, in the United States the use of conscription is relatively recent. America's refusal to resort to conscription for so long is interesting in itself. The United States had flirted briefly with conscription in the Civil War, along with the use of substitutes, but rapidly abandoned the idea in response to riots and the refusal of large numbers of people to comply with the law.[6] Conscription once again received brief authorization during World War I, but few conscripts ever reached the battlefields in time, and it was never extensively used in practice. It finally came into extensive use during World War II as a response to global conflict and a grave military threat. It was dismantled once again immediately after the war. The degree of American demobilization after the war was unprecedented. But Soviet actions between 1945 and 1948 again prompted national conscription,

and it was used from 1948 through 1973, including the Korean War and almost
ten years of the Vietnam War. In contrast, the Soviet Union has had an unbroken
tradition of conscript service since its institution in 1699 by Peter the Great.[7]

In 1973, the United States returned to its basic tradition of a volunteer force,
but even when the conscription system was in force, a large number of men—
certainly over half of those serving—were volunteers. In its time-honored militia
tradition, conscription was viewed primarily as a way of augmenting standing
military forces which were usually filled by volunteers. Thus, the current confrontation between the United States and the Soviet Union pits a large standing
army organized along traditional lines through conscription and universal service
strongly linked to citizenship against a small "peacetime option" army organized
along modern lines through voluntarism and econometric modes of motivation
and organization. In a sense, the armies in which the Soviet soldier and the
American soldier serve represent a confrontation of modes of military organization, thought, and doctrine that are literally worlds apart.

Manpower

The differences between the Soviet and the American armies show up most
clearly in a comparison of their respective manpower and equipment. In terms
of military manpower alone, the Soviet ground forces exceed the total of all four
U.S. services by almost a half million men. Indeed, total Soviet ground force
manpower is more than twice that of the United States: 4,832,000 compared to
2,041,000. In addition, active Soviet military regulars, even excluding their
security forces, exceed the size of the entire U.S. military establishment, including its civilian and reserve forces. If Soviet paramilitary and reserve forces
are counted, the amount of Soviet military manpower available to pursue military
objectives is more than four times the total available to the United States.[8]

What has stimulated the growth of Soviet forces and limited that of the United
States? The turning point in the expansion of the Soviet Army seems to have
come in the 1960s when one of the necessary requirements for the Soviet military
buildup, an industrial plant capable of supporting it had been established.[9] By
1960, much of the war damage had been repaired, many new factories had been
built, and the Soviet Union had developed a whole range of new military technology. These conditions provided sufficient background for the expansion of
the Soviet military machine.

The most immediate stimulus to the Soviets' military expansion was the Cuban
missile crisis of October 1962 when for the first time, Soviet and American
forces faced each other in a confrontation that threatened to escalate to nuclear
proportions. The confrontation revealed severe weaknesses in Soviet military
strength, most notably in its navy, air force, and logistical services. As was
noted at the time, the Soviets counted the guns, saw they were outnumbered,
and withdrew from the brink of war. However, the trauma of the crisis triggered
a movement within the Soviet defense establishment, led by the armed forces
themselves to increase Soviet military capabilities so that never again would they

be at a disadvantage when dealing with the United States. At the same time, the increased influence of the armed forces in the decision-making process was demonstrated in 1964 when Khrushchev was removed with the complicity of the military.[10]

The Cuban missile crisis also propelled a new breed of military technocrats to greater policy influence. These men had earned their spurs in World War II but only as young officers. When they came to power in the early 1960s they did so as a group of military technocratic managers in charge of redesigning the Soviet military machine and modernizing it. These men continue to occupy positions of high authority today. Indeed, the average tenure of the highest level Soviet General Staff officers is fourteen years compared to only five months in the American Army.[11] U.S. intelligence analysts have explained much of the Soviet expansion of its military capabilities as reflecting the increased influence of the Soviet military in the decision-making process, accompanied by the rise of a new breed of "iron men" whose careers are closely tied to the production and implementation of the new policy.

While the Soviets were increasing their military capability, the United States was fighting its ten-year war in Vietnam and was unable to match those increases. Although the Vietnam War provided limited opportunities to test new tactics and weapons, in general it precluded any long-term investment in and modernization of the American Army. While the United States was tied down with Vietnam, busily expending stocks of equipment, manpower, and money that could have been used to remain abreast of increases in Soviet strength, the Soviets were able to increase their own military forces unhindered by the threat of competition. Accordingly, by 1980 U.S. intelligence analysts believed that the Soviet expansion of its ground forces was nearing completion. The gap in the military power between the two armies reached alarming proportions in the Soviets' favor. For example, in the 1970s the Soviet Union's active service military manpower increased by 280,000, while that available to the United States decreased by 566,000. Following the high point of 1968 when American ground forces reached 1,570,000, by 1980 that total had been reduced to the 758,000-man army that is the spine of the American ground force. At the same time, the ground forces available to the Soviet Union increased from 1,420,000 to approximately 1,680,000.[12]

Military manpower does not tell the whole story. The organization and equipping of that manpower are crucial elements in fighting ability. Since 1970, the United States has remained organized into essentially the same sixteen divisions it had a decade before. American standing forces are organized into four armored divisions, six mechanized infantry, four infantry, one heliborne division, and one airborne division. Counting only Category 1 and 2 divisions—those divisions that are 90 percent and 75 percent up to strength and ready to deploy—the Soviets increased the number of available divisions by almost 10 percent. In 1970, it had seventy-three Category 1 and 2 divisions, and by 1980, eighty. Twenty-six were armored divisions, forty-seven motorized rifle divisions, and seven airborne divisions. When Category 3 and 4 divisions are considered—that is, those divisions that would have to be filled out within the first twenty days of battle—the United States has half its force, eight divisions, in these categories. For its part, the Soviets have increased the number of Category 3 and 4 divisions from eighty-six to ninety-three, or an increase of seven divisions since 1970. Of these Soviet divisions, twenty are armored, seventy-two are motorized rifle, and one is airborne.[13] Clearly, then, the gap in ground force power available to the United States and the Soviets has widened considerably, with the Soviets able to field about 1.6 million ground troops to 758,000 for the United States. Moreover, as the above figures show, it can field far more battle units as well.

The gap between Soviet and American military manpower is more evident from the following statistics. Since 1970, the United States has not increased the number of total deployable divisions (including National Guard and reserve divisions) available to it, while the Soviets, beginning with 159 deployable divisions in 1970, have increased that number by fourteen, for a total of 173.[14] By any standard it is clear that the Soviet Union can bring to bear in a short period of time, say, within thirty days of the outbreak of war, a substantial advantage in terms of deployable manpower and divisions.

Weaponry

The Soviet Army also enjoys a considerable advantage in certain types of weaponry, and here the Soviet emphasis on mobile and heavily armored forces is evident. The Soviet Army currently has over 49,000 tank vehicles in its inventory, 47,000 of which are heavy and medium tanks and 2,000 light tanks. By comparison, the American Army has 16,100 tank vehicles, of which 10,160 are light tanks.[15] Even more impressive is the fact that in the period of 1965 to 1980, the Soviets were able to deploy and bring into production three new prototype tanks: the T-62, T-72, and the most recent prototype, the T-80, which is already undergoing tests. By contrast, the American Army has been able to deploy only one major tank prototype, the M-60, with the XM-1 just beginning to enter production. Sustaining the ability to field massive tank armies is the fact that Soviet tank production is roughly ten times that of the United States. At this time, the Soviets can produce and deploy about 4,000 tanks a year compared to only 400 for the United States.[16] The Soviet emphasis on armor which is discussed in detail later is readily apparent, as is its advantage of almost four to one in armored vehicles that would have to be engaged on the battlefield.

A Soviet numerical advantage is also evident in the deployment of armored personnel carriers (APCs). Because the Soviet Army is configured to move large masses of armor in a high tempo rapid attack, large stocks of APCs are vital if infantry forces are to keep pace. Since 1967, no Soviet infantryman has been required to walk into battle; since then, all ground forces have been fully mechanized, so troops could move through battle areas in their APCs accompanied by tanks. So thorough and complete has the mechanization of the Soviet Army been that all eight airborne divisions are now equipped with the new BRD light air droppable APC.[17] The disparity in APCs between the two armies is clear enough, with the United States maintaining 14,122, a small increase from the 11,870 it had in 1970. The Soviet Army has 60,000, up by 30,000 from what it deployed only a decade ago.[18] By most intelligence estimates, the quality of Soviet armored vehicles is far better than American prototypes, with the Soviet versions being more heavily armored and less susceptible to breakdown, and providing full capability for movement through and survival on a nuclear and chemical battlefield. The deployment of large numbers of these vehicles is fully consistent with the Soviet emphasis on mobile mass armored warfare that has typified its employment doctrine over the last twenty-five years.

The Russian experience in World Wars I and II in which massive casualties were suffered from artillery is too well known to warrant elaboration here. It is a canon of Soviet thought that artillery is truly the "king of battle"—and rightly so when it is recalled that fully 60 percent of all battle casualties taken in warfare since the invention of gunpowder have been inflicted by artillery. The introduction of nuclear battlefield munitions may well increase this number. Soviet doctrine reflects this concern for deliverable artillery munitions. Compared to the American Army which has 4,650 artillery pieces, the Soviet Army can deploy 24,000 pieces of artillery, up almost 8,000 from the number it had in 1970.[19] The Soviet Army views the integration of armored and artillery forces as vital to conducting successful operations on the modern battlefield. By any measure, the American Army is severely outgunned in its ability to deliver large numbers of rounds on target by artillery. Another reason why the Soviet advantage in artillery tubes is important is that long-range artillery is absolutely vital to the ability to deliver both nuclear and chemical munitions. Soviet doctrine presumes both types of munitions to be a normal part of the tactical deployment of the Soviet Army at war.

In one area, anti-tank guided missiles, the American Army has made rapid progress. A decade ago it had almost none in its inventory; today it has 14,650 precision guided missile (PGM) launchers. Despite this substantial increase, the Soviet Army has outpaced the United States in this area, moving from 5,000 launchers in 1970 to over 22,500 PGMs as of 1980.[20] As demonstrated by the Arab-Israeli War in 1973, the PGM will play an increasingly important role on the modern battlefield. Such weapons are simple to operate, very reliable, accurate, and very deadly. When firing from a defensive position, the probability of achieving a first-round hit against an armored vehicle exceeds 90 percent. In addition, PGMs are relatively cheap, costing in most instances under $3,000 per missile. Whether examined from a defensive or offensive posture, the Soviet Army's ability to wage anti-tank warfare with PGMs is substantially greater than that of the American Army.

Adding to the awesome Soviet artillery force are heavy mortars capable of delivering a wide range of special munitions. Once again the Soviet Army demonstrates a clear and significant advantage, having some 3,000 more mortar tubes than the American Army. The Soviet Army has approximately 8,000 mortars compared to 2,745 that can be mustered by the American Army. So it is, too, with regard to surface-to-surface missiles (SSMs). The U.S. Army has only 226 SSMs in its inventory compared to 1,330 for the Soviet Army.[21] More importantly, the Soviet Army has functionally integrated SCUD and FROG rocket battalions into its forward combat formations, so that the combat application of SSM missile power does not have to stand on its own as it must in the American Army. Rather, this element is functionally integrated into the entire frontal area battle plan.

One area in which the Soviet Army thoroughly outnumbers and outperforms the American Army is air defense. The American Army is far behind the Soviets in air defense missile launchers, maintaining approximately 1,100 launchers compared to the Soviets' 3,300. In addition, American anti-aircraft guns number only 5,500 compared with 8,700 for the Soviet Army.[22] Moreover, Soviet anti-aircraft artillery is normally self-sufficient, mounted on self-propelled chassis or at least can be rapidly towed into battle. Most Soviet guns have a radar direction and multifire capability, and are expected to deploy rapidly alongside advancing armored units and APCs. The capability of the Soviet air defense forces to provide effective security in the battle area for deploying ground and armored forces borders on the awesome and exceeds anything that the American Army would be able to bring to bear.[23]

Numbers, of course, do not tell the whole story in comparing the combat power of any army. Many other factors come into play, one of which is the quality of weapons, which each side can deploy. It may be a peculiar American penchant to put its faith in machines and, as is the case for some commentators, to suggest that an American advantage in technological quality can spell the difference on the battlefield. However, on balance, with regard to inventory items used most in ground war, Soviet military technology is, at worst, equal to that of the United States and, in many cases, better. For example, the Soviet T-72 tank seems to enjoy every advantage over the M-60—larger gun, smaller silhouette, simpler to maintain, longer range, an automatic gun loader, and even better armor. Soviet APC's are, by any standard, better armored, faster, easier to maintain, carry more firepower, and able to function in a nuclear environment and cross rivers better than the U.S. version. The Soviet soldier's rifle and personal equipment—gas masks, boots, cold-weather gear—are widely agreed to be better than their U.S. equivalents. To be sure, the United States enjoys an advantage in micro-circuitry, acquisition radar, some missiles, and battlefield computers. While the subject of who has the technological advantage will remain a matter of debate for some time, it seems fair to suggest that even if the United States does enjoy a certain technological edge in some areas, it is at least outweighed by the Soviet advantage in numbers.

In view of the large manpower and equipment imbalance between the Soviet and American armies, some observers believe that the 1980s may be the most dangerous decade for the United States in dealing with the Soviet Union. It is feared that during the decade the Soviet economic machine will reach its peak along with its military machine, giving the Soviet Union such an advantage that it may be tempted to engage in a reckless antagonistic course toward the West. The term *window of vulnerability*, while invented to describe the increased nuclear vulnerabilities of America's strategic nuclear deterrent, has also been applied to the balance between the two conventional forces. Never in the history of U.S.-Soviet relations has the gap between two armies been greater or more in favor of the Soviet Union than in the early 1980s.

Doctrine

With regard to the mix of weapons and their employment, the American emphasis has traditionally been placed upon infantry, while the Soviets have shifted from infantry, characteristic of its operations in World War II, to armor. The reasons for each army's doctrinal emphasis are complex. Yet, it might be suggested that the United States, which has historically maintained only a small force and has been free from the need to fight battles on its own soil, has found it necessary to maintain the kind of military force that would maximize maneuverability and flexibility relative to its size. This has meant the development and emphasis on infantry. Infantry units are cheap to deploy, they cost little to maintain, and, most importantly, they can be easily tailored for duty on foreign battlefields with a minimum of support and transportation facilities. Moreover, infantry forces can be easily reconfigured to fight in many types of battlefield environments. Throughout its history, American projections of military power have always been beyond its own borders to battlefields as different as Vietnam to the plains of Central Europe. For these reasons, the American stress on infantry units remains basic doctrine.

For their part, the Soviets have tended to stress the use of armor. Historically, the Soviets have fought most of their wars on their own soil. The battlefields of the Soviet Union are marked by great distances and plenty of room for maneuver. These elements require highly mobile armored or rail vehicles in order to move military forces in significant numbers. Furthermore, during the early development of the Soviet Army, the impact of Marshall Mikhail Frunze on Soviet doctrine cannot be understated. Frunze was very impressed with the power of the tank and clearly saw the need to modernize the Soviet Army along armored lines. This stress on modernization, coupled with the desire to construct a first-rate heavy industrial plant, led to the Soviet emphasis on armor. By World War II, the Soviet Union had become accustomed to fielding large armored formations along with its infantry. These were capable of rapid movement through the wide expanses of the Soviet Union. Russia is ill fit geographically to be defended by infantry. This historical reality has also played its part in the development of doctrines that stress the deployment of large armored and mechanized infantry units.

While all armies teach their commanders to seize the initiative and to take the offensive, the realities of force mix and deployment often telegraph other messages. So it is with the doctrines of the American and Soviet armies. By 1965, there was a complete change in the deployment and doctrines that supported both armies, and, in effect, both armies switched roles. Under Stalin, throughout World War II and immediately thereafter, Soviet ground forces were regarded as essentially defensive in nature, a condition that revealed itself in all its short-comings in the Cuban missile crisis of 1962. By contrast, American doctrine has always stressed the employment of highly mobile infantry forces always on the offensive. By the end of the Vietnam War, the great disparity between the two armies in terms of strength began to emerge. As the increased inability of American forces to fulfill their stated missions in Central Europe became evident, the doctrines of both armies began to shift.

The Soviet Army is presently positioned to take the offensive, as is reflected in their military doctrines. Soviet doctrines stress offensive action and increasing the tempo of battle even to the point of not replacing units that have been badly damaged. Soviet units are not expected to be replaced in battle but are augmented by fresh units which absorb the remnants of the battered unit and continue the attack. Moreover, the Soviets make little distinction in battle tactics between nuclear, non-nuclear, chemical, and nonchemical battle environments. Regard-less of how a war begins, the Soviets have configured their forces to achieve absolute victory at all levels of combat.[24] If a war begins in Central Europe, at least at the tactical level, it will be initiated by the Soviets by delivering a first-strike massive attack. They will utilize surprise, seize the initiative, and increase the tempo of the attack, always carrying the battle to the enemy and never relinquishing the offensive.

The realities of life in Central Europe are that the American Army has little choice but to fight a defensive war. This reality is stated in the new battle operations manual, FM 100-5, published in 1979.[25] The manual specifies that the American Army must be prepared to "fight outnumbered and win" in any battle in Central Europe. Accordingly, the configuration of American forces is essentially defensive. The army has neither the manpower nor the equipment in either a nuclear or non-nuclear scenario to carry the war to the Soviets. Most realistic scenarios of the American military role in Europe require a Soviet attack to which the United States will respond in a very orchestrated way, absorbing the tempo of battle and trading ground for time. Eventually, limited nuclear weapons will be employed. In this sense, American Army employment doctrine reflects a clearly defensive orientation instead of an offensive one. Only fifteen years ago, exactly the reverse was true. The doctrinal debate was not over how to start a war with the Soviets; we have never planned a "first-strike" conven-tional war. Rather, the doctrinal change surrounds how we would fight it once a ground war in Europe broke out, presumably as a result of a Soviet attack. In the past, U.S. doctrine called for American ground forces to carry the war to the enemy in an offensive style reminiscent of World War II. Today, U.S. doctrine foregoes the offensive and concentrates on defending territory already in our possession. This shift in doctrine represents a very significant difference between the two armies.

The two armies also differ in terms of the degree to which they are able to maintain battle momentum and sustain their forces. The American emphasis has always been on its ability to land a long-range punch, to be able to deploy ground forces abroad, and to sustain them for long periods. World War II with its 3,000-mile supply line, Korea with its 8,000-mile supply line, and Vietnam with its 12,000-mile supply line are textbook examples of American doctrine in operation. By contrast, a common critique made of Soviet forces by intelligence analysts is its supposed inability to sustain its ground forces for sufficiently long periods. This fact is ostensibly reflected in the Soviet doctrine of trying to finish up a war in Europe in thirty to ninety days. There is some truth in the criticism insofar as the Soviets do not emphasize sustainability to the degree that the Americans do. Indeed, its "tooth to tail ratio"—the proportion of fighting soldiers to logistical ones—is much greater than for the American Army. In addition, the Soviet supply system is organized along the lines of a "push" rather than a "pull" system. Material is, therefore, delivered from the rear to the front on the basis of anticipated loss schedules rather than in response to requests from fighting units. This "pushes" the forward units into battle, minimizing their responsibility for repair and maintenance, and freeing local commanders of responsibility for supply problems so that they can continue to fight.[26] The American Army uses a "pull" supply system in which fighting units have direct supply and maintenance functions, thereby absorbing some of their battle strength. Quite frankly, the Soviets are not particularly interested in sustainability in the sense that they are prepared to maintain ground forces in battle for a period of years. The Soviets see the ability to win as depending on the tempo of battle, great momentum, shock action, and massive firepower so that they can bring the war to a rapid conclusion. Soviet doctrine is not unlike that which characterized general European military thinking prior to World War I, in which it was held that the nation that mobilized the fastest and delivered the quickest and heaviest blow would carry the day in a relatively short period of time.

Reserves

In the final analysis, of course, active forces in any kind of sustained warfare require the addition of large numbers of troops to remain effective. Thus, any war in Central Europe is likely to be heavily influenced by the ability of both armies to bring its reserve forces into play. The ability to mobilize one's reserve power and to deliver it to the point of battle becomes a crucial variable in appreciating the differences between the capabilities of the American and Soviet ground armies.

In the Soviet Union, a history of conscription has led to a long tradition of sustaining large reserve forces. The Soviet Army has improved considerably on the Tsarist ability to bring those forces to bear in a short time, and the Tsarist ability was considerable in itself. The Soviet Army maintains an awesome reserve manpower pool that is readily available for deployment on short notice.

Approximately 2.5 million men a year reach draft age in the Soviet Union.

Of these, all but about 12 percent serve on active military duty for two years, and all are assigned to reserve units until age fifty.[27] Although there is a question of how good reserve training is once the soldier leaves active service, individual soldiers in these units are periodically called to active service for training, in some instances for periods as long as two years. The manpower reserve system is enormous. If one counts only those soldiers who have been released from active service in the last five years, the ready reserve force of the Soviet Army exceeds 10 million trained men on rapid call. The Soviet ready reserve force is approximately five times as large as that of the American Army; this does not count the paramilitary and irregular forces that could be thrown into battle in an emergency.[28]

The large number of Soviet Army reserves speaks well for the Soviet Union's preparation for war, but how well can the army mobilize and deploy its reserves? The answer appears to be very well indeed. Every soldier in the reserve has his age, draft status, and medical records computerized and stored at the local draft commissariat, so that reserve manpower can be quickly located and notified. Estimates suggest that within twenty-four hours the Soviets could mobilize and move into their active ranks almost 3 million reservists. Furthermore, they could double that number in forty-eight hours.[29] This means that at D (battle date) plus thirty days the Soviets could deploy over 400 Category 1 and 2 divisions in the field ready to fight.[30] Along with these troops, the Soviets would be able to deploy support facilities in the form of civilian transportation. The ability of the Soviet Army to double its active ground forces within such a short period of time represents a significant military advantage in its own right.

The Soviets' ability to mobilize reserve forces has been adequately illustrated in the invasions of Hungary, Czechoslovakia, Poland, and, most recently, Afghanistan. In all of these instances, reserve units were used alongside regular units. Afghanistan provides an interesting case study of the Soviet ability to use reserve forces. Of the eight divisions initially deployed in Afghanistan, only two were regular divisions while six were reserve divisions. In the invasion of Afghanistan, the Soviets demonstrated a clear capability to bring up their reserve divisions in a short period of time—less than ten days—mobilize their equipment, place them in the field, and keep them there for at least ninety days before replacing them in normal rotation. Indeed, the Soviet Army's ability to mobilize and deploy its reserve forces is probably the best in the world.

In contrast, the reserve forces available to the American Army are thin and ill organized. Part of the problem is related to the adoption of the "total force" concept as an adjunct to the AVF.[31] The total force concept views forces in being as only a "peacetime option" and sees the necessity to augment those forces rapidly in the event of war by drawing heavily upon reserves. As a consequence of this policy, emphasis is placed upon maintaining substantial reserve and National Guard units that can rapidly expand active forces to needed strength levels. Corollarily, along with transferring the main manpower function to the reserves, many of the crucial logistical and medical functions that any army needs to operate have been transferred as well. The number of reserves available to the American Army is disastrously small when compared to those of the Soviet Army. Under ideal circumstances, no more than 2.8 million men could be mobilized from the reserve forces, and that is 1 million short of the 3.8 million that the army requires.[32] These shortages would be spread by more than a half million men in the active forces, a quarter million in National Guard units, and another quarter million in reserve units. Since 1972, overall available reserve manpower forces have declined by at least 19 percent, while ready reserve forces have declined by over 50 percent of required strength. In the last decade, ready reserve force strength dropped from 2,494,000 to 1,222,000. The individual ready reserve is itself almost 500,000 men short of required strength.[33]

These shortages take on even more ominous proportions when it is realized that under the total force concept many of the vital tasks required of an effective combat army are poorly positioned. They are in the reserve structure rather than in the active forces themselves. Thus, 54 percent of the total combat forces of the U.S. Army is located in reserve.[34] The shortages are even greater when examined in terms of specific force allocations. Accordingly, 56 percent of the army's total deployable forces are in reserve units, as are 37 percent of its aviation forces and 49 percent of its Special Forces groups. Also located in reserve are 52 percent of its infantry and armored battalions, 57 percent of its field artillery battalions, 65 percent of its combat engineer battalions, and 67 percent of its tactical air support units.[35] In the best of circumstances, if the U.S. Army had to go to war, more than half its combat power would be found in reserve units. More importantly, fully two-thirds of its logistical support and 60 percent of its combat medical support is also deployed in reserve.[36] The sixteen standing divisions of the American Army are not really a ready force in being, and they are not ready to fight with what they have in a "come as you are" war. Instead, they are designed to join battle only after they have been substantially augmented by reserve units. The American reliance upon reserve forces to deliver or absorb a first blow is much higher than in the Soviet Army and probably much too great in any case.

The difficulty in using reserve forces in an emergency is compounded by the fact that the United States has no real experience at rapidly mobilizing its reserve forces. Beginning in World War II, continuing through Korea, and even in Vietnam, the American solution to increased manpower demands was always to increase draft levies rather than systematically mobilize its reserves. Never have our reserves been systematically and completely mobilized. Moreover, given their state of readiness, it is unclear whether mobilizing existing reserves would help very much. In the Army National Guard, for example, in a nationwide test only 6 percent of its units were regarded as "fully ready"; 25 percent were "substantially ready"; 37 percent "marginally ready"; and 32 percent "not ready." The Army Reserve itself had only 14 percent of its units fully ready, 24 percent substantially ready, 27 percent marginally ready, and 35 percent not ready at all.[37] When an evaluation of Army Reserve combat battalions was conducted, five of ten combat battalions were found to be incapable of performing their missions, four of ten to have difficulty of such magnitude as to limit severely their ability to accomplish their mission, and only one in ten to have difficulties that would only marginally limit its performance. No battalion was found to be fully capable of performing the mission for which it was organized.[38] More than half the Army Reserve unit commanders responding to a study stated that the quality of the enlisted men in their units was much lower than that needed to accomplish their mission. Moreover, of reserve company-size units, 35 percent were not ready to perform their mission, and 27 percent were only marginally ready. The Army Reserve consists of about 3,000 company-size units, including 1,618 combat-support companies, 1,018 training companies, and 321 combat companies. None of these units is truly combat ready by even the most marginal definition of the term.[39]

One of the major reasons why these units are not fit for combat is the critical shortage of trained personnel in important military operational specialties, shortages that seem to be unknown in the Soviet Army. When examined as a percentage of required battle strength, these shortages are enormous. For example, the reserves are 17 percent short of infantry troops, 43 percent short of combat engineers, 52 percent short of field artillerymen, 59 percent short of air defense artillerymen, 20 percent short of medical personnel, 35 percent short of communications specialists, 20 percent short of armored personnel, and 27 percent and 30 percent short, respectively, of supply and transportation personnel.[40] Thus, even within those few units that exist, most cannot be relied upon to perform adequately because of critical area shortages. The army's reserve forces are only a hollow shell of what they would have to be to fullfil their role under the total force concept.

Reserve forces are useless unless they can deploy to the battle area. If one examines the readiness of what the army calls "early deployers," units that are expected to be immediately available for deployment, it is clear that many cannot perform their missions. Fully 29 percent, or almost a third of the units designated as early deploying units, are not ready to deploy. Only 21 percent are regarded as "fully ready," 26 percent as "substantially ready" and 24 percent as "marginally ready."[41] If the affiliated units which would be required to deploy with the early deploying units are examined, 88 percent of these units are either "marginally ready" or "not ready" at all to deploy; only 2 percent were designated as "ready to deploy."[42] From almost any perspective, then, American Army Reserve forces in being are inadequate not only in size, but also in training, qualified manpower, and ability to deploy.

In contrast to the Soviet Army which can double its available forces within a matter of days, the American Army has a low capability to realistically augment its standing forces. It is estimated that it would take the Selective Service about seven months or 200 days to register, draft, train, and ship the first new recruit once war had begun.[43] Even if Selective Service were to perform very well, the fact remains that the Army Reserve mobilization system is ill equipped to deliver troops and materiel to the frontlines in anything approaching an adequate amount of time.

Experience

Since the end of World War II, Soviet ground forces have not seen any significant action against a formidable enemy. Soviet ground forces have been used several times to suppress unrest in the satellites, most recently in the 1968 invasion of Czechoslovakia. In all instances where these troops have been used, they have been used effectively and in mass and have demonstrated a capability for rapid deployment. Only in Afghanistan have large numbers of Soviet troops been committed against an even moderately tenacious enemy, and the available data again demonstrate their ability to mobilize, deploy, and sustain reserve forces for sufficient periods.

In contrast, the American Army has had considerable combat experience since World War II, first in Korea and then in Vietnam. It has also seen short-term service in the Dominican Republic and in the small and ill-fated operations in North Vietnam, Cambodia, and Iran. On balance, the performance of American troops during and since Vietnam leaves much to be desired. The Vietnam War saw the army shaken from within as its units showed lack of cohesion and poor performance. Problems such as high rates of desertion, AWOL, combat refusal, mutiny, drug use, and even the assassination of officers have been documented far too often to be taken lightly.[44] Equally to the point is the fact that many of the problems that brought about the army's poor performance in Vietnam appear systemic to the army's organizational structure and may still lurk within it. Important, too, is the fact that the AVF itself has in many ways hampered the army's ability to deal with these problems and has even added to them. With regard to its combat commanders, although the army spent ten years in Vietnam, it probably is no better off in terms of NCO or officer quality. Although many officers saw service in Vietnam, most were demobilized in 1972 and 1973. In these years, approximately 70,000 combat-trained officers, mostly captains, lieutenants, and warrant officers, were involuntarily demobilized from active service. The generation of leaders that would have comprised today's senior colonels and battalion commanders was largely lost through the process of demobilization and reduction in force.

On balance, the combat abilities of the Soviet Army are obscured by the lack of significant combat experience, and the ability of the American Army to fight well is in doubt as a consequence of its severe manpower and equipment shortages as well as poor reserve and mobilization capability.

While it is important to understand the organizational structure in which the Soviet and American soldier must fit, the fact remains that armies win or lose wars largely on the strength of the quality of their soldiers. The basic question at issue is, to what extent can the American and Soviet soldier adequately perform the tasks assigned to them with the equipment they have available to them? It may be said that all combat is small combat, all war is small war. The multiplicity

of forces arrayed against the soldier only makes sense in terms of his own narrow
horizon, and much of that horizon exists only in his mind. Thus, the attitudes
and values—the pictures—which exist in the mind of the Soviet and American
soldier are all important to his ability to perform under the stress of modern
combat. While the organization and equipment that the soldier have at his disposal
are important, in the end it is the individual soldier who will stand or fall. It is
to the nature and quality of the Soviet and American soldier that this analysis
now turns.

Notes

1. Richard Gabriel, *The New Red Legions: An Attitudinal Portrait of the Soviet Soldier*
(Westport, Conn.: Greenwood Press, 1980), p. 121.

2. Ibid., pp. 31-34.

3. William E. Odom, "The Militarization of Soviet Society," *Problems of Communism* (September 1976), pp. 34-51.

4. For an excellent history overview of conscription and military service in the United
States, see Robert L. Goldrich, "Historical Continuity in the U.S. Military Reserve
System," *Armed Forces and Society* 7 (Fall 1980): 88-112. Also by Goldrich, see
"America and the Draft," unpublished paper, May 6, 1980.

5. Ibid., p. 103.

6. Much of the domestic opposition to the draft during the Vietnam War was predicated on precisely this argument, namely, that the executive was abusing his powers
and part of that abuse was conscription of the unwilling.

7. Gabriel, *The New Red Legions*, p. 34.

8. John M. Collins, *The US-Soviet Military Balance, 1960-1980* (New York: McGraw-
Hill, 1980), p. 89.

9. Richard A. Gabriel, "The Reasons for the Soviet Arms Build-up," paper presented
before Massachusetts Chapter of the National Military Intelligence Association, Fort
Devens, Massachusetts, on November 8, 1980.

10. Ibid.

11. Louis Sorley, "Turbulence at the Top: Our Peripatetic Generals," *Army* (March
1981): 17.

12. Collins, *The US-Soviet Military Balance*, pp. 90-91.

13. Ibid., Table 12, pp. 470-71.

14. Ibid.

15. Ibid.

16. Ibid.

17. Ibid.

18. Ibid.

19. Ibid.

20. Ibid.

21. Ibid.

22. Ibid.

23. Lieutenant-Colonel William P. Baxter, "A Formidable Anti-Aircraft Defense,"
Army (December 1980): 31-33.

24. See *Soviet Military Operations* (U.S. Department of the Army: Army Intelligence

and Security Command, April 1978 (entire work) and "The Soviet Threat" (no author, special issue), *Army Reserve Magazine* (Spring 1980).

25. See Army manual FM-100-5, "Operations," Washington, D.C.: U.S. Department of the Army, July 1, 1979, p. 1-1.

26. For an interesting overview of Soviet logistical operations, see Lieutenant-Colonel William P. Baxter, "Logistics with a Difference," *Army* (November 1980): 30-32.

27. Collins, *The US-Soviet Military Balance*, p. 94.

28. Ibid., pp. 89-91; see also Annex A, Graph 1, Table 4.

29. Harriet F. Scott and William F. Scott, *The Armed Forces of the USSR* (Boulder, Colo.: Westview Press, 1979), p. 236.

30. Gabriel, "The Reasons for the Soviet Arms Build-up," p. 3

31. For a discussion of the total force concept under the AVF, see Report of the Comptroller General to the Congress, entitled "Critical Manpower Problems Restrict the Use of National Guard and Reserve Forces" (July 11, 1979), pp. 1-22.

32. "An Overview of the Manpower Effectiveness of the All-Volunteer Force," Report by the Comptroller General (April 14, 1980), p. 3.

33. The estimates vary somewhat. See "Status of the Individual Ready Reserve," News Release, Washington, D.C. Office of the Assistant Secretary of Defense (Public Affairs), January 30, 1980, p. 3. Also see GAO Report of July 11, 1979, dealing with manpower problems in the reserve forces cited earlier and the GAO Report of April 14, 1980, dealing with the AVF manning problems, also cited earlier.

34. GAO Report of July 11, 1979, "Critical Manpower Problems Restrict the Use of National Guard and Reserve Forces," Washington, D.C., p. 4.

35. Ibid.

36. Ibid.

37. Ibid., p. 56.

38. Ibid., p. 24.

39. Ibid., pp. 48-58.

40. Ibid., p. 50.

41. Ibid. p. 58.

42. Ibid.

43. Collins, *The US-Soviet Military Balance*, p. 93.

44. See Richard A. Gabriel and Paul L. Savage, *Crisis in Command: Mismanagement in the Army* (New York: Hill and Wang, 1978).

2

The Soldiers

In any study of armies, the tendency is to assume that all soldiers are pretty much alike. This assumption has not served us well, for it has often prevented a focus upon the very substantial differences among soldiers in different armies that might affect the way an army is able to perform. The American Army has always tended to compare the American soldier with his Soviet counterpart in precisely the terms in which American society is often compared to Soviet society. It has been argued, for example, that the American soldier shows a greater degree of initiative than the Soviet soldier, or that he comes from a better social background, or that he has a greater stake in the political system, or that he enjoys a higher standard of living. This type of analysis has often led to the assumption that certain ''social types'' will fight better than others. But to assume that differences among soldiers basically reflect the societies in which they live is only partially correct. This type of macro-analysis tends to obscure a more pointed focus on the differences among soldiers that flow from the roles they must play within their respective military organizations and the degree to which these differences relate to the soldier's ability to carry out his mission.

The American Soldier

Immediately following the end of the Vietnam War, the United States abandoned conscription and returned to its traditional way of raising an army, the all volunteer force. Even the designers of the AVF knew that it would be impossible to generate a standing force of 1.2 million men by pure voluntarism; accordingly, American ground forces were reduced to slightly under 800,000.[1] The argument for reinstating a volunteer force had nothing to do with military requirements. What really propelled the institution of the AVF was political pressure emanating from the politically powerful middle class of American society. This social segment no longer wanted to risk their sons being drafted to fight on some foreign battlefield, and the United States returned to voluntarism as a way of quieting them.

The AVF concept, based as it was upon econometric models, proposed to offer large pay raises and increased benefits to attract sufficient manpower to the military. The Gates Commission, which recommended the establishment of the AVF, based its recommendation on several assumptions. It assumed that (1) there would be an adequate manpower pool upon which to draw; (2) the quality of manpower would be sufficient to learn and retain reasonable military skill proficiency; (3) attrition rates for those enlisting in the AVF would be smaller than for the draft army; and (4) the retention rate of those already in military service would remain stable or increase. If all of these assumptions held, there would be no need to resort to conscription in order to sustain an army of about 800,000. The commission did not consider whether such an army was sufficiently large to meet projected defense requirements.

Representativeness

The AVF was established as a reaction to the perceived discrimination of the draft during the Vietnam War. It was frequently pointed out that those who were conscripted for service in Vietnam were essentially the poor, the nonwhite, the uneducated, or the cumulatively disadvantaged of American society. In point of fact, the data dealing with the draft during Vietnam reveal that under conscription, as biased as the system was, almost all racial, religious, ethnic, and socioeconomic groups saw military service in approximate proportion to their strength in the society as a whole, with the single exception of those were were white and had three years of college or more.[2] Although the draft exempted a substantial number of the white college-educated middle class, by and large selection by draft was relatively equitable during the Vietnam War. Nonetheless, the popular perception at the time was that the draft was excessively discriminatory towards the poor. In an effort to quiet the campuses (whose students, paradoxically, were largely draft exempt by 1969), President Richard M. Nixon returned to an all volunteer force on the grounds that such a force would be more closely representative of American society and more equitable in levying the burden of military service.

The AVF turned out to be the opposite from that was intended. Since 1973 the American soldier has become less representative of mainstream America than he was under the draft. Indeed, the AVF may constitute the most discriminatory social institution in the United States since slavery.[3] At least 36 percent of the soldiers in the army are black, and if Pentagon projections hold, by 1985 over 50 percent of the enlisted strength of the army will be black.[4] Blacks are over-represented in the armed forces by a number three times as large as their proportion of the population at large. Some combat units have an even higher number of blacks, in some instances exceeding 50 percent. While blacks comprise three times their fair share of soldiers in the enlisted ranks, they comprise only slightly more than half (7.3 percent) of their share of officers and slightly more than one-third (5.9 percent) of their statistical share of warrant officer ranks.[5]

While reliable data about the percentage of other minorities serving in the AVF are hard to come by, at least one prominent sociologist, Charles Moskos, has suggested that over 40 percent of the army is being drawn from minority groups.[6] From the perspective of racial and ethnic minority representation, the AVF draws disproportionately from lower status black and minority groups to fill its ranks. If the army were to go to battle, these groups could be expected to suffer a greater number of deaths than they would suffer under a reasonably equitable draft.

The AVF is an army of America's poor, its minorities, and its educationally disadvantaged. It is comprised largely of those who are unable to function successfully within a society whose economy is increasingly complex and requires sophisticated skills. Unable to make their way in this economy, many seek the last available outlet: they enlist in military service. There is no doubt that America's army is demographically unrepresentative of American society. Viewed in this light, the AVF is not really a volunteer army at all. A form of conscription is already operating; it is conscription by poverty, by lack of opportunity, by disadvantage, and by race. Its great advantage is precisely that it exempts those of the middle and upper classes and takes those who are socially and economically marginal into military service.[7]

Mental Ability

It might be suspected that because the army draws disproportionately from the lower strata of American society that the quality of raw recruit material might be somewhat lower than what we would find under a draft. With conscription, the law of large numbers would operate, and the military could be expected to draw fairly evenly from all intelligence levels. The average recruit in the AVF is truly representative of the lower strata of society and tends to have definable intellectual and behavioral shortcomings which present great difficulties in transforming him into a good soldier.

One of the most obvious difficulties is a clear decrease in the mental skill levels which recruits bring to military service. This decrease can be examined through several indicators. The most important is the number of high school graduates attracted to military service. According to the army's own studies, the possession of a high school diploma is one of the key predictors of whether a soldier is likely to successfully complete his tour of duty and perform his job adequately. The soldier with a high school certificate is unlikely to have as many adjustment and disciplinary problems as the soldier without the degree.[8] The available evidence demonstrates that the number of high school graduates in the army is falling disproportionately below that of the population at large. At a time when over 83 percent of American youth obtain a high school degree, only slightly more than 42 percent of the army's soldiers have obtained this degree legitimately.[9] Even this figure may be inflated by increasing numbers of women, almost all of whom have a degree upon entering the military. Moreover, the data are somewhat distorted by the large number of black soldiers who, on the average, tend to have higher educational achievement levels than white soldiers, the only area in American society in which blacks surpass whites in status.[10]

Beginning in 1976 and ending in 1980, the army has attracted ever-declining numbers of high school graduates. The figures went from 105,543 in 1976 to 85,825 in 1980, and the trend continues downward.[11]

The demographic imbalance of the AVF is reflected in another figure: the number of soldiers with some college education. In 1973, 10.9 percent of the army's enlisted force had some college experience. This figure was slightly greater than the number of soldiers who were allowed by law to fall into Category 4, the army's lowest mental skill-level category. By 1980, the number of soldiers with some college education had dropped to 8.9 percent, while the number of college graduates had fallen from 3.0 percent to 1.9 percent.[12] Under the AVF, all three indicators of educational achievement of its recruits have declined steadily as those with the educational skills to function in the economy systematically avoid volunteering for military service.

A better indication of the low quality among raw recruits under the AVF is found in the army's own qualification tests. These tests, the Armed Forces Qualification Tests (AFQTs), measure math and verbal skills. During the Vietnam era when a draft was operating, less than 10 percent of the troops in the army fell into Category 3B or below. Category 3B is reserved for anyone who scored 31 percent of a possible 100 on the test, and Category 4 is for those who scored less than 20 percent. In 1980, the number of soldiers in Category 3B or below was at least 59 percent.[13] Moreover, there is evidence that the army may have "misnormed" these scores to its own advantage. Until 1980, the Pentagon commonly cited the figure of 9 percent as the number of soldiers falling into Category 4. In that year, Secretary of the Army Clifford Alexander ordered a comparison of AFQT scores under the AVF with those from World War II, Korea, and Vietnam. The analysis showed that the scores were "misnormed," that is, they had been misinterpreted against their original data base. When the AFQT scores for the army were corrected, an official report noted that the number of Category 4 soldiers had risen from 9 percent to fully 46 percent! Moreover, the corrected scores showed that 37 percent of the soldiers also fell into Category 3.[14] By the army's own estimate, then, the number of soldiers in Category 3B or below was off by as much as 500 percent. The new data demonstrate that 83 percent of the soldiers in the army in 1980 were Category 3B or below. This fact suggests that the quality of raw recruit material is far below what we would expect to find through the use of conscription. Further examination of the data shows that in the 1964 draft army 35 percent of the soldiers ranked above the sixty-fifth percentile in intelligence tests, whereas in 1979, the figure fell to 84 percent *below*.[15] Because it draws from the lower strata of American society the AVF has succeeded in attracting to it mostly the economically and educationally marginal members of the society. This marginality is reflected in performance on general intelligence tests. Moreover, the ability of these recruits to learn military skills is also in doubt.

The decline in educational and intelligence levels is also evident when reading skills are examined. In 1973, the average American soldier read at the eleventh grade level, or about the equivalent of a high school graduate. In 1981, the average reading level had dropped to the fifth grade level, or about one grade level for each year since the AVF was established.[16] This decline has forced the army to undertake prodigious efforts to rewrite many of its training and instructional manuals for less literate troops and on many posts to establish remedial reading programs. Moreover, the need to read and comprehend becomes crucial if soldiers are to be able to understand, operate, maintain, and repair increasingly sophisticated weapons. In addition, the soldier's ability to understand his environment, the regulations that govern him, and his mission depends upon his ability to read and expose himself to information.

Attrition

Because many soldiers cannot adapt to military life and are unable to acquire the skills required for successful military performance, a substantial number of first-term soldiers never finish their tour of service. In 1980, 37 percent of enlistees failed to complete their first tour of service.[17] The rate of attrition approaches four soldiers in every ten, a rate that has increased the already high levels of "personnel turbulence" found in most army units. This high attrition rate has also reduced military strength. Since the establishment of the AVF, the army has fallen short of its required strength by 10,000 to 20,000 recruits. However, Pentagon officials acknowledge that as the recession of 1982-1983 takes hold, the AVF will be able to meet its manpower goals as more and more recruits turn to the military as a way of finding a job. In addition, the quality of recruit can also be expected to rise in response to the same forces. Nonetheless, such solutions to the manpower problem are likely to disappear rapidly once economic recovery begins. Total strength, moreover, includes almost 65,000 women who are not expected to serve in combat. The low quality of recruit material drawn from the lower strata of society is apparently making it difficult for other soldiers to adjust to military life and even to acquire the skills necessary to sustain them in battle.[18]

Perhaps the most disturbing aspect of the attrition picture is that most losses are coming from combat arms units. The highest rate of attrition is found in infantry units, where 13 percent of the army's total attrition occurs. Another 7 percent comes from artillery units.[19] Attrition is plaguing the army at its most vulnerable point: it is attacking the strength of its vital combat power.

Attrition often occurs for what the army calls "adverse reasons." Many of the social habits, values, and behavior patterns found among those in society's lower strata are similar to those in a true poverty culture. Accordingly, these strata are often resentful of authority, unskilled, ill disciplined, and even drug-ridden. With so many recruits drawn from these strata, the army tends to statistically recreate within its enlisted ranks and barracks life many of the habits of the street culture. It becomes almost impossible to retain large numbers of these soldiers because of their severe adjustment problems. An examination of the reasons associated with attrition shows that the most common reason for attrition is inability to perform adequately.

Of those soldiers who left the army by attrition in 1978, 17 percent were permitted to leave under training discharge programs and another 25 percent under the expeditious discharge program.[20] Both programs are bureaucratic euphemisms concealing the fact that a large number of soldiers cannot perform at even the lowered military standards of the all volunteer army. Thus, 42 percent of all those who left, or four in every ten soldiers, did so largely because of marginal performance. Another 7 percent were found to be unqualified for active service for mental, moral or physical reasons—this in 1978 before the army discovered its intelligence test scores were misnormed—and another 15 percent were discharged for "the good of the service," usually a cover term for some disciplinary offense. Another 7 percent were discharged for drug abuse, a figure below the actual drug-use rate, and 4 percent were discharged because of hardship.[21]

The attrition rate is closely related to the low quality of recruit and his inability to learn military skills or adjust to military life. This implies that the American soldier is likely to be alienated not only from military life per se but also from the very society that produced him.[22]

Another consequence of the low-quality army is that military jobs which require a certain amount of mental ability to master are going unfilled at critical levels. The areas in which shortages appear seem to be directly related to the mental ability to perform them successfully. Furthermore, because the attrition rate and rate of assignment turnover are so high, shortages in critical military operational specialties (MOS) have been further exacerbated. The combination of high mental skill requirements, high attrition rates, and high rates of assignment turnover has created severe shortages in important military job areas.

These shortages show up in the following areas. In 1979, the army was 51 percent short of its authorized radio operators, 95 percent short of its heavy anti-armor weapons crewmen, 44 percent short of its cavalry scouts, and 29 percent short of its authorized armor crewmen for its M-60 tanks.[23] Even in the essential combat arms units, shortages are evident. If one examines the more highly skilled areas of specialist operations, the number of critical MOS shortages increases. For example, the army is 73 percent short of the chemical operations specialists it needs to go into battle, 66 percent short of medical specialists, 70 percent short of operating room specialists, 84 percent short of clinical specialists, and 63 percent short of its authorized electronic warfare specialists.[24] The high mental requirements in the increasingly technological areas of military operations have resulted in grave shortages in the army's combat and combat-support structure. The paradox is that at precisely the time when the U.S. military structure is attempting to modernize its forces and is making major investments in new sophisticated weaponry, the soldier's overall mental ability to handle these weapons is declining relative to the intelligence levels of the larger society.

By the simple literacy standard, the American Army falls short. Far too many

of its recruits belong to Category 3B or 4. Their reading comprehension levels
have fallen to about the fifth grade, which is lower than the standard used by
the United Nations to define illiteracy. The number of high school graduates
attracted to military service has declined substantially in the last seven years.
Taken together, the facts suggest that the soldier produced by the AVF is unqualified and ill prepared to use the military's complex weapons and high technology. If the present decline in mental quality continues and the ''scissors''
effect is exacerbated further by continually rising technological requirements for
high mental skills, the result will be an inability to field effective battle units.

Military Life

Life for the modern soldier under the AVF is dramatically different from that
of the American soldier in World War II, Korea, and Vietnam. The change has
to do with the transition away from conscription. The AVF is based firmly in
econometric models wherein military service is seen as the equivalent of any
other occupation in civilian society. The military is forced to compete with other
civilian enterprises in order to attract adequate manpower. Thus, the soldier's
''working conditions'' had to be changed radically in order to compete. Traditional emphasis on service to country, sacrifice, and citizen duty has been replaced
by economic attractions. The econometric approach has forced the army to
restructure itself along the lines of the business model.

One of the major changes is the increase in pay and benefits provided the
average soldier. In 1983, an army recruit received $6,612 a year compared with
the average civilian per capita salary of $9,489. In contrast, the Soviet recruit
earns about 3 rubles a month and the average civilian worker 180 rubles a month.
In order for the army to compete with business on economic grounds, it had to
move away from the subsistence pay normally accorded conscripts. A raise in
pay and benefits was thought necessary if a truly professional force was to be
created. The pay raises were ''front loaded,'' however, so that major pay increases came not in the senior or middle NCO ranks as much as in the initial
entry ranks. Ranks E-1 through E-4 were the primary beneficiaries of increased
pay. This approach created severe morale problems in the NCO corps. Traditionally, the NCO measured his standard of living not against the larger society
outside the military but against those with whom he served, mainly soldiers of
lower rank and less service experience. By this measure, the NCO's standard
of living has dropped considerably, while that of his subordinates has risen
dramatically. The policy of increased pay and benefits has been less than a
success for the NCO corps.[25]

The better pay was accompanied by changes in ''working conditions.'' Enlisted soldiers are now allowed to live in private apartments off the military post,
a condition that has given rise to the ''nine-to-five syndrome.'' Over 40 percent
of enlisted soldiers do not reside on the military posts to which they are assigned.
Although they report for ''work'' every morning, they live in private quarters
off base and away from the controlling arm of the military. Off-post living was

made possible by increased salaries and the deliberate policy, begun in the 1960s, of refusing to construct adequate numbers of military quarters. Instead, it was decided to stimulate local economies near military posts by subsidizing the construction of housing units that could then be rented to soldiers. In any case, off-post living represents a major change in the military environment. The soldier is no longer confined to his barracks and company area every night where once he was subject to the constant discipline and ambience of military life. Instead, the soldier reports to work at 7:30 in the morning and is gone by 4:30. While on the military post he is subject to military discipline, but when he leaves at the end of the working day he is literally beyond its control. As a consequence, the American soldier has much better working conditions but is continually exposed to civilian values and habits which, in many cases, may be corrosive of the good habits and discipline required by an effective military force.

The "nine-to-five" syndrome is characteristic of most civilian enterprises. It implies that one's loyalty to one's occupation or, in this case, to the army is predicated upon one's expertise and economic function. No one truly expects working for a civilian corporation to be a "way of life" or a vocation; it is merely a job, and in return for performance one receives pay. This business psychology has deliberately penetrated the American Army.

The "nine-to-five syndrome" separates soldiers from one another, removes them from consistent discipline, severs the link between citizenship and military service, substituting for it mere economics, and breaks down unit identity and cohesion. Thus, the syndrome hinders the creation of any kind of larger loyalties to the military or even to one's unit. It replaces such loyalties with pay and other economic considerations that cannot sustain cohesion.

The new military life-style has helped dismantle major institutional structures that have traditionally helped build strong bonds among men and units. One institutional change, off-post living arrangements as opposed to barracks living, especially hinders cohesion. Barracks life continually demonstrates to the soldier that he and his comrades are all in the same boat. In reinforces a crude social equality among soldiers from divergent backgrounds; it subordinates all personal experiences and qualifications to the singular common denominator of being a soldier; and it forces individuals to understand that those who live together are crucially dependent on one another for both pleasures and punishments received at the hands of military authorities.[26] As the Soviets have proven, barracks living is an important social institution in building unit cohesion.[27] In contrast, once the American recruit leaves his basic training, there is no true barracks life left in the army.

Today, American soldiers are assigned to two-and three-man private apartments. They may decorate and arrange these rooms in any manner they choose, and, on some military posts, after certain hours not even military authorities may enter without permission or a warrant. Aside from its effect on common bonding, official studies show that apartment living is one of the strongest institutional supports for drug use. The ground breaking study by Dr. Larry

Ingraham of the U.S. Army Medical Center at Walter Reed, *The Boys in the Barracks*, demonstrates that private rooms provide the privacy necessary for drug use to be sustained and to spread.[28] According to Ingraham, three-man apartments are particularly dangerous, for often two occupants are drug users; the third man must often choose between refusing to participate or risking isolation from his roommates. This kind of focused peer pressure often results in drug use.[29] Finally, the soldier's isolation from the mainstream of military life and from his unit is itself a factor in drug use, a problem that is addressed later.

Another major change in the army has been the elimination of most group formations and inspections, which were once constant features of the army. The purpose of group formations and inspections is not harassment; rather, they are mechanisms for testing whether troops can perform certain functions adequately, and, more importantly, for submerging the soldier into the collectivity of the unit and instilling a sense of cohesion and pride. Formations required all soldiers to be present in order to bear witness to their collegiality and their requirement to observe the same rules. So it is with inspections, especially when company or unit punishment follows failures. In other armies, individuals who fail to integrate well into the unit are marked by their comrades for informal punishments, additional help, or even "talking sessions" to increase their performance. The dismantling of military formations and inspections has been yet another blow to effective military discipline, unit cohesion, and battle performance.

The dismantling of traditional institutions has helped weaken disciplinary standards. With the decline of barracks life, only the rare NCO lives in the barracks, nor do many unmarried officers live on post. At the end of the day, military posts are greatly depopulated, including the NCOs and officers who have traditionally maintained order and discipline in the units. As a result, crime on military posts, once the safest places in the country, has risen greatly.[30] There are no officers and NCOs left to ensure that the troops behave correctly once the sun goes down.

Changes in military life-style have therefore, affected the way in which individual soldiers live. The average first-term soldier has far more money than he is used to, he is now allowed to live off-post, he is normally not required to attend formations or early morning inspections, and he no longer lives in the barracks with his comrades but lives in his own room with one or two roommates where he is free from control and discipline by officers and NCOs. These changes have transformed the soldier into an employee, and he is beginning to show many of the same problems of the civilian employee.

An important problem for the American soldier which is addressed in detail later is the degree of alienation he demonstrates.[31] Instead of structuring military life around ways to increase peer identification, unit cohesion, and group discipline, many of the army's reforms under the AVF have done just the opposite. American units are now full of soldiers who are strangers to one another, who do not care for their comrades, or who are not willing to depend on them. Whether such units can display the required cohesion to sustain themselves in battle is unlikely, for an army that cannot sustain unit identification and cohesion in peacetime is not likely to be able to magically build such bonds during war. When such units are placed under high combat stress, they will likely fragment. Such was the experience of some American units in Vietnam which were comprised of strangers rather than comrades.[32]

Another major change in military life-style is the proportion of enlisted men who are married. With increased salaries and advertisements selling the military as a stable career, the number of young soldiers who marry has increased dramatically. The trend for young soldiers to marry runs contrary to the trend toward later marriages evident in the society at large.[33] Between 1965 and 1976, the proportion of married enlisted men increased from 36.4 percent to 56.9 percent.[34] The increase came almost entirely among junior, first-term soldiers. Under the draft, about one-quarter of junior enlisted soldiers were married; today that number exceeds 34 percent. Few first-term soldiers were married under the draft simply because pay levels were too low to support a wife. Among soldiers today, almost one in three is married during his first tour of service.[35]

Married soldiers find that their pay is still inadequate in most instances to support a wife and child. The large majority of married first-term soldiers are under twenty-two years old. Many of the difficulties which young marrieds experience are exacerbated by the military life-style, low salaries, separations due to military duty, and even general poverty.[36] The number of soldiers reporting recent marital and family problems *that are service related* has been steadily rising since 1976 when it went from 50 percent to 60 percent.[37] Among first-term soldiers, the increase has been even more significant, from 35 percent to 45 percent.[38] Married soldiers create all sorts of problems for the military, ranging from discipline to refusal to leave their families to attend exercises. The increased number of married soldiers has changed the composition of the enlisted ranks and has created a range of new problems. In one official study, Human Readiness Report No. 5, family problems were listed as the third most important of thirteen problems identified by unit officers and commanders as affecting their troops. Among officers in troop units, 83.4 percent reported that family problems were among the major problems affecting their troops.[39]

The married soldier's frequently poor living conditions merits greater attention here. While single soldiers have adequate financial means, the married soldier is usually forced to live in more expensive off-post, rented housing which is often exploitative in cost and substandard in condition. Because of the general cost of living, inflation, and the fact that when a soldier is posted to a foreign station his wife is often not "command sponsored" and, therefore, not entitled to additional benefits, soldiers find themselves living in conditions that resemble urban ghettos. Indeed, a substantial number of married American soldiers in the United States receive welfare payments or food stamps.[40] Lieutenant-General Julius W. Becton, Jr., commanding general of the 7th Corps in Germany, has discussed conditions for some married soldiers:

I'm just wondering whether the American public fully appreciates the conditions under which some of our soldiers are living. I've seen a lot of ghettos in my life—Philadelphia, Washington, New York, and Baltimore—but some of the ghettos we have here for our people to live in are just as bad as some of the worst you'll find in some American cities.[41]

The married American soldier is unable to provide for his family in a manner even moderately comparable to the rest of society. Those who joined the AVF to escape the problems of the larger society and to obtain better jobs and living standards certainly have been sorely disappointed.

What has been the overall effect of restructuring the army from a draft to an all volunteer force? What have been the results of trying to "sell" the notion of military service on economic grounds rather than as a duty of citizenship? What are the effects of the lowered quality of recruit as well as the changes in military life-style? The army's own studies indicate that all three changes have lowered his morale, reduced his motivation, and increased his general alienation from the military. The data show that the ranks are comprised of soldiers with low motivation, who do not bond well with their peers, and who are alienated from both society and the military. Under these conditions, the ability of units to withstand battle stress is open to serious doubt. Human Readiness Study No. 5, an armywide study of 3,000 officers and men, found that 84.4 percent of officers in troop units identified low troop motivation as the most serious problem for their units. Similarly, 74.4 percent of troop unit commanders thought that motivation was a major problem, as did 59.1 percent of all officers surveyed armywide.[42]

Consistent with these views are the perceptions that the soldier has low ability. Among the officers who commanded units, 74.4 percent thought that low-ability personnel was a major problem with which they had to deal "in the past six months."[43] Officers in TO&E (Table of Organization and Equipment units, which are usually combat and combat-support units) units shared this view; 83.3 percent of them felt that low ability was a major problem.[44] Even commanders of combat arms units thought that the ability of their men was a problem; 86.5 percent of them said that low ability was a major problem.[45] Armywide, 70.4 percent of all officers surveyed identified the problem of low soldier ability as a major problem with which they had to deal.[46] Low ability was the second most frequently mentioned problem seen afflicting troops in the Human Readiness Study.

One difficulty of the American soldier is his apparent inability to take pride in his unit or the army. When asked, "are soldiers in your unit proud to be members of your unit," only 36.2 percent of first-term soldiers responded positively.[47] Among enlisted men armywide, only 37.9 percent agreed.[48] This failure to identify with one's unit is significant inasmuch as strong indentification represents the successful development of cohesion; without these bonds, units cannot be expected to perform well in battle. The fact that American soldiers do not seem to identify with their units positively suggests that the army is having only marginal success in integrating its soldiers into military life.

American soldiers also reflect fairly high levels of alienation from society as well as from the military.[49] In an original study done in 1979, Major Stephen Westbrook interviewed 425 soldiers in the grades of sergeant through private who were assigned to eight infantry companies, one armored battalion, one mechanized infantry company, and two airmobile battalions stationed in the United States. His sample, though small, is generally representative of soldiers serving in combat arms units. He concludes that junior enlisted men in particular "are evidencing extremely high levels of alienation directed toward society and life in general."[50]

Alienation is a condition of estrangement or separation that includes cynicism, mistrust, and lack of confidence; isolation, a condition in which the values held by the individual differ from those held by the rest of society; and meaninglessness, a condition in which the individual lacks clear goals.[51] The causes of alienation are systemic and tend to be found among lower status groups. Alienation affects the abilities of soldiers to identify with their comrades and units and even with the society for which they may be asked to suffer the ultimate sacrifice. Westbrook's study, the first of its kind, found that 86 percent of the soldiers surveyed believed that "most people will take advantage of me if given the chance." Another 61 percent said that there were "few dependable people," while another 11 percent were unsure. Sixty-nine percent felt that most people "are not concerned about others," and another 16 percent were uncertain; 51 percent thought that "most people cannot be trusted." In examining isolation, Westbrook found that a significant portion of the sample lacks belief in such critical areas as due process of law and promotion based on merit. He notes that 47 percent of the soldiers believed "a person generally does not receive fair treatment under the law," while 54 percent thought that "luck and who you know" mattered more in getting ahead than merit and hard work. Twenty-eight percent believed a person "must do what is best for himself even at the expense of others." Similarly, a substantial number of soldiers evidenced attitudes of meaninglessness toward society and life in general. Thirty-four percent believed that "there are no right or wrong ways to make money, only easy and hard ways," and 54 percent thought that "ideas change so fast that there is nothing to depend on." Thirty-three percent believed that "there are no rules to live by and everything is relative," and 51 percent that "the government is not concerned with people like me."[52]

A very large number of these soldiers are also alienated from the military establishment in which they serve. For example, 43 percent of those surveyed did not think they were accomplishing anything as soldiers, while another 9 percent were unsure. A very disturbing statistic was the 44 percent who did not believe their units "would make every effort to reach them if they were cut off in battle"; another 31 percent were uncertain if they would try.[53] The soldier's general alienation cannot be separated from that which he feels toward military life. Westbrook's study is unclear as to whether the soldier brings his alienation into the military or whether he acquires it while in service. Since alienation tends to be found most commonly among the lower social strata, the fact that the AVF draws disproportionately from that segment of the population suggests that some degree of alienation is evident in the soldier prior to his military service. On the other hand, his interactions as a soldier are likely to be conditioned by those perceptions, and over a period of time, his military experience would lead him to become alienated from the military.

The problem is more immediate from the military perspective than from the sociological one. The problem is not to discern if the soldier brings his feelings of alienation with him, for if the AVF continues to draw disproportionately from the lower social strata the army can do little about it. Nor, indeed, is the problem to discern if the soldier is being alienated from the military per se. A number of practices are necessary to the military that may alienate any number of civilians. The real problem from the military's point of view is how is it possible for officers and NCOs to mold alienated soldiers into effective combat units? There is no doubt that social alienation has a major negative effect on general military efficiency. As Westbrook observes, "any army that possesses large numbers of alienated soldiers is susceptible to total distintegration in the event of war."[54] Westbrook has uncovered a major problem among the enlisted corps of the American Army: their tendency toward alienation and their inability to forge strong bonds with their fellow soldiers so that the military experience can produce cohesive battle units. The ability of such "associations of strangers" to perform well in the battlefield is very much in doubt. The performance of American soldiers in Vietnam is replete with instances of desertions, failures to engage, mutinies, and even assassinations of officers—all of which suggests that whenever men in groups cease to think of themselves as part of the larger group, the ability of combat units to perform declines.[55] That these conditions pertain to many American soldiers in the AVF is beyond dispute.

Because of the overrepresentation of the lower strata, on the battlefield the deaths of America's poor and minorities would be far disproportionate to their number in the larger society. It is ironic that the AVF should have been adopted largely as a reaction to the perceived inequality of the draft, only to establish a far more discriminatory social institution—one that selects who will endure military service and who must ultimately bear the risk of death on the battlefield. The cure has proven worse than the disease.

The Soviet Soldier

As noted earlier, the Soviet Army relies almost exclusively upon conscription, the first conscription law in Russia having been promulgated in 1699 under Peter the Great.[56] The conscription system developed much as it did in the West, expanding to national conscription by 1860 and remaining intact through World War I. By 1920, as the Communist hold on the Russian state tightened, another conscriptiion law was introduced requiring terms of military service for all workers and peasants reaching the age of twenty-one. In 1925, Marshall Frunze, commissar of The Red Army, again reformed the conscription law to make terms of troop service more specific, and in 1927, the conscription law underwent yet another change. Until then, conscription had involved primarily the "Slavic races" of the Soviet Union. Other nationalities were either exempt or were used in territorial militia units on a volunteer basis. The new conscription law extended military service to all nationalities and for the first time fully integrated them into the Soviet armed forces.

The system introduced in 1927 remained unchanged throughout World War II. In 1947, the new Constitution of the Soviet Union was introduced, and conscription was enshrined in the Constitution itself. The document decreed that general military service be levied upon all males between the ages of nineteen and forty-nine years. After a tour of duty, the conscript was assigned to a reserve unit. This system remained in force until 1967 when the General Law of Universal Military Service was promulgated. This law required military service of all eighteen-year-old males. The conscription cycle operated on a semiannual basis, with two-year tours of duty mandatory. Upon completion of active service, soldiers were required to remain in reserve units until age fifty. While in these units, soldiers are subject to training and periodic call to active service as circumstances warrant.[57]

Training for the armed forces starts before the recruit begins active duty. The 1967 law also established a compulsory system of premilitary training for all men and women between the ages of sixteen and eighteen. This training is controlled by an organization directly under the Ministry of Defense called the Voluntary Society for Cooperation with the Army, Aviation and Navy, more commonly referred to by its Cyrillic initials, DOSAAF. DOSAAF designs, manages, and conducts all premilitary training, and is a system of military commissariats paralleling governmental jurisdictions from the republic level down through the *rayon*, a governmental unit equivalent to the urban ward.

Premilitary training begins at the high school level but is also provided to working youths in factories. It gives future soldiers the equivalent of basic training and has reduced the training time required for new recruits once they enter active service. The standard program provides about 140 hours of instruction in military organization, courtesy, regulations, civil defense, first aid, and firearms training. Typically, students spend about two hours of their work or school week studying topics related to the military. In addition, workers in factories attend three one-week long special training sessions. Along with classroom exercises, trainees participate in field exercises held at military camps, which last from five to fifteen days.

Besides premilitary training and basic skills, the DOSAAF system provides special training in a range of military skills such as glider pilots, motorboat and motor vehicle operations, radio repair, and marksmanship. Individuals trained through the DOSAAF program are screened for special aptitudes and skills, and are assigned to units that can utilize their particular talents. Finally, the DOSAAF system is responsible for conducting training in physical education and conditioning. Although attention is given to building military-related skills, the program improves the conscript's general physical condition so that each year fewer and fewer are rejected for military duty. We do not have sufficient data for comparative rates of rejection for physical reasons, but the rejection rate is probably far lower than that in Western armies.[58]

The Soviet Union has about 60 million males between the ages of seventeen and forty-nine, about 80 percent of whom are fit for military service. Each year approximately 2.5 million young men reach the age of military registration, that is, the year in which they turn seventeen. At the very least, three-quarters of them are inducted when they reach eighteen. Those who are not called immediately to active service may obtain deferments based on education, hardship, or personal reasons. If deferred, they are assigned to reserve units where they are required to participate in reserve drills, exercises, and training. If they are deferred beyond their twenty-seventh birthday, the last point at which they may be conscripted, they must remain assigned to reserve units and are subject to periodic training and even extended recall until age fifty. Very few succeed in escaping some form of military service, probably no more than 12 percent.[59]

Soviet authorities make strenuous efforts to emphasize service in the military as a universal condition of citizenship to be shared by all. The Soviet soldier knows why he must serve, and he has ample evidence that all social strata share the burden of conscription. The Soviet soldier is very representative of his society. Since the literacy rate, over 93 percent, and the general educational level of the population is fairly high, a universal conscription system statistically produces a relatively high-quality recruit. The Soviet soldier does not apparently suffer from the critical deficiencies in aptitude skills, verbal and math skills, and reading skills that plague the American soldier today.[60] The reason must be traceable to conscription. By drawing upon all segments of the society in rough proportion to their numbers in the general population, the conscription system ensures that a proportionate mix of aptitudes and skills will be be projected into the military.

The conscript system seems to work rather well insofar as it provides the military with a regular, sufficient supply of good-quality manpower. The two-year term of service is generally shorter than that found in other armies, and the massive size of the Soviet Army means that at least twice a year the personnel structure undergoes extreme turbulence as new soldiers move in and old soldiers depart.[61] As a consequence, the time and effort that would normally be used for training must be devoted to the integration of large numbers of conscripts into main force units, while simultaneously discharging large numbers of others. The problem is complicated by a very low retention rate for Soviet conscripts beyond their required tour of duty. Yet, the conscript system is able to marshal large manpower pools for use by the army.

What does the Soviet soldier think about conscription, and how does he view his military service? Family support of his military service is an important element in the mind of the Soviet soldier. Soldiers were asked, "How does your family feel about your going into the military?" Only 6.2 percent of the respondents felt that their family approved of their military service because it was "my duty," while 5.3 percent said their families thought military service "was a good thing." Less than 1 percent (0.9 percent) felt that their families "were proud that I was serving my country." These results do not suggest a particularly deep sense of familial support for conscription, despite the ideals of patriotic duty stressed by Soviet authorities. Exactly the reverse seems to be the case. Only 1.8 percent of the respondents indicated that their families "had no real feelings" about their military service, and 6.2 percent said their families were "generally not happy with my going into military service."[62] The most common feeling of the families of Russian soldiers is resignation: 76.1 percent of the soldiers indicated that their families were "resigned because military service could not be avoided."

The Soviet soldier was also asked about support for his military duty among his friends and peers. Specifically, "did your friends think that going into the military was a good thing, something to be proud of, or something that could not be avoided?" Only 4.4 percent of the respondents felt that it was a "good thing," while 5.3 percent indicated that their friends thought military service was "something to be proud of." The vast majority, 88.5 percent, said that their friends believed that military service was endured because "it was something that could not be avoided." In interview after interview, the soldiers suggested that the general view of conscription was that it was a hardship to be endured because it could not be avoided. The almost universal view of military service was that it was a waste of time. This is not to suggest that the Soviet soldier is dragged kicking and screaming to the draft commissariat. Clearly, however, the punishment for failing to register for or attempting to avoid the draft is very severe indeed. While conscripted military service does not have strong social support, it is not socially condemned. In general, the civilian populace treats the soldier relatively well because "by and large the people feel sorry for them; they can imagine their own sons and relatives who had to go into the Army."[63] Moreover, there is no lack of respect attached to military service, although career officers and NCOs are not held in high esteem.[64]

Why, then, does the Soviet soldier conform so readily? Certainly, the fear of punishment has some effect. The most probable reason, however, is that he has internalized a social requirement. Military service is seen as one more requirement in a society that has strict rules for everything. Any portrait of the Soviet soldier being shackled against his will on the verge of revolt is extremely inaccurate and, moreover, overlooks Russian history. On the other hand, the Soviet authorities' portrait of the soldier as highly motivated by the ideals of patriotism, duty, and service to country is also grossly inaccurate. The Soviet conscript most likely views military service much as do the youths in West Germany today or American youths during the draft years before the Vietnam War.

When conscripts are asked, "Do you think that you got anything good out of going into the military," only 27.4 percent said that they had; 69.4 percent responded they had not. These responses are consonant with those given to the question, "At the time you were in the military did you think it was a waste of time?" Most of the soldiers (83.2 percent) agreed that it was a waste of time;

only 14.2 percent thought they obtained something positive from it.[65] If both questions are combined, a rough index of support for military service can be developed. On this basis, about 30 percent of those who served admitted generally positive feelings about military service; this is about the same level found in the American Army if we use the first-term retention rate as an indicator of positive approval of military service. What would happen if conscription were not so rigorously enforced? The answer can be surmised by responses to the question, "If you could have avoided going into the military like some people did would you have avoided it?" The data indicate that there may be little genuine support for conscription and that if most soldiers were given a choice, most would not have voluntarily entered service. Some 69 percent of the respondents said they would have avoided military service if they could have, and 29.2 percent indicated they would have served even if they could have avoided it. These findings are not particularly surprising in light of the experience of those Western countries that have abandonded conscription. The experience of Britain, Canada, and the United States suggests that once conscription is abandoned, the size of military forces will decline largely as a result of the inability to attract sufficient manpower through volunteers. Even in the United States with its extremely attractive pay and benefit inducements, the AVF does not attract as many as one in five of the available manpower pool. This figure is intriguing in that it is below the 29.2 percent that the Soviets could theoretically expect to attract if they abandoned conscription.

Military Life

Throughout Soviet military history, Russian soldiers have endured almost incredible hardships. One of the most important reasons for the harshness of Soviet military life is the maintenance of military organization that emphasizes traditional mechanisms of control. In fact, the tendency to overdiscipline and overregiment the soldier, the limit his freedom, and to carefully control his movements is typical of all traditional European armies. The hallmark of the traditional army, prior planning and unquestioning obedience to orders, remains very much the key motivational form in the Soviet Army. This element is manifested in such policies as the control of the individual on post and of the money he has, the restriction of passes and furloughs, very difficult training schedules, and other practices designed to ensure maximum control of the soldier.

The harsh quality of life at the conscript level is also due to the traditional Russian doctrine that units will perform well in combat only if training conditions are even more rigorous in peacetime than in war.[66] The doctrine of "difficult in peace, easy in war" has long marked Russian military thought and does so no less so today. Yet another reason for the harshness is that the quality of life in the military reflects the shortages and maldistribution that plague the economy as a whole.

Military life does not command as much social prestige in the Soviet Union as it does in other societies.[67] This finding is consistent with the earlier finding that the families and peers of conscripts do not have high regard for military life.

A chronic complaint among Soviet soldiers concerns the poor quality of rations. Their standard diet consists of kasha, porridge, and bread, supplemented with fish, a little meat as a source of protein, cabbage, potatoes, farina, macaroni, butter, and jam. The food is often poorly prepared, and the same dishes are served repeatedly. One soldier revealed in a personal interview that his unit was the victim of bureaucratic bungling and was forced to subsist on kasha and fish for thirty consecutive days. This brought the troops to the point of open revolt. The problem is complicated by the food requirements of the ethnic minorities; often, Moslems are forced to choose between eating pork as the only available meat or going without any meat at all. Yet another problem is the tendency to substitute one food for another. Generally, the diets posted in official documents do not accurately reflect the Soviet soldier's actual caloric intake; the intake appears to be lower. In addition, the food does not seem to be adequate in terms of its caloric and vitamin content, a condition that results in a range of diet-related illnesses among the troops.[68] The majority of soldiers believe that military food is worse than in civilian life, and, in general, military rations are considerably below the quality and preparation available to Soviet citizens. With the soldiers' intense training schedule, it is questionable whether the food meets basic physiological requirements. The average weight gain of the Soviet conscript during his military service hints that it is not.[69]

Another aggravating problem is low pay. The Soviet conscript earns 3 to 5 rubles a month or about the equivalent of $10 (U.S. dollars), while the average Soviet civilian earns 180 rubles a month. Low pay, of course, is a very effective way for the regime to force savings within the military economy and to extract services from the civilian economy at very low cost. Soviet military compensation is too low to meet the soldier's needs; 77 percent of the soldiers indicated that their pay was not enough for their needs. Soviet press articles often indicate that the soldier becomes a financial burden upon his family while in military service.[70] The old Western tradition of joining the military and sending one's pay home to help one's family is absent in the Soviet Union.

Inadequate pay apparently affects Soviet morale. The Soviet press has printed articles urging the soldier to endure the sacrifices of military life by getting by on what he has rather than asking for money from his family.[71]

The Soviet Army maintains very strict leave policies. While pass policies are generally left to the local commander, it appears that most commanders are genuinely hesitant to issue passes for fear that soldiers will get into trouble. The unavailability of passes and furloughs is a particularly sore point for the soldier who finds himself constantly restricted to his company area. Technically, the soldier is allowed by law to have his Sundays free, but this is rarely the case. More often, on Sundays he has more indoctrination classes, additional duties, further specialized training, or mandatory athletics. Formal regulations require that the soldier also be granted at least one ten-day leave for every two years of service. The normal procedure, however, is not to grant leave at all but to give the soldier a ten-day "early drop" or release from service. He uses his ten days as travel time to his home or to complete the necessary bureaucratic outprocessing and paperwork. Home leaves are relatively rare in any case, and young conscripts often begin to feel like prisoners in their garrisons. It is not unusual for a soldier to spend the full two years of his enlistment without a leave or furlough long enough to visit his home.

Some idea of how restrictive furlough policies are can be gained from the responses of Soviet soldiers to the question, "In the whole time you were in the military how many times were you allowed to leave the base for your own recreation?" Some 54 percent of the soldiers were allowed only one pass a month. Most often this was not an overnight pass but consisted of a few hours in a local town or on a guided tour. Overnight passes are granted only rarely, and when they are the soldier probably will find himself part of a group, usually in the company of a supervising sergeant or officer.

In general, the Soviet soldier's life is far harsher than that of the American soldier. In the Soviet Army, the emphasis on communal living and communal hardship seems designed to force the individual to become part of the *mir* (the community) and to endure with his peers. In the American Army, the individual soldier is regarded as exactly that, an individual. The Soviet soldier at least has the comfort of knowing that he is not enduring hardship alone. While the American soldier is subjected to less physical hardship, he may pay a much higher psychological price, for he most often endures alone and at best, shares his concerns with one or two others who occupy his room. Because of his isolation, the American soldier often does not feel he is part of a cohesive military unit. Far more than the Soviet soldier, he tends to be a member of an association of strangers.

Conclusions

The Soviet and American armies display significant differences. For example, the Soviet Army does not suffer the extremely high attrition rates so characteristic of the American Army. More than one-third of U.S. soldiers fail to complete their first three-year tour of military service, leaving the military for a range of reasons. Soviet attrition is either insignificant or is associated with the normal biannual troop rotation.

The Soviet soldier's mental skills are likely to be much higher than those of the American soldier, being about the same as that of the population at large. With the USSR's excellent educational system, by the time a conscript has reached the draft age of eighteen he is most likely to have completed twelve years of schooling, much of it in the areas of science and engineering. Since the conscription system is all-inclusive, the Soviet Army is a demographic microcosm of the larger society in terms of race, ethnicity, language, religion, and education. In contrast, in the American Army these levels are devastatingly low.

The Soviet Army has no critical shortages in the combat arms such as result in the U.S. Army because of the soldiers' inabilities to master military skills. The Soviet shortages are the normal types one would expect to find in an army trying to fill critical MOS positions with large numbers of people who turn over on a semiannual basis.

The evidence suggests that the DOSAAF system of premilitary training has done a good job in preparing the Soviet soldier for military life. It has insured a relatively high level of trainability for the Soviet soldier and has provided the military with large numbers of soldiers already trained in technical military skills. The DOSAAF system has been very successful in producing soldiers capable of learning and mastering military skills faster than they had been able to without DOSAAF training.[72] Partially as a result of this success, the mandatory tour of service was reduced from three to two years in 1967.

Another interesting difference between the Soviet and American soldier is that few Soviet soldiers are married. Most Soviet soldiers are inducted into the army at age eighteen, a fact which encourages people to plan for marriage after mandatory service. In addition, the Soviet Army does not permit the conscript soldier to take his wife with him. The Soviet soldier has no family worries to affect his performance. Moreover, he is not allowed to live off-post, and, thus, he is not allowed to live in civilian ghettos where he can be exploited or exposed to a range of habits and temptations that erode military discipline and perform- ance. The Soviet soldier spends almost all his time within a rigorously controlled military environment. His level of discipline is likely to be somewhat higher than that of his American counterpart, a subject that is addressed in more detail later. In any case, the social isolation and family difficulties that seem to plague the young American soldier are in most instances absent in the Soviet Army.

On balance, the Soviet soldier is far less severely affected by certain problems than his American counterpart, namely the problems of attrition, mental ability, ability to learn new skills, quality of premilitary training, number of married soldiers and the difficulties they face, barracks life, esprit de corps, motivation, and general alienation.

Notes

1. "This Is Your Army, 1981," Information paper, U.S. Department of the Army, Washington, D.C., December 29, 1980, p. 1.

2. Richard A. Gabriel, "About Face on the Draft," *America* (February 9, 1980): 95. See also Charles Moskos, "How to Save the All-Volunteer Force," *The Public Interest* (Fall 1980): 74-89; see also by Moskos, "Surviving the War in Vietnam," in Charles Figley and Seymour Leventman, eds., *Strangers at Home: Vietnam Veterans Since the War* (New York: Praeger Publishers, 1980), pp. 71-84.

3. Gabriel, "About Face in the Draft," p. 95.

4. Ibid.

5. "This Is Your Army, 1981," p. 7.

6. Moskos, "How to save the All-Volunteer Force;" Gabriel, "About Face on the Draft."

7. It will be recalled that the introduction of the AVF in 1973 was not done in

response to military criteria (the military opposed it) but to quiet the vocal middle-class segments of American society restive over sending their sons to war in Vietnam. For more on the class origins of the AVF, see Gabriel, "About Face on the Draft," pp. 95-96.

8. "This Is Your Army, 1981," p. 7. See also Robert B. Pirie, Jr., "Why Military Aptitude Tests Really Do Matter," *Armed Forces Journal* (July 1981): 70; also see Juri Toomepuu, *Soldier Capability and Army Combat Effectiveness*, U.S. Army Recruiting Command, Washington, D.C., 1981, pp. 11-12.

9. Gabriel, "About Face on the Draft," p. 95. Note that the army's official figures for 1980 show 72.3 percent soldiers had high school degrees. However, this figure includes those who have been awarded a degree *after* entering service, degrees obtained through at least eleven programs operated or recognized by the army. Many of these equivalency programs require much less than a "genuine" high school degree.

10. Moskos, "How to Save the All-Volunteer Force," p. 77.

11. "This Is Your Army, 1981," p. 2.

12. Ibid., p. 7.

13. This is a conservative estimate. Hard data are found in John J. Fialka, "25% of Recruits in Low Intelligence Category," *The Washington Star*, March 11, 1980, p. 3; see also a staff study prepared by Congressman Robin Beard, file paper, 1980. Finally, see *Aptitude Testing of Recruits*, Washington, D.C.: Office of the Assistant Secretary of Defense (Manpower), (July 1980), pp. 1-12.

14. *Aptitude Testing of Recruits*, p. 9.

15. "GI Bodies and Brains," *The Washington Star*, March 12, 1980, p. 14 (editorial).

16. Toomepuu, *Soldier Capability*, p. 27.

17. Staff study prepared for Congressman Robin Beard, 1980, p. 3.

18. While a later chapter is devoted to the problems associated with training the American soldier, it is worth noting at this point that no less an authority than General Don Starry, commander of the Army's Training and Doctrine Command (TRADOC)—the agency responsible for overseeing training—has pointed to the great difficulties in training the American soldier as a consequence of the soldier's low mental abilities.

19. GAO Report, "Active Duty Manpower Problems Must Be Solved," November 26, 1979, pp. 1-29.

20. Ibid.

21. Ibid.

22. This is the conclusion of a study of American soldiers by Major Stephen Westbrook, "The Alienated Soldier: Legacy of Our Society," *Army* (December 1979): 18-23.

23. "Active Duty Manpower Problems Must Be Solved," p. 29.

24. Ibid.

25. As a result, NCOs are leaving military service in growing numbers. While the exact totals are subject to some debate, the American Army is at least 11,000 short of the number it feels it needs to operate effectively.

26. Frederick the Great instituted barracks life structured around the small unit, with the express purpose of building unit cohesion. By forcing men to live together, eat together, and be punished together, he felt they would fight well together.

27. "Though there are a lot of bad things to be said about barracks living, it certainly adds to unit cohesion, helps instill discipline, and makes for a more deployable force. The Soviets, of course, have all their first-termers in the barracks where they are making a total commitment to soldiering." From Mitzi Leibst, "Comparative US/Soviet Man-

power," quoted in John M. Collins, *The US-Soviet Military Balance, 1960-1980* (New York: McGraw-Hill, 1980), p. 98.

28. Major Larry H. Ingraham, *The Boys in the Barracks* (Washington, D.C.: Walter Reed Army Institute of Research, July 1978.)

29. Ibid., Chapter 3.

30. Official army statistics note a decrease in criminal activity on military posts. However, the practice of "managing" the disciplinary rate is followed, that is, a large number of criminal offenses are dealt with through either expeditious discharges or other administrative remedies that make it unnecessary to prosecute. Thus, official army data are highly suspect in this area. Most military policemen and army prosecutors tend to agree that the rate of actual criminal activity has increased.

31. Westbrook, "The Alienated Soldier."

32. Richard A. Gabriel and Paul L. Savage, *Crisis in Command,: Mismanagement in the Army* (New York: Hill and Wang, 1978).

33. Human Readiness Report No. 5, (Washington D.C.: Office of the Deputy Chief of Staff for Personnel), (August 1979), pp. 20-21.

34. Staff study prepared for Congressman Robin Beard, 1980, p. 2.

35. Human Readiness Report No. 5, p. 21.

36. See Lieutenant-General Julius W. Becton, Jr., "First Class Army. . .4th Class Living Conditions," *Army* (November 1980): 22-26.

37. Human Readiness Report No. 5, p. 21.

38. Ibid.

39. Ibid., p. 5.

40. The Association of the U.S. Army Defense Report No. 25 of August 1981 shows that 25,500 military families receive food stamps.

41. Becton, "First Class Army. . .," p. 26.

42. Human Readiness Report No. 5, p. 5.

43. Ibid.

44. Ibid.

45. Ibid.

46. Ibid.

47. Ibid., p. D-7

48. Ibid.

49. Westbrook, "The Alienated Soldier," pp. 18-23.

50. Ibid., p. 19.

51. Ibid., p. 18.

52. Ibid., p. 19-20.

53. Ibid.

54. Ibid., p. 21.

55. Gabriel and Savage, *Crisis in Command*, Chapter 2.

56. Richard A. Gabriel, *The New Red Legions: An Attitudinal Portrait of the Soviet Army* (Westport, Conn.: Greenwood Press, 1980), p. 34.

57. Ibid., p. 35. For an excellent description of the Soviet conscription system, see *Handbook on the Soviet Armed Forces*, Defense Intelligence Agency, Washington, D.C.: U.S. Government Printing Office, February 1978, pp. 5-1 to 5-14.

58. Some limited data do exist. Collins notes that the rejection rate for military service in the U.S. Army is about 16 percent for physical reasons and 4 percent for moral reasons, or about 20 percent across the population. The Soviet rate is only 10 percent. A common

estimate heard among intelligence analysts is that the rejection rate does not exceed 12 percent. See Collins, *The US-Soviet Military Balance*, p. 96.

59. Ibid.

60. Toomepuu, *Soldier Capability*.

61. This would, of course, place the planned turbulence rate among Soviet troop units at 50 percent a year, considerably below that of the American Army which suffers at least 89 percent annual personnel turnover.

62. Gabriel, *New Red Legions*, pp. 39-40.

63. Ibid.

64. Richard A. Gabriel, "Combat Cohesion in Soviet and American Military Units," *Parameters* 8, No. 4 (December 1978): 16-26.

65. Gabriel, *The New Red Legions*, p. 42.

66. This concept is basic to Soviet and Tsarist military thought and permeates most of the literature dealing with military training. A strong sense of how it affects even teaching techniques in the military can be gained by reading a collection of articles edited by A. M. Danchenko and I. F. Vydrin, *Military Pedagogy: A Soviet View* (Moscow: Government Printing House, 1973).

67. For an interesting comparison of the military as a career relative to other occupations in Soviet society, see Zev Katz, "Sociology in the Soviet Union," *Problems of Communism* (May 1971).

68. My information on diet-related illnesses, especially those related to high carbohydrate strep infections, was garnered in a series of conferences with the medical and nursing staff of St. Anselm College, Manchester, New Hampshire.

69. In the West, the average weight gain for a young man between the ages of eighteen and twenty is approximately 12 pounds. For the Soviet soldier in the same age group, the average weight gain is 6 pounds. See "Life in the Soviet Army," *Time*, May 4, 1970.

70. *Bloknot agitatora*, No. 12 (June 1971).

71. Ibid.

72. Collins, *The US-Soviet Military Balance*, p. 99.

3

The NCOs

Combat-effectiveness is largely a function of leadership, and strong primary group bonds develop within small battle units. The NCO as the leader closest to the troops is crucial to the development of these bonds and to fostering the transmission of combat skills. History is full of examples of armies which, despite bad officers, fought well largely because of a professional NCO corps that could fill the gaps in leadership and training. Bad officers can often be ignored if an army has NCOs who are confident and well trained, have strong attachments to their men, set good examples, and are willing to bear hardships and risks with their men.

The noncommissioned officer is the leader most responsible for building interpersonal bonds which are so vital to cohesion. Bonds of trust, confidence, ability, and concern are central to good performance in battle. Combat ability does not consist of technical expertise alone; even more important is the human "cement" which bonds men in battle units together and increases their ability to withstand combat stress. Without this psychological element, fighting units could not endure the stress of combat.[1] The NCO is central in engendering these attachments because he is the most visible leader, interacting most frequently with his men on a day-to-day basis.

Soldiers in most armies leave their training schools with only a minimum level of military skill. It is left to the NCOs in the unit to develop these skills and to raise their level of proficiency. The NCO must also be the exemplar and socializer, the counselor, the problem-solver, and, far more than a unit's officers, the unit's true leader on a daily basis as well as the manager of everyday problems. He is the "backbone of the army" upon which the rest of the structure depends. If he does not perform his job well, his unit will not perform well.

The American NCO

The model for the American NCO corps is found in traditional European armies, which, indeed, are also the Soviet NCO corps' model. Both armies want a professional NCO corps that can act as a basic transmitter of values and military techniques to the soldier. Such a corps is expected to be a stable, career, long-term corps that will not be overly subject to personnel turbulence or attrition. The classical model draws heavily upon the British, French, and German experience and has, in fact, served these countries well. Its adoption by the U.S. Army is not a recent phenomenon. Because the American Army has historically relied upon a volunteer system to fill its ranks, it has tended to stress the development of a stable professional NCO corps to act as the primary organizers and managers of military skills and values at the small-unit level. In time of war, these NCOs form the basis of an experienced training and combat cadre needed to rapidly train large numbers of conscript soldiers.

The American Army had very little difficulty maintaining a career NCO corps either in the volunteer period prior to World War II or in the draft armies of that war, Korea, and Vietnam. However, since the return to the volunteer system following the Vietnam War, personnel problems have greatly affected the quality of the NCO corps. Recently, the American NCO corps has been unable to attract and maintain sufficient numbers in the corps itself. The army is short approximately 11,000 noncommissioned officers when measured against its authorized strength of 259,064.[2] Many of these shortages occur in the "top five" zone, that is, among the most senior NCO grades above E-5 rank. These experienced NCOs are crucially important to the operation of any army.

The difficulty in retaining NCOs is obvious from the following figures. Prior to 1973, 65 percent of first-term soldiers who reenlisted stayed on to become NCOs. In 1981, that number declined 45 percent.[3] Perhaps more damaging is the number who were already NCOs and who chose to leave service rather than reenlist. In 1973, the percentage of career NCOs that reenlisted and remained on active service was 82.2 percent; that percentage has fallen to only 55 percent,[4] and it appears likely to continue to decline. This shortage has grave implications for the American Army's performance in battle. In one of its official studies on readiness, the army concluded that the single most important factor in low unit readiness was the lack of qualified NCOs within units.[5]

Attempts to deal with NCO shortages have created additional problems. Because of the armywide shortage of NCOs, the practice has been to strip units on duty within the United States of their noncommissioned officers in order to maintain units in Europe and Korea at full strength.[6] As a result, the assignment rotation time for NCOs between unit assignments has decreased. Career NCOs frequently find themselves shuttled between overseas stations, often unable to bring their families, with little more than sixty or ninety days between assignments. Moreover, stripping units in the United States of their NCOs has resulted in some of these units being as much as 50 percent short of their required NCO strength. What would happen to these units if they were to go to war on short notice? NCO shortages overburden officers who are required to assume many NCO duties. This situation has led many officers to lose trust and confidence in the NCOs in their units. As pointed out in Chapter 2, one of the major problems facing the AVF is the disproportionate number of recruits from the lower social strata. This problem is beginning to make itself felt within the NCO corps. The overall quality of the American NCO corps expressed in terms of its ability to learn and train its troops has dropped off considerably. There are several reasons for this decline. In an attempt to meet the shortage of NCOs there has been an acceleration in promotion within the corps itself and diminished time in grade.[7] As a consequence, NCOs are less well trained and less experienced than they were before. Few NCOs have had sufficient time in grade to acquire the experience and skills they are expected to transfer to their men.[8] The Rosenblum Report undertaken in 1979 for the Army's Training and Doctrine Command (TRADOC) revealed that the amount of training and experience that the NCO receives is considerably below that found in the armies of Great Britain, France, Canada, and West Germany where promotion is much slower and where the future NCO has much greater opportunity to learn his skills before being moved up in rank.[9]

The NCO's mental ability level is dropping considerably, reflecting the same lowered levels in the AVF at large. The reasons seem related to accelerated promotion and to the pool of soldiers from which NCOs are selected. Since first-term reenlistments in the AVF have been declining for years, the problem centers in the type of people who do stay in long enough to reach the rank of NCO. A series of studies shows that soldiers in the lowest mental skill categories, namely, Category 3B and 4, tend to remain in the military more than any other group once they have completed their first tour.[10] It is from this group that most future NCOs will come. Because low-ability soldiers seem more willing to reenlist and stay in service, a transmission belt has been created between this pool of low-ability soldiers and the NCO corps. As a result, the overall quality and mental ability of the army's NCO corps has been dropping over a ten-year period.[11]

Evidence of this decline is presented in the Rosenblum Report which documents the problems of quality in the NCO corps. The report notes that the decline in NCO quality has required the introduction of self-pacing instruction, even in the once-prestigious NCO academies.[12] The soldiers who move through these academies and are rapidly promoted to the rank of NCO are known derisively throughout the army as "shake and bake" NCOs. (The derisive description is drawn from an analogy with an American food product in which cheap quality meat can be made tasty after a quick treatment with a coating of ersatz flavoring so that the meat will appear better than it is.) It is said of those "shake and bake" NCOs that they "look like NCOs and smell like NCOs," but they are not very good noncommissioned officers. The Rosenblum Report also notes that throughout the army the reputation of the prestigious NCO academies has declined. Self-pacing instruction was clearly a response to low-quality material. Paradoxically, the report points out that self-teaching and self-pacing have not worked well, and that, compared to European armies, the quality of the American NCO in terms of training and skill levels has continued to decline.[13] In addition, self-pacing seems to have increased both discipline and attrition problems within the NCO corps.[14] This suggests that the army has come up with solutions that may be more damaging to the corps than the original problems they were designed to treat.

The difficulties the American NCO corps has in training its soldiers are reflected in the Army Training Study of 1980.[15] This study noted that one of the major problems in training the soldier adequately can be traced to the poor quality of his sergeants and corporals. They generally know little more about military subjects than those they are trying to train.[16] NCO quality and training are further reduced by the long list of extraneous duties and frequent assignment rotation that is both a cause and effect of the overall NCO shortage. Thus, the shortage of NCOs coupled with low-quality NCO recruit material and poor training and trainability of NCOs has led to a situation where many NCOs are unable to perform the critical function of any NCO corps, the training of their own troops.

This inability shows up in the performance levels of the soldiers themselves. The Army Training Study presents evidence that the performance ability of many soldiers is very low. With regard to tank crews, for instance, it notes that the ability of units who have left training school and integrated into units to learn or improve their skills once with their units is "essentially flat."[17] Despite the fact that soldiers have been in their units for some time under the tutelage of sergeants whose job it is to improve their performance, a substantial number of soldiers do not improve at all. As a result, the inability of sergeants to train their soldiers often means that many soldiers, especially in tank units, leave their initial training centers with the highest level of skill performance that they will ever attain throughout their three-year period of military duty. NCOs are having great difficulty bringing units to adequate levels of training and performance readiness because they do not have the skill to do so themselves. In the words of the Army Training Study, many of the NCOs "do not appear to be any more proficient than lesser experienced individuals" and, thus, have great difficulty in training their troops well.[18]

As new and more sophisticated and complex equipment enters the army's inventory, the skills to operate and maintain that equipment have to be continually updated, sometimes on a yearly basis. The inability of NCOs to train their men in the skills of war represents a major shortcoming not only of the NCO corps but also of the units themselves.

Why has the NCO corps had problems of quality and training? After all, the United States has fought two major wars since World War II. The NCO corps, if properly managed, should, therefore, be among the best and most experienced in the world. The opportunity to create a corps of experienced professionals has certainly been present.

In 1978, the army undertook a study to assess the causes of the decline in NCO quality.[19] The study identified four basic causes for the decline. The first and perhaps most important was the number of NCOs who were "lost" during Vietnam and who were replaced by less experienced men. When one talks about the "loss" of NCOs during Vietnam, three things are implied. A substantial number of NCOs were killed during that war. As with any battle environment, Vietnam took its toll among junior NCOs, many of whom would normally have been retained in service and been promoted to NCO. Perhaps more important were the NCOs who were "lost" to attrition. Vietnam occurred at a time when two categories of NCOs would have normally reached retirement age. Large numbers of thirty-year career sergeants who had joined during or immediately after World War II reached their normal retirement. After a tour in Vietnam or, perhaps, even to escape it, these men left military service. The same was true for the twenty-year group which entered the military during Korea or immediately thereafter. The continuation of the Vietnam War for ten years ensured that both groups would reach normal retirement sometime during that war.

Finally, a number of NCOs were lost because the duration and unpopularity of the war made it very difficult to convince individuals to remain in military service especially when reenlistment virtually guaranteed another tour in Vietnam. At that time, the army was populated with a large number of NCOs who had already served in Vietnam two or three times. Moreover, the virtual certainty that men would see battle if they remained in service made it difficult to retain first-term soldiers, the source of future junior NCOs. Thus, the Vietnam War was responsible for a considerable loss in the number of NCOs whom the army would normally have retained.

This loss of sergeants created difficulties even during the Vietnam War. It meant that those who left service had to be replaced, more often by "shake and bake" NCOs with little experience or training. General George S. Blanchard, commander of the U.S. Army in Europe, commented on this problem at the time when he said, "We almost lost our noncommissioned officer corps in Vietnam. I arrived at the First Cavalry Division in 1966 and when I said my goodbyes a year later I realized that the platoon sergeant, E-7 in many cases, had been placed by a staff sergeant. When I returned to the division after another year, I discovered that many buck sergeants E-5 were replacing staff sergeants."[20] In short, these younger NCOs had been promoted too rapidly to senior grades and without proper training and experience. The result was an overall decline in the quality of army NCOs as well as a decline in their numbers.

Another reason for the decline in quality has to do with the introduction of the AVF itself. As noted earlier, the general quality of recruits has declined, but those who stayed were likely to be in the lowest mental categories. Thus, the NCO corps began to attract soldiers of much lower intelligence.[21]

In the pre-AVF army, a senior NCO typically made seven times more than the new recruit. As a consequence of front-loading, under the AVF in 1981 senior sergeants made three times as much as new recruits. In 1983, the base pay of a recruit was $551.40 a month, while that of a sergeant with twenty-two years of service was $1,578, or slightly less than three times more than the recruit. Historically, sergeants have measured their standard of living and pay and success not against the larger society but against the men with whom they serve. With the front-loading of increased benefits, many NCOs as well as those who considered staying in service and obtaining NCO rank perceived that their standard of living relative to both the society and the other ranks was declining. Many, therefore, left service. The attempt under the AVF to change the military along the lines of the occupational model accelerated the attrition of high-quality experienced noncommissioned officers.

Still another reason for the decline in NCO quality has been the emphasis placed on altering the army's "tooth to tail ratio."[22] As the AVF came into being and as pressures on manpower increased, the army attempted to restructure its force so as to reduce the number of support troops required to sustain the combat soldier in the field. In order to free more troops for combat assignments, a large number of support functions were either done away with or recombined. Some were even transferred to civilian firms hired to do specific jobs. The result was the reclassification of large numbers of NCOs out of their MOS in which they were trained and experienced, and their reassignment to other MOS areas without benefit of additional training or experience.[23] This seems to have been particularly true for senior and middle-grade NCOs. Hence many NCOs were thrown into positions of leadership that required skills with which they were thoroughly unfamiliar. They were expected to lead and to assume responsibility for training their men, but they often lacked both the skills and experience to do so. Many floundered, and the perception that the NCO corps was filled with unqualified soldiers increased.[24] Paradoxically, the tooth to tail ratio was not significantly reduced, and, under manpower pressures for retention, the quality of the NCO corps was reduced even further, especially so in the eyes of the officers with whom they had to serve.

A final factor contributing to the decline of the NCO corps was the growing perception on the part of the officer corps that the quality of NCOs was in fact declining.[25] As a consequence, the officers, especially during Vietnam when the corps itself was bloated to almost 16 percent of total strength, began to protect itself by assuming more and more functions of the NCO corps. The American officer understood that, with the efficiency rating system by which his career was judged, mistakes could be very costly. As he began to trust his NCOs less, he assumed an increasing proportion of the NCO functions as a way of ensuring that the job was done correctly. The system began to feed on itself: the officers did not trust the NCOs because of their declining quality, while the NCOs, lacking the trust and responsibility that they deserved from the officers, began to distrust the officers until a gap developed between officers and NCOs. As the NCO corps fell in the eyes of its officers, it also fell in the eyes of the troops which witnessed the officers usurping the NCOs' tasks. Today's army officers continue to view the NCOs negatively—so much so that the NCO corps' morale and prestige have been affected. Thus, what was once the most experienced and battle-hardened NCO corps of all the Western armies has slipped precipitously.

In 1979, the army published Human Readiness Report No. 5,[26] which addressed itself to the problem of quality NCO leadership. When officers were asked what they thought was the most severe problem facing their units over the five-year period of the study, they most often identified the quality of leadership at both the junior and senior NCO ranks.[27] Both officers in troop units (84.4 percent) and unit commanders (85.2 percent) throughout the army cited the low quality of junior NCO leadership as the first-ranking problem.[28] As to senior NCO leadership quality, the data are not significantly better; 69.8 percent of the officers in troop units regarded senior NCO quality leadership as a major problem in their units, as did 64.9 percent of commanding officers generally.[29] The army's own studies reveal that the officer corps—especially those officers in troop units who hold positions of command—considers the quality of the NCO corps to be low.

In the view of commanders in all types of units, the perceptions of NCO quality are even less complimentary. When commanders were asked which of the following they thought was the "greatest personnel problem" in their units, 46.5 percent of these commanding officers identified the low quality of junior NCO leadership as the major problem. Indeed, 68.3 percent of the commanders armywide interviewed over a five-year period identified the quality of their NCOs as the "greatest personnel problem" with which they had to deal.[30] When the data are stratified by type of unit, the same dismal picture emerges. Among commanders of combat arms units, the army's most important units, 58.3 percent identified the low quality of junior NCO leadership as being the greatest problem with which they had to deal. Another 9.2 percent noted that senior NCO leadership was a problem. Combined, 67.5 percent of the commanders of combat arms units felt that the general quality of NCO leadership was a serious problem. With regard to other types of units, namely, support and noncombat units, 68.8 percent of the commanding officers in these units identified low-quality NCO leadership as a major problem.[31] Of these commanding officers, 28.6 percent found senior NCO leadership quality to be a serious problem, while 40.2 percent thought junior NCO quality was a problem.[32]

The army study attempted not only to discern the degree to which NCO quality was a problem but also to assess whether that problem was getting better, worse, or remaining stable over time. When officers were asked to assess whether the quality of NCO leadership in their units "in the past six months" had increased or decreased, the data suggested that things were generally getting worse. Among commanding officers of all types of units armywide, 64.9 percent felt that senior NCO leadership was a major problem, and 23.9 percent that the problem was getting worse within their units.[33] With regard to their perceptions of junior NCO quality, 85.2 percent felt that it was a problem in their units, and 39.1 percent that the problem was increasing as well.[34] Officers in troop units shared the same views; 69.8 percent saw senior NCO leadership quality as a problem in their units, and 30.8 percent perceived that the problem was growing worse. At the same time, 84.4 percent of these officers saw low-quality junior NCO leadership as a problem, and 45.4 percent thought the problem was increasing.[35] Unfortunately, the problem is not even stabilizing, but is growing worse as the AVF continues to draw heavily upon low-quality recruits.

The responses of officers in combat arms units to questions about the quality of their NCOs suggest that there are serious problems within the corps of sergeants who man the combat units. Among officers in combat units, 67.7 percent identified low-quality NCO leadership at the senior level as a major problem and 29.2 percent thought that the problem was getting worse.[36] Their perceptions of junior NCO quality were no better; 86.7 percent of the combat arms officers thought junior NCO quality was a problem, and 46.8 percent perceived that the problem was getting worse. When analyzed armywide, 56.4 percent of all officers identified low senior NCO quality as a problem, and 23.3 percent said the problem was increasing; 64.4 percent identified junior NCO leadership as a problem, and 32.4 percent said the problem was getting worse.[37]

The fact that the quality of junior NCO leadership is invariably perceived as worse than that of the senior NCOs is most disturbing, for many of these junior NCOs, through attrition and promotion, will eventually reach the senior ranks. Thus, the overall quality of the American NCO corps is likely to deteriorate even further. The NCO corps is unlikely to get appreciably better soon. Without an effective NCO corps the task of building up effective combat units is likely to be very difficult indeed and based on present data, will be even more difficult in the future. The problem cannot be solved without a major change in the way the army obtains, trains, and promotes its manpower.

Two official reports, a single section of Human Readiness Report No. 5 and the study undertaken by Major Steve Westbrook dealing with soldier alienation,[38] address three crucial dimensions of NCO leadership. First, troops must always believe that their NCOs truly care about them; soldiers who feel they are being misused by their NCOs or officers will quickly become indisciplined and not regard their leaders as worth following. Second is trust; soldiers must feel that their leaders are genuinely concerned about them and will do what they can to make their lives easier and, above all, will not squander them in battle. Finally, there must be a belief in the NCO's military competence. A good leader must convince his men that he has good judgment in battle; troops must believe that if they follow their NCOs in battle their chances of survival are as good as or at least equal to that of their leaders.

The American NCO does not do well on any of these three dimensions. For example, the armywide study revealed that only 45 percent of the soldiers felt that "NCOs care about the welfare of their men."[39] In the Westbrook study, when soldiers were asked what they felt about their NCOs, 52 percent believed they could not count on their NCOs "to look out for the soldier's interest." Another 20 percent were unsure if they could count on their NCOs. In the very best of circumstances, then, at least 60 percent of the soldiers felt that they could not be sure if they could depend on their NCOs. Moreover, 37 percent of the soldiers believed that their senior NCOs "are not concerned about them personally" and 15 percent more were unsure.[40]

Study of trust as a leadership quality reveals much the same negative picture. Fully 28 percent of the soldiers believed that their senior NCOs "cannot be trusted," and another 23 percent were unsure. More importantly, only 49 percent believed that "most NCOs can be trusted."[41] While the data are incomplete, they do tend to indicate that the American NCO may not have been very successful in building strong bonds of trust with the men he leads. This condition cannot have anything but negative effects on the NCOs' ability to mold cohesive battle units.

Of concern, too, is the extent to which troops believe that their NCOs will be good men to go into battle with and the extent to which they trust their judgment and leadership under fire. In the Westbrook study once again, 32 percent of the soldiers studied did not believe that in battle their NCOs would be willing "to go through anything that they made their men go through." Another 18 percent of the troops were unsure. Thus, 50 percent of the soldiers interviewed were uncertain that their NCOs would endure the dangers of battle equally with them.[42] Very disturbing in this regard are the responses to a survey which the Columbia Broadcasting System (CBS) conducted in 1979 among troops of the Berlin Brigade. The Berlin Brigade is nicknamed the "tip of the lance" because it is a fully ready combat brigade deployed in Berlin for immediate action. Members of the brigade understand that it is outnumbered and surrounded and in the event of battle is likely to be crushed forthwith. Nonetheless, it is expected to have the best morale, the best NCOs, and certainly very high motivation and thorough training. When CBS researchers interviewed soldiers of the Brigade, they found that 53 percent said they would not trust their NCOs or officers in battle. Most soldiers lacked confidence in their officers, NCOs, and even their peers.[43] Yet, it is at the small-unit level where the effect of good or poor quality NCOs is more seriously felt. If NCOs are not perceived as competent, it is unlikely that they will be able to help build effective battle units.

When viewed along the three crucial dimensions of leadership identified above, the American NCO corps has not succeeded very well. The men who must be relied upon to follow NCOs into battle appear to have serious reservations about the quality of their leaders. The NCO's low quality is probably most damaging at the small-unit level, precisely in those units that are expected to bear the stress of battle.

If the data presented thus far are combined it would seem that the American NCO corps is suffering from considerable difficulties. At one time it was the most battle hardened and experienced corps in the world, certainly more so than the Soviet NCO corps. This is no longer the case. Most of the experienced NCOs who saw combat in World War II, Korea and even Vietnam have left service. Some Vietnam veterans remain but their numbers are small and many are reaching retirement within the next five years. On balance the American NCO corps is no longer more experienced and battle hardened than most Western armies today.

The NCO corps is also plagued by low strength and high rates of attrition. The transition of the military to an all volunteer force has forced it to compete for manpower in the open market, and it has not been very successful in attracting enough quality soldiers. The high attrition rate among NCOs can essentially be traced to the conditions of life in the military, especially the constant turnover in assignments resulting from personnel shortages, as well as frequent separations from their families. Moreover, as already mentioned, the practice of front-loading pay and benefits has reduced the comparative standard of living for senior NCOs, making a career in the military less attractive. It is difficult to assess the degree to which separating military service from citizenship has affected the career soldier, but anecdotal evidence suggests that he is acutely aware that the society now pays him less respect and less attention. All of these factors have had detrimental effects on the total number and quality of the senior NCO corps.

Many of the NCO corps' difficulties are beyond its control. It is not responsible, for example, for the rapid turnover resulting from manpower shortages, nor is it directly responsible for the army's high attrition rates. It cannot legitimately be held responsible for the generally low quality of the American soldier or for accelerated promotions or self-paced instruction. The best in the corps may be said to be victims of larger systemic forces. Many of these forces were initiated and are sustained by civilian authorities more than military ones. Nonetheless, regardless of who is responsible for the conditions that have developed over the last fifteen years, these conditions have produced an NCO corps that lacks many of the critical traits, techniques, values, and habits that have been historically associated with effective noncommissioned officers and that are vital to producing cohesive combat units.

The Soviet NCO

The Soviet noncommissioned officer's place in the structure of the Soviet Army is quite different from that of his American counterpart. Since the creation of the Soviet Army, Soviet authorities have attempted to build a career NCO corps as part of the traditional structure of that army. The goal was to establish an NCO corps that would constitute a highly stable and professional element within the authority structure of the army, a structure that would closely parallel that found in traditional nineteenth-century European armies. Overall, Soviet efforts to create such a corps have failed.

This failure represents one of the major differences between the Soviet Army and most Western armies. The Soviet failure is quite clear: less than 5 percent of Soviet noncommissioned officers are career soldiers compared with an average of about 26 percent in Western armies, particularly in the American Army whose NCO strength tends to run above 28 percent.[44] In 1978, the Soviets launched a major effort to correct this problem by introducing a warrant officer program, but it has not succeeded.[45] Some of the failure to sustain a long-term, stable career corps is directly related to the manner in which NCOs are selected. In Western armies, a soldier does not usually achieve NCO rank until he has already completed at least his first term of service, often three years, and has signed on for another term.[46] Thus, most NCOs in the armies of the West have at least three years of experience before entering the bottom rungs of the NCO corps. Exactly the reverse is the case in the Soviet Army. The local Commissariat often selects NCOs even before they enter active military service, on the grounds that a conscript may have special training or show a particular aptitude during his DOSAAF training. Those not selected in this manner are often selected after they have completed their basic training and have been in active service for as little as two or three months.[47] Upon selection, they are removed from their units and sent to an NCO training school which lasts about six weeks. They are then reassigned to another unit as sergeants. It is not unusual for a conscript who has been in the military for less than two years to attain the rank of three-stripe sergeant, a condition virtually unknown in the American Army and most armies of the West. The predictable result of this recruitment system is a large number of minimally qualified noncommissioned officers who must occupy important positions of small-unit leadership.

Along with its recruitment problems, the Soviet NCO corps is continually subjected to a tremendous amount of personnel assignment turnover. Every six months, as a consequence of the biannual conscription cycle, the Soviet Army must absorb a massive influx of new conscripts. Thus, every six months, approximately one-quarter of the NCO corps leaves active service to be replaced by new conscript NCOs coming directly from civilian life. In addition, the small number (less than 5 percent) of conscripts who remain on active service usually move up in rank or change assignments. The NCO corps is in a state of constant turnover as this cadre of small-unit leaders moves in and out of their positions at all levels except the most senior ones. Instead of a stable cadre of career professionals capable of providing leadership and continuity within Soviet units, the Soviet NCO corps is comprised almost totally of inexperienced amateurs subject to frequent assignment turnover. It is the antithesis of the NCO corps found in traditional nineteenth-century European armies.

The Soviet Army has a major problem in retaining qualified NCOs beyond their mandatory term of service. Although a soldier can achieve NCO rank rapidly and although rewards are offered for those who reenlist for extended service, the Soviet Army has been unable to convince significant numbers of conscripts to remain in service beyond their initial tour of service. The problem is a serious one: approximately 26 percent of Western armies, on the average, are comprised of professional career noncommissioned officers compared with only 5 percent for the Soviet Army.[48] Moreover, those who remain within the Soviet Army for a career in the ranks often reach top NCO rank relatively quickly, which means that most of the experienced NCOs are positioned at the senior NCO level. The lower level NCO leadership, made up of squad leaders, element leaders, platoon sergeants, and even company sergeants—the most critical leadership posts in terms of cohesion and small-unit battle performance—is left in the hands of a new biannual corp of conscripts turned sergeants. These NCOs have no more dedication to the military profession or to developing unit spirit and leadership than does the average conscript.[49]

The Soviet NCO component is quite large compared with the American. The American Army sustains approximately 26 percent of its total strength as noncommissioned officers, a figure roughly approximated in other Western armies. While we have no precise data on the size of the Soviet NCO corps, it is probably quite large by Western standards: it probably accounts for 30 to 33 percent of the Soviet Army's strength.[50] Control at the NCO level is further buttressed by an officer corps that is considerably larger than that found in Western armies. Hence, in the Soviet Army many tasks which in Western armies would be left to NCOs are performed by officers.[51] Close supervision and overcontrol of NCOs, which is the rule in the Soviet Army, emerged as a constant complaint in interviews with noncommissioned officers. This tendency toward overcontrol, which many sergeants see as being based in a lack of trust, further reduces the level of professionalism. Thus, although the Soviet NCO corps is considerably larger than the American NCO corps, it has considerably less professional standing.

How does the average soldier perceive his NCO? Soviet soldiers were asked, "How would you rate the quality of noncommissioned officers you came in contact with while in military service?" A total of 20.4 percent of the soldiers in the ranks thought their NCOs were "extremely good" or "good," at what they did; 35.4 percent rated them "fair," "poor," or "very poor" (13.2 percent of these described them as "poor" or "very poor"); and 44.2 percent, rated their sergeants as only average.[52] Overall, the Soviet NCO's rating by his men is not all that bad considering the disabilities under which the corps labors. The fact that about one-quarter of the troops saw their NCOs as of "good" quality speaks well of the corps. A high number, however, thought their sergeants were "poor." Most Soviet NCOs are at least perceived as being able to do their job adequately.

With regard to how Soviet sergeants perceive their fellow noncommissioned officers, 31 percent rated their brother NCOs as "fair, poor, or very poor." Of all rank levels, the NCOs themselves had the lowest number of respondents who rated their NCOs as being "extremely good or good." Only 17.2 percent of the sergeants themselves placed their brothers in this category, compared to 20.3 percent of the soldiers and 26.4 percent of the officers who rated their NCOs highly.[53]

The manner in which the Soviet officers perceive their sergeants in terms of quality is unclear. On the one hand, 26.4 percent of the officers rated their NCOs as "extremely good or good," the highest number of any rank level including the NCOs themselves. On the other hand, 36.9 percent of them rated their sergeants as "fair, poor, or very poor," the highest number of any rank level to give the NCO corps such low ratings. Like other ranks, the largest number of officers placed the NCO in the "average" quality range. The data for all ranks—soldiers, NCOs, and officers—taken together suggest that most ranks see their sergeants as adequate to the tasks they perform, with the remaining numbers more likely to give them lower than higher ratings on quality. There is little evidence, then, that his men, his officers, or even his brother NCOs see the NCO as a first-rate military professional.

A disparity emerged in the perceptions of enlisted and officer commanders. Only 17.6 percent of enlisted commanders rated their sergeants as "good or extremely good," compared with 41.6 percent of commanding officers who gave their NCOs this description.[54] It is difficult to account for this disparity in views. Whatever the reason, however, less than one-fifth of enlisted commanders rated their sergeants as being of high quality. This implies that large numbers of Soviet NCOs may not be competent to perform small-unit leadership tasks. When these tasks are related to combat, the implications for the effectiveness of their units may be serious. The commanders who are in the best position to judge, namely, enlisted commanders, do not give their NCOs high grades for quality. The unit subleaders' general view of the Soviet sergeant is that he is not a good soldier. It is a view we would expect to find of an NCO corps comprised largely of inexperienced conscripts enduring short-term service. The Soviet NCO corps consists largely of amateurs, and its amateurism seems to be reflected in the levels of quality it demonstrates in the eyes of its officers and men.

Among the more interesting questions is the degree to which the Soviet NCO corps has improved over time. Table 1 shows Soviet NCO quality over a forty-year period, as measured by the perceptions of Soviet officers who served with the corps during that period.[55] During the 1940-1952 period, 26.0 percent of the NCOs were rated by their men as being of high quality. By the 1964-1978 period, this figure had declined to 20.4 percent. As the number of top-quality NCOs has declined since World War II, the number judged in the lower categories has increased markedly. The reasons for this decline are not clear. During the last forty years, the Soviet Army has generally improved: it has become more professional, it has better equipment, it is better prepared for battle, it has greater influence in domestic policy, and certainly it should feel more secure from any threats of "direct action" by the political regime. Yet, the perceived quality of the NCO corps has dropped off dramatically. As shown in Table 1, twice as many respondents (40.8 percent) judged the NCOs to be only fair to poor than those (20.4 percent) who rated them of high quality.

Table 1
Perceptions of Soviet NCO Quality, 1940-1978

Time	Extremely Good	Good	Average	Fair	Poor	Very Poor
Prewar	1.	0	3.	1.	0	0
1940-1952	4.3%	21.7%	47.8%	13.0%	4.3%	8.7%
1953-1957	0.0%	19.0%	33.3%	33.3%	14.3%	0.0%
1958-1963	0.0%	15.4%	76.9%	0.0%	7.7%	0.0%
1964-1978	0.0%	20.4%	38.3%	24.5%	10.2%	6.1%

As of 1981, the Soviet objective of creating a high-quality, professional, NCO corps with some stability of service, which would be the basis on which to build and train the rest of the conscript army, had not been achieved. With the failure of the warrant program, this condition is not expected to change. Instead of a professional NCO corps in the style of the European model, the Soviets have a cadre of short-term conscript sergeants who are not regarded very highly by their officers, their commanders, or the soldiers they lead. This failure represents one of the major institutional weaknesses of the Soviet Army.

The Soviet NCO has apparently not provided leadership to the small unit. When soldiers were asked whether they thought their NCOs "always set the example for their men," only 16 percent agreed and 65.5 disagreed. More specifically, soldiers were asked whether they felt their NCOs presented "a good example to young soldiers." Only 23 percent of the soldiers said yes, whereas 61.1 percent thought they did not.[56] Among those in command positions, 50 percent of the sample felt that NCO served as good examples; only 25 percent of the officers felt this was the case. Among the NCOs themselves, only 23.1 percent thought that their fellow noncommissioned officers served as good exemplars for young soldiers.[57]

Much the same conclusion emerges when we examine the commanders' opinions of their NCOs as models. Thirty-seven percent of the enlisted commanders felt their NCOs set a good example for young soldiers. Since NCOs interact most with enlisted commanders on a day-to-day basis, these commanders are likely to have accurate assessments of their sergeants. If anyone is likely to be close to the Soviet soldier, it is his enlisted commanders, the element leaders, fireteam leaders, and squad leaders. The fact that more than two-thirds of these commanders fail to perceive their NCOs as good exemplars suggests that the Soviet NCO corps may lack competence in an important leadership element. This suspicion is reinforced by the number of commanding officers who felt their NCOs failed to provide good examples for their men; only 14.3 percent of the commanding officers agreed that their NCOs provided good examples.[58]

How are these conditions to be explained? For one thing, the fact that the NCO corps is a conscript corps may have some relevance. Because noncommissioned officers are drawn from among the conscript population, they are usually no more motivated to leadership than the average conscript. Like his subordinates in the ranks, the Soviet NCO seeks only to complete his military service with a minimum of difficulty and trouble. Accordingly, he is likely to feel very strongly that he is bearing up under the burdens of a military service and a position of responsibility that he would gladly have avoided if he could have. If the conscript has a generally negative attitude toward military life, most of the conscript NCOs will probably share these attitudes and often with good reason. Like conscripts in the ranks, noncommissioned officers are forced to live in overcrowded barracks, endure bad food, suffer through long training schedules, and participate in compulsory indoctrination classes. Membership in the NCO ranks has some advantages, but for the conscript NCO they are more often seen as heavily outweighed by the increased responsibility and the chance of being held heavily accountable for a mistake. The conscript NCO is likely to feel that military life is just as hard on him as it is on any other conscript in the ranks. The problem is, of course, that the conscript in the ranks generally does not believe that his NCOs share the hardships of military life. In this case, the troops' perceptions are far more important to unit morale and cohesion than the objective facts of the matter.

The degree to which small-unit leaders are willing to take risks on their own initiative and to encourage their peers and subordinates to do likewise is an important aspect of military leadership. An NCO corps that is practiced in seizing the initiative and taking risks is likely to be an effective corps on the battlefield. Conversely, a corps that restricts its own initiative and that of other leadership elements is likely to become highly bureaucratic, inflexible, and dedicated to its own prerogatives and the minimization of error to the point of ossification. In order to measure initiative, soldiers were asked whether they felt their NCOs "stifled the initiative of others." Fully 35.3 percent of the soldiers and 63.6 percent of the enlisted commanders agreed that this was the case.[59] The fact that almost two-thirds of the enlisted commanders felt that their NCOs failed to encourage initiative suggests that the Soviet NCO may demonstrate the inflexibility and remoteness so evident in the officer corps. By any standard, the Soviet NCO apparently is not a risk-taker himself and tends to discourage this quality in his subordinates as well. The fear is that if something went wrong, the NCO would be held responsible. Such a fear only stunts the development of vital leadership qualities within the NCO ranks.

In order to discern and measure yet another quality of NCO leadership, it is important to know the degree to which NCOs are perceived as unselfish by their troops. When soldiers were asked whether their NCOs were selfish, 50.2 percent agreed they were. When enlisted commanders were asked the same question, their perceptions of the NCO corps were devastating: 92.3 percent said yes.[60] The fact that far too many NCOs are perceived by subordinates as self-serving can only retard the development of strong interpersonal bonds between soldiers and small-unit noncommissioned officer leaders.

With the evidence indicating that the NCO scores poorly in terms of setting an example, sharing hardships, exercising initiative, and pursuing his responsibilities unselfishly, it is difficult not to conclude that the Soviet NCO may have failed to develop and practice many of the basic leadership traits historically associated with small-unit effectiveness.

Many NCOs reflect the same negative conditions of military life as do the conscripts themselves. In the first place, the Soviet NCO is a conscript soldier; he is not a professional like the career warrior. He is merely a citizen-soldier barely prepared in a short six weeks for NCO rank. As a consequence, he has more affinity with the conscript ranks from which he came than with the professional NCO corps. Probably no more than one-third of the NCO corps can be judged to possess the leadership qualities that one would expect in a truly professional corps. In this sense, its rate of professional capacity (or incapacity) is about the same as that found in the American NCO ranks.

Crucial to developing bonds of unit cohesion among soldiers in small combat units is the degree to which troops perceive their leaders are close to them and genuinely care about them and their problems. In an attempt to measure this quality, soldiers were asked whether they felt their NCOs were "genuinely interested in their men's personal problems." Only 15 percent of the soldiers agreed, whereas 44.3 percent felt that their NCOs often "treated people in an impersonal manner; like cogs in a machine."[61]

In the case of the Soviet NCO, it seems that his distance from his men is deliberate and self-imposed. When soldiers were asked whether they felt their NCOs "drew too strong a line between himself and his men; he was too distant," 34.5 percent agreed. More importantly, when enlisted commanders were asked if their NCOs deliberately removed themselves from their men, 46.7 percent agreed.[62] Whatever the degree of distance between the Soviet noncommissioned officer and his men, and it seems substantial, his superiors believe that that distance is self-imposed.

The degree to which NCOs are capable of establishing strong personal ties with their men is vitally important to unit effectiveness. Unless soldiers are convinced that these strong personal ties exist, they will not likely constitute strong primary groups. Among common soldiers, 55.5 percent said that their NCOs "never developed close personal ties with their men." More damaging was the finding that 41.7 percent of Soviet officers also agreed that NCOs rarely established close ties with their troops. Even worse, the NCOs themselves admitted that they rarely established such ties; 72.7 percent of the NCOs agreed that their fellow NCOs never established close personal bonds with their men.[63] This failure is regarded as the normal course of events by most soldiers. This seems true of enlisted commanders, 62.5 percent of whom agreed that their NCOs failed to establish personal attachments to their troops. Officers who held command positions also agreed; 30 percent of them believed that their NCOs never established such ties.[64] The Soviet NCO has generally failed to convince anyone—his men, his peers, and his officers—that he has established close bonds with the men he leads. Interestingly, the military authorities appear willing to tolerate a much greater degree of remoteness of their NCOs from the troops than most Western armies.

The NCOs themselves were asked about the degree to which they established personal ties with their men and developed feelings of unit pride in their units. When NCOs were asked, "How close to your fellow soldiers did you feel when you were in the military," 31 percent felt that they had established moderately close ties. However, 37.9 percent believed that they had not established any close bonds at all or "felt few bonds with their men."[65] Thus, from the perspective of the NCO himself, at least one-third admitted that during their time in service they had not established any strong bonds with the men they were expected to lead.

A further dimension of the problem emerged when NCOs were asked, "How

strongly did you develop feelings of pride and affection for your military unit?''
Only 3.4 percent felt that they had established ''strong ties'' to their units, but
not a single NCO admitted to having ''very strong ties.'' Another 13.8 percent
thought they had established ''moderate'' ties with their units, while 31.0 percent
believed that whatever ties they had established ''were not strong at all.'' A
surprising 17.2 percent of the NCOs admitted that ''unit pride did not concern
me very much,'' while 34.5 percent indicated that they had developed ''no
feelings of pride at all.''[66] If the responses in the last three categories are combined, 82.7 percent of Soviet NCOs indicated that they had never established
strong feelings of unit pride or, at best, had developed such attachments to only
a marginal degree. Clearly, in his two short years of military service, the conscript
NCO is not acquiring the sense of dedication, attachment, and pride that we
would expect to find in a truly professional NCO corps.

Whatever the positive or negative qualities of the Soviet NCO, they are most
meaningful insofar as they contribute or retard the development of individual
and unit combat performance. Important in this equation is the degree to which
NCOs know their men, both their capabilities and their limits. NCOs who do
not have this knowledge are likely to commit grievous errors on the battlefield.
When soldiers were asked if they felt their NCOs ''truly knew their men and
respected their capabilities,'' only 17.7 percent agreed.[67] Therefore, a large
number of soldiers at all rank levels felt that their NCOs were insufficiently
informed about their men and their capabilities. The impact on the combat ability
of Soviet units is certain to be negative.

Another important facet of small-unit leadership is the extent to which soldiers
perceive their leaders to be good men to have around when the shooting starts.
When Soviet soldiers were asked for their views, 15.1 percent thought their
NCO would ''be a good man to go into combat with.'' However, the over-
whelming majority 84.9 percent admitted that they would not trust their NCOs
to lead them into battle, a rate considerably higher than that (53 percent) reported
by American soldiers.[68] As one moves up in rank, the degree of trust which
soldiers are willing to place in their noncommissioned officers changes only
marginally. For example, 24 percent of Soviet officers thought their sergeants
would be good men to go into battle with. The NCOs themselves had only
slightly greater faith in their combat abilities; only 33 percent of the sergeants
themselves felt that their peers would make good men in battle, while 40 percent
of their commanding officers expressed a similar opinion.[69] Apparently, few
people at any rank have sufficient faith in the ability of the Soviet NCO to
perform well under fire, and this includes his peers.

Judgment is a basic quality of good combat leadership at the small-unit level.
Combat commanders who lack judgment on the battlefield are dangerous to
themselves, their men, and their mission. When Soviet soldiers were asked
whether they felt their NCOs ''had the kind of judgment I would trust in combat,''
only 14.2 percent thought they had. The number of soldiers who rated their

NCOs positively was even lower than the 15.1 percent who felt that their NCO "would make a good man to go into combat with." The Soviet NCO is viewed to be devastatingly short in both combat ability and combat judgment.

Because enlisted commanders and commanding officers must deal with NCOs daily and depend upon them so heavily in combat, their viewpoints assume great importance. When enlisted commanders were asked if they felt their sergeants had the kind of judgment they would trust in combat, 50 percent reported that they did. By implication, however, at least half these crucial small-unit leaders did not trust their NCOs' judgment. More importantly only 37.5 percent of the commanding officers felt they could trust their sergeants' judgment in battle.[70] These data suggest that, in the view of his superiors and subordinates, the Soviet NCO may be seriously deficient in this vital quality of leadership.

The Soviet NCO corps may be failing to develop many of the skills and characteristics traditionally associated with highly effective combat leadership. The Soviet NCO does not seem to know his men well and to appreciate their capabilities and limitations, and neither his subordinates nor superiors consider him a good combat leader. Most seriously, he is reported to lack combat judgment. The Soviet NCO corps may be suffering from severe leadership deficiencies that could make themselves felt with a vengeance if Soviet units were forced to battle.

Conclusions

Both the Soviet and American NCO corps have significant weaknesses. The Soviet's most glaring failure is its inability to retain significant numbers of conscripts beyond their mandatory tour of duty. As a result, the Russians have not been able to develop and sustain a stable corps of military professionals at the small-unit level. Without such a corps to sustain the army under battle stress and train its troops, the Soviets' abilities to perform in battle are cast in doubt. Moreover, because of the biannual conscription cycle, nearly 25 percent of the army turns over every six months. With such instability, one may have serious reservations about how well such a corps would perform in battle.

In an attempt to compensate somewhat for these difficulties, the Soviet army has expanded its officer corps and assigned many NCO duties to junior officers. Data presented in Chapter 4 suggests that this effort is not working well. The amateurism of the NCO corps also makes it difficult to build unit cohesion, for precisely the same reasons as it does in the American Army—namely, no one is on station long enough to create and sustain the strong interpersonal attachments required to maintain unit cohesion. Indeed, with the biannual conscription cycle, no one is in place longer than eighteen months, a period that most Western armies have long recognized as too short to build effective units. The assignment turnover rate is generally much higher, at least in the ranks, than even in the American Army, although the gap seems to be narrowing somewhat.

The Soviet system of NCO recruitment and training has serious disadvantages, and no major advantages, from the point of view of military prepardness or unit effectiveness. It continues to exist primarily because of its *political* advantages: the two-year universal conscription system funnels everyone through the military, a system which is designed to inculcate the habits of obedience and attention to authority, habits which a totalitarian regime needs to control the larger civilian society. The notion is not unique to the Soviets; it worked rather well for almost a century for the conscript armies of Europe. But unlike these armies, the Soviet Army has failed to sustain a stable NCO corps. Thus, a major weakness of the Soviet Army is that its NCO corps is made up of conscripts who must train and lead other conscripts. Fears that such a corps may not perform well under battle stress are not without foundation.

The American NCO corps shares many of the same problems that afflict the Soviet NCO corps, albeit for different reasons. The rates of attrition and assignment turnover in the American corps are only slightly less than those in the Soviet Army, but are still high enough to raise serious questions about the corps' effectiveness. While the American Army has been more successful than the Soviet Army in retaining career NCOs, the quality of the corps has declined and continues to do so. Moreover, the American NCO is too distant from his troops and, much like his Soviet counterpart, is not held in particularly high regard by either his men or his officers. This problem shows up most seriously in the average soldier's lack of trust in his NCO and his lack of faith in the NCO's combat judgment.

The one major advantage of the American NCO corps, its extensive combat experience, has pretty well evaporated as the army moves into the 1980s. Most World War II and Korean veterans have left service, and gone, too, for the most part are the Vietnam veterans. If the American NCO corps still enjoys an advantage in combat experience, it does so only marginally.

Much of the damage that has been done to the American NCO corps is the result of a system that, like the Soviet conscript system, cannot truly be justified in terms of military effectiveness. The AVF has been accepted for its political viability and not its military applicability. Simply stated, the AVF does not threaten the lives and careers of the politically powerful and vocal middle and upper middle classes. The burden of military service has been placed upon the lower strata of American society who, if not entirely politically powerless, are at least mostly silent. As a consequence, the AVF has not been able to provide an adequate corps of good quality soldiers from which to build a professional NCO corps.

While both the Soviet and American NCO corps have serious problems, the American Army may be at a greater disadvantage because of the Soviet superiority in manpower, equipment, and deployment. On a man-to-man, one-to-one basis, the American NCO may in some aspects actually be somewhat worse than the Soviet NCO.

Notes

1. Edward A. Shills and Morris Janowitz, "Cohesion and Disintegration in the German Wehrmacht in World War II," *Public Opinion Quarterly* 12 (1948).

2. Human Readiness Report No. 5 (Washington, D.C.: Office of the Deputy Chief of Staff for Personnel), (August 1979), p. 8.

3. Ibid., p. 9.

4. Ibid.

5. Don Hirst, "Revised Criteria Cited in Readiness Reports," *Army Times*, November 10, 1980, p. 5.

6. John Fialka, "US Shell Games Cover Up Serious Lack of Readiness," *The Washington Star*, December 17, 1980, pp. 6-7.

7. Lieutenant-Colonel Ernest L. Webb, *NCO Corps: Is It Really Back on Top? Army*, (July 1978), p. 27.

8. See John Fialka, " Army Views Manpower Situation As Possible Crisis," *The Washington Star*, March 31, 1980, p. 6.

9. The Rosenblum Report is a two-year study undertaken by TRADOC in 1978-1979 on the quality of troop training and NCO quality. It formally emerged in a briefing given in 1979 under the title "Comparative Training Strategies." The information contained here and attributed to the Rosenblum Report was obtained from John Fialka's notes and memoranda on that briefing. The official version of the report is unobtainable. Citations from here on in will refer only to the Rosenblum Report.

10. John Fialka, "Re-Enlistments Higher Among Low IQ Recruits," *The Washington Star*, January 24, 1981, pp. 1 and 4.

11. John Fialka, "GI Proficiency at Low Level, New Study Says," *The Washington Star*, February 3, 1980, p. 2; see also the Rosenblum Report which makes the same point.

12. The Rosenblum Report, 1979.

13. Ibid.

14. Ibid. See also John Fialka, "Army Views Manpower Situation As Possible Crisis, *The Washington Star*, March 31, 1980, p. 4.

15. Cited in Fialka, "GI Proficiency at Low Level New Study Says, p. 2.

16. Ibid.

17. Ibid.

18. Ibid.

19. Webb, *NCO Corps*.

20. Ibid., p. 27.

21. Ibid.

22. Ibid., p. 28.

23. Ibid.

24. Ibid.

25. Ibid.

26. Human Readiness Report No. 5.

27. Ibid., p. 5.

28. Ibid.

29. Ibid.

30. Ibid.

31. Ibid.

32. Ibid.

33. Ibid., p. C-3.

34. Ibid.

35. Ibid.

36. Ibid.

37. Ibid.

38. Major Stephen Westbrook, "The Alienated Soldier: Legacy of Our Society," *Army* (December 1979).

39. Human Readiness Report No. 5, p. 12.

40. Westbrook, "The Alienated Soldier."

41. Ibid.

42. Ibid.

43. *CBS News Report*, September 15, 1979.

44. These figures are extrapolated from my own data. However, I can find no serious disagreement with them as estimates from intelligence agencies.

45. Again, the assessment of the failure of the Soviet warrant officer program is generally shared by most intelligence analysts, although official studies on the subject remain classified.

46. This is far more the case in the Canadian, British, German, and French armies than in the U.S. Army where it is not uncommon for a soldier to reach the rank of corporal in his first term.

47. Gabriel, *The New Red Legions,: An Attitudinal Portrait of the Soviet Army* (Westport, Conn.: Greenwood Press, 1980), p. 120.

48. Ibid., p. 119.

49. Ibid., p. 121.

50. This estimate was gained from conversations with army intelligence analysts.

51. Gabriel, *The New Red Legions*, p. 122. .

52. Ibid., p. 123.

53. Ibid.

54. Ibid., p. 124.

55. Ibid., p. 125.

56. Ibid., p. 127.

57. Ibid.

58. Ibid.

59. Ibid., p. 130.

60. Ibid., p. 131.

61. Ibid., p. 132.

62. Ibid., p. 133.

63. Ibid.

64. Ibid.

65. Ibid., p. 134.

66. Ibid., p. 134-35.

67. Ibid., p. 146.

68. Ibid., 146.

69. Ibid.

70. Ibid., p. 148.

4

The Officers

Officer leadership is most important at the small-unit level. All large battles are really collections of hundreds of skirmishes and contacts involving small-size (battalion, company, and platoon) units. Personal leadership remains critical, despite the popular notion that the killing power of sophisticated weaponry and the overall destructiveness of the modern battlefield have made traditional leadership skills less important, if not obsolete. In this view, all officers do is serve as "managers of the conflict," selecting options orchestrating the application of technology within the battle environment. But the human and psychological elements that bond soldiers together and to their officers and NCOs have little to do with technology, or even the type of battle. Indeed, the intensity of modern warfare has increased the need for the human psychological factors which help the soldier and his leaders withstand the horrors of modern combat.[1]

The officer is the crucial link in performing many functions necessary to effective combat operations. The officer corps is also the institutional memory of an army, the living repository of its history, its experiences, and, above all, its lessons. It is within the officer corps that the values, habits, and characteristics of the military profession are most clearly demonstrated. If the corps is corrupt or incompetent, then the profession will be corrupt; if the corps is of high quality, then it will be possible to shape a good army. The officer has two chief functions: to provide example and to provide judgment. Without example, effective combat units cannot be built because there are then no role-models for the young officers to follow and no exemplars for the men to emulate. Without an officer corps that sets the example for behavior in battle, an adequate corps cannot be retained since there is no clear line stretching from the existing corps to the one that must be built to meet the future. With regard to judgment, an officer corps that is incapable of good battlefield judgment will find itself unable to sustain itself or its units in battle.

The American Officer

The ten years of war in Vietnam are invaluable to any analysis of the American officer corps. The weaknesses and strengths shown in that war can be used as standards against which to measure the officer corps' character and performance today. The mode of analysis in this chapter is simple: if the difficulties that emerged during Vietnam are still evident today, then these same difficulties could well portend continued poor performance. If the difficulties have disappeared or at least lessened, then more optimistic prognoses are justified.

The American officer's performance in Vietnam is well documented in a number of books and articles written by scholars, military men, and the military establishment itself.[2] Almost all these assessments conclude that the quality of officer leadership in Vietnam, especially at the small-unit level, left much to be desired. Most studies point to the serious problems which emerged within American battle units that can be traced directly to poor officer leadership. Among these problems were high rates of desertion, refusal of units to engage the enemy, a series of mutinies, a consistently high drug-use rate and, most serious of all, the assassination of a considerable number of officers at the hands of their own men.[3] These events are mute testimony to the American officer's general inability to perform up to standard in Vietnam.

The difficulties in officer performance cannot be easily dismissed as reflecting the unique character of the war or the lack of homefront support. Most analyses of officer performance trace the difficulties to the officer corps' own behavioral patterns, values, institutions, practices, and policies, many of which had their origins in Secretary of Defense Robert S. McNamara's "reforms" of the 1960s.[4] By 1970, Secretary McNamara's restructuring of the military produced an officer corps that was unable to perform well and produced combat units that, in some instances, displayed such diminished capacity to function that they were virtually useless in battle. The collapse of small-unit cohesion characteristic of many American units in Vietnam can be traced to several systemic and institutional practices of the army itself and its officer corps. These policies helped erode the ties that bond men together in combat. Thus, the erosion of unit cohesion, the decline in combat-effectiveness, and the poor performance of the officer corps are not properly seen as aberrations of the system as much as logical consequences of the system's operation. Several analysts have identified these policies and have concluded that an "institutional rot" affected the officer corps, which in turn affected its ability to perform well.[5]

What, then, are some of the institutional and systemic problems that continue to plague the American officer and to make it difficult for him to be an effective leader? Undoubtedly, among the most serious is the rotational turbulence that affects the entire corps. The rapid and continual turnover of officers in leadership assignments was a characteristic of the Vietnam War, and it continues today. It often became impossible for an officer to remain with his unit and men long enough to gain their confidence and build cohesive units, or for the American officer to adequately train his troops. The exaggerated emphasis upon short-term performance has contributed to the emergence of the "ticket puncher," the officer who moves through a number of command assignments, remaining in each only long enough to impress his superiors with short-term gains and then moving on.

The problem worsened in Vietnam when the disruptive practice of having troops serve with their units in battle for twelve months was established, while officers served only six months after which they rotated back to the safety of staff assignments.[6]

Another problem that emerged in Vietnam was the perception that the officers were remote from their men and unwilling to share the burdens of combat and death. The troops may well have been quite accurate in this regard.[7] Because the officer corps was in constant motion, it had very little time to get to know the men and because units did not train as units and then deploy as units with stable officer elements, it was nigh impossible for officers and men to develop close ties. As to the failure to share the risks of battle with their men, the casualty figures again suggest that the troops were correct in their perceptions. Representing over 17 percent of total strength, officers took less than 7 percent of total battle casualties.[8] This, coupled with the shorter tour of duty for officers, quickly led the average soldier to feel that his officers did not care for him. That soldiers reacted to these perceptions is clear enough; over 1,000 officer and NCO leadership elements were assassinated by their own men, and there is some evidence that the rate may have been even higher.[9]

During the Vietnam War, the American Army had too many officers: they accounted for over 17 percent of total strength. With such a large officer corps, far too many of them were employed in unnecessary staff and noncombat assignments. At the same time, they were highly visible to the troops who bore the brunt of the combat risk. At the peak of American involvement in the war, more than 645,000 soldiers were deployed in the country, but no more than 88,000 soldiers were ever involved in combat operations.[10] Thus, a larger number of officers and men were in staff and support roles, and, most importantly, large numbers of safely ensconced troops and officers were visible to the combat troops. Combat soldiers would foray into the bush for a few days in search of the enemy, only to be met upon their return to camp by large numbers of officers assigned to staff positions, wearing starched fatigues, living in air-conditioned huts, and, most importantly, bearing no real risk of death.

The size of an officer corps is historically associated with its ability to perform well. There may even be an optimum size for an officer corps that is associated with successful armies. Generally, a corps that ranges between 3 and 6 percent of total strength seems most effective in battle. Examples abound and include the Roman Army, the Waffen S.S., the German Army in World Wars I and II, the British Army, the French Army in Indochina, and the present Israeli Army. In the American context, marine units fought better than army units in Vietnam in part because the percentage of marine officer strength never exceeded 6.4 percent, while army officer strength exceeded 15 percent.

The relation of size to good officer leadership is not difficult to discern. A small officer corps recognizes that leadership is a rare quality. When rigorous intellectual and physical standards of leadership are set, only a small number of men can meet them. Historically, successful armies have tended to utilize only the available qualified talent in their officer corps rather than to dilute standards in order to expand size. The American effort in Vietnam was marked by exactly the opposite policy, a deterioration in the quality standards for officers in order to meet inflated numerical requirements.

The size of an officer corps contributes to good leadership in another sense. A small corps is likely to develop a sense of being a brotherhood rather than just another organizational instrumentality. A sense of brotherhood, besides creating a sense of esprit, establishes within the corps an information network through which knowledge of an officer's reputation and abilities can be passed. In such a network, bureaucratic incompetence cannot easily be camouflaged. Members of a small corps are likely to know one another more intimately, making it easier to develop a sense of trust and to judge the competence of one's brothers. In short, many of the interpersonal relationships that contribute to corps and unit cohesion seem to develop more easily in a small officer corps.

Another aspect of small size is related to the willingness of officers to assume responsibility. In a small corps, known to one another, well trained, and imbued with a sense of brotherhood, small numbers of officers must assume direct responsibility for the task of leadership. Larger corps have a proliferation of formal authority but a diminishing sense of acceptance of responsibility. A large corps tends to diffuse responsibility rather than focus it upon individual officers, to blame the "system" for failures, and to utilize the bureaucratic process to avoid responsibility.

The prominence of managerial values and entrepreneurial ethics contributed greatly to the American officer's inability to perform well in Vietnam. In 1960, with McNamara's appointment as Secretary of Defense, the army set out to change its image. No longer was the army and military service, especially service as an officer, to be regarded as a special calling requiring special men to accomplish special tasks. Instead, it was to be regarded as only another occupation reflecting many of the same practices and values found in any business organization. Thus began the rise of what has been called managerialism, the tendency to see the officer as no different from other civilian managers and to regard their tasks similarly. Unfortunately, managerialism and its attendant entrepreneurial ethics cut completely across the idea of an officer corps as a brotherhood of professionals. Furthermore, they force officers to make decisions in terms of the impact they will have on their own careers rather than on the basis of military experience or expertise. The result has been a transition of the military away from its traditional values of duty, honor, country, service, and sacrifice toward a military rooted in managerial self-interest, careerism, and promotion. These conditions have given rise to the "ticket punching syndrome," a condition describing the officer in continual assignment rotation, avoiding risk, focusing upon the short-term gain, and moving on before he can be made accountable for his failures. In short, many American officers during Vietnam and since have made a career out of avoiding responsibility.

An examination of the American officer's actual battlefield performance in

Vietnam reveals additional shortcomings. The officer corps was infected with managerial careerism, forced into constant rotation between units, and bloated by its own size. As a result, the troops saw their officers as concerned primarily with career and self-interest and unwilling to share risks with their men. These attitudes may perhaps be directly linked to the fact that over 1,000 officers and NCOs were assassinated by their own men, a rate of military murder which is unique in the American Army and perhaps even in Western armies. Modern military history perhaps offers no other instance of as many as 20 percent of officer casualties being attributed to their own men.

Officer casualty figures are another indicator of the failure of the officer corps to perform credibly and to develop effective leadership in battle. As mentioned above, although the officer corps comprised over 17 percent of total troop strength in Vietnam, it absorbed only 7 percent of the casualties.[11] The number of officers who actually met their deaths at the hands of the enemy decreases rapidly as rank rises.[12] In a war of battalion, rapid officer rotation and transfers allowed for the presence of over 1,600 battalion commanders over a ten-year period. In a war in which the battalion was the primary maneuver and combat element, only eight battalion commanders met their deaths through hostile fire.[13] Finally, only three general officers died of battle wounds in the Vietnam War, two flew their helicopters into fog-shrouded mountains, and one was killed by enemy fire. Hence, it seems that the American officer corps neither bore its fair share of the burden of death nor was able to establish strong bonds with its men. Throughout Vietnam, the American officer corps suffered from a range of institutional and systemic difficulties that crippled its effectiveness. Evidently, the officers who took the field of battle in that war did not lead very well.

Ten years after the end of American involvement in Vietnam, many of the problems that emerged during that war concerning the officer corps remain, and with the introduction of the AVF, many of these problems have become more serious. One of the largest problems is the shortage of officers. The army has a total of 84,447 serving officers, or 11 percent of total force strength (down from 17 percent during Vietnam). Curiously, however, as the strength of the officer corps relative to enlisted strength has tended to decline, the ratio of general officers to troop strength has increased by 31 percent since the Vietnam War.[14] The army has more general officers serving relative to the number of troops than it had during the war. Today the American Army troop strength is less than half what is was during Vietnam. Although the number of officers as a percentage of total strength has declined to 11 percent, this number still represents an officer corps that is far too large as well as maldistributed in rank. Generally, in effective field armies the ratio of officers to men almost never exceeds 5 percent.[15] By this standard, the American officer corps is twice as large as it has to be. Moreover, its ratios are maldistributed. During Vietnam, the army fielded one officer for every 8.5 soldiers, a ratio that was far too high and that exceeded the World War II ratio of one officer for every 9.4 soldiers. Today that ratio is even more disproportionate, with the army fielding one officer for every 6.8 soldiers.[16]

Despite its large size, the officer corps suffers from an acute shortage of officers in certain ranks, most noticeably in the junior ranks from which the commanders of small combat units are drawn. The army is having great difficulty retaining young officers, especially combat arms officers. In 1975, 70 percent of the serving young officers expressed a willingness to remain in service beyond their existing tour. By 1980, this number had declined to 44 percent. Across the board the army is retaining only 60.5 percent of its officers beyond their first tour of duty, the lowest retention rate since 1975, and the rate continues to decline.[17] Although retention is slightly better (66.7 percent) in the combat arms, it still represents a five-year low.[18] Curiously, the retention of officers has declined steadily since the introduction of the AVF and improvements in salaries and benefits, although exactly the opposite was expected.

The magnitude of the officer shortage is serious. According to official army projections, the corps requires the entry of approximately 10,500 new junior officers every year. In 1980, that number fell to about 8,000 actual entrants from all sources, including ROTC and West Point. Thus, the army is short approximately 2,000 officers, or about 20 percent of the force complement that the army regards as necessary to man a force of 700,000.[19] The overall in-service officer strength is also short. These shortages are felt most importantly at the junior ranks. There are no shortages of field grade officers; only excessive overages. The army does not lack general officers, nor is there any evidence of shortages in the major, colonel, or lieutenant-colonel ranks. The shortages are most acute and most damaging at the lieutenant, first lieutenant, and captain ranks, precisely at those points where officers are needed to train and command killing combat units of platoon and company size. In 1980, the army projected that it would be short 5,900 captains, a rank that normally occupies critical combat leadership positions.[20] By accelerating promotions and reducing the experience required for its first lieutenants, the army estimated that by 1982 it could reduce the shortage of captains from 5,900 to 3,740.[21] This would, of course, precipitate an even greater shortage of first and second lieutenants, a shortage that would have grave consequences since the army is already 20 percent short of the number of lieutenants it says it needs to man the force. Moreover, by reducing the time in grade requirements by accelerating promotion to the rank of captain in order to solve the captain shortage, the quality of captains will likely decline along with the decline in the training and experience of lieutenants. At the end of the Vietnam War, the army released over 74,000 young combat-trained officers, most of them lieutenants and captains, as part of the overall reduction in force. Today, a decade later, it is critically short of these manpower skills.

The shortage of junior officers is a serious problem in the American Army as it would be for any army. While it tolerates excessive numbers of field grade and general officers—few of which ever serve in combat positions—it finds itself acutely short of those junior officers who actually command combat units. The result is an overall decline in experienced leadership at the company and platoon level a decline which most certainly ramifies upon the battalions as promotion of young officers is accelerated as an inducement to remain in service. In short, the army officer corps is still too much tail and not enough teeth, just as it was in Vietnam. Ten years have brought few changes in this regard.

Stability of assignments is an important variable in the equation of combat-effectiveness for battle units. The period of assignments of officers has ranged from the extremes of the Roman Army's twenty years to the modern Canadian and British armies' five years. The greater the stability of officers in command positions, the greater the likelihood that they will develop a close knowledge of their men and their units' abilities.[22] When allowed to remain with a unit for long periods, officers can develop, learn from mistakes, and grow in ability. But when an officer has only eighteen months with a unit (a common occurrence in the American Army), every decision and mistake becomes crucial to his evaluation and his career. These conditions are intensified by an evaluation system which expects officers to be almost perfect to qualify for their next promotion or command assignment. Under these conditions, officers rarely learn from their mistakes, for few dare admit they made any.

Officer corps stability is also important to the development of unit cohesion without which combat-effectiveness cannot develop. The bonding of men together in battle can occur only when subordinates see their officers as competent, trustworthy, and dependable. Such perceptions require time to develop, which means longer tours of officers with their units.

The American officer corps is afflicted by excessive personnel turnover. In 1980, 81 percent of the army's officer and enlisted personnel changed assignments. A 1975 study of the 2nd Armored Division in Europe found that in a seven-month period the turnover rates were 119 percent for platoon leaders, 113 percent for company commanders, and 98 percent for platoon sergeants.[23] At the staff level of the same division, assignment change ranged from the 177 percent characteristic of the S-3 section—the crucial operations planners for the division—to the 217 percent found among senior staff officers and noncommissioned officers. The average assignment turnover rate in the entire division at all ranks ranged from a low of 177 percent to a high of 388 percent.[24]

What these figures imply is that when positions change at a rate of 100 percent soldiers have to adjust to two new leaders in a single year; at a 200-percent rate, three new men; and at 300 percent, four new leaders. In 1977, the Army Research Institute examined a "typical" company in the field and found that in a normal period 24 percent of the men had left their units, either departing service or going to other units, and that another 24 percent changed squads or staff assignments. The average rate within this "typical" infantry company was 15 percent per month, or 180 percent each year.[25] Not surprisingly then, it is difficult to engender any sense of confidence and cohesion in such units. They are comprised of and led by men who are strangers to one another.

The turnover of general officers is equally rapid. For the 1960-1980 period, as Louis Sorley points out, the average length of time on station for a four star general in the American Army was only twenty months; for a lieutenant-general, it was twenty-one months but rapidly declining to nineteen months. For most lower ranking general officers, the average assignment time was less than twenty-four months.[26] Even at the highest staff levels, the rotation in assignments was excessive. Over the same twenty-year period, Sorley analyzed key staff positions at the highest level of the army General Staff. He found that the average time in which all these people were on station together so that they could function as a complete staff unit was only 4.8 months, a finding consistent over a twenty-year period of analysis.[27] Although this figure is up somewhat from the 3.8 month average found during the Vietnam War, the rate of assignment instability is still excessive. The comparable figure for the Soviet General Staff during the same twenty-year period was fourteen years. Thus, even the major planning mechanism of the American Army at its highest levels is in a state of continual turbulence.

An example of the extent of turnover as it affects field units is provided by a letter written by General George S. Patton, Jr., commander of the 2nd Armored Division in Germany. General Patton noted that in the twenty-six months in which he was that unit's commander, he witnessed the turnover of five assistant division commanders or a rate of 400 percent. During the same period, he witnessed the changing of three chiefs of staff for personnel, three chiefs of staff for intelligence, three chiefs of staff for operations, and four chiefs of staff for supply. Focusing on his field commanders, General Patton had six different brigade commanders, three divisional artillery commanders, and two different division support commanders. In addition, he saw the turnover of three maintenance battalion commanders, four cavalry squadron commanders, and two engineer battalion commanders.[28] With the rate of assignment turnover among officers so high, their ability to train and prepare their units to fight effectively has become questionable.

The severe assignment turnover is the logical consequences of certain institutional practices which require that the officer corps change assignments frequently in order to function within the bureaucratic environment. One major cause is that the army has too many officers to begin with and far too many field grade and general officers. As pointed out earlier, the officer corps is twice as large as historical standards of military effectiveness suggest. The increased number of staff officers, coupled with the unrealistically short twenty-year retirement system, forces an officer to move from one assignment to another. Within a twenty-year career, the "successful" officer will move through almost twenty-two different assignments in order to qualify for general officer promotion. The army does not allow captains, majors, or lieutenant-colonels to serve long periods without necessarily competing for promotion and new assignments. This "up-or-out" policy forces an officer to pass through a number of "gates" or "tickets" in order to qualify for promotion or even to qualify for his retirement benefits.[29] An officer cannot remain in a specific job or assignment for long periods, as he can in the Canadian, British, German, French, Israeli, and even the Soviet Army, and continue to perform effectively in that assignment. The great emphasis, rather, is upon a number of different assignments rather than upon long-term service in a few stable positions. Moreover, command positions are very desirable and since there are far fewer command positions than officers, in order to ensure that every officer gets an opportunity to command, the tenure of command assignments is reduced to the lowest time possible. The tremendous competition to acquire these assignments adds to the instability within the officer corps.[30]

Yet another factor compelling assignment turnover is the emphasis upon managerialism. Over the last two decades the officer has acquired the image of the managerial expert. This image has been molded by sending great numbers of officers to the army's large number of staff schools as well as to civilian universities to obtain advanced degrees, mostly in administration. As a result, there are too many staff officers with high expectations. The army fails to select a percentage of officers from the great mass who would qualify for promotion and to allow the rest to serve long periods in their assignments. For example, in the early 1960s, no more than 18 percent of army officers were selected to attend the Command and General Staff College. It was clear to all officers that those chosen would constitute a pool for selection to the highest ranks. Those not selected generally understood that they would probably not achieve rank higher than lieutenant-colonel. Today, however, virtually every officer attends the Command and General Staff College, and those who are not selected to attend directly must complete the course by correspondence. Even Army Reserve officers must complete the course to qualify for promotion.

Because of the great personnel turnover, officers are rarely able to establish bonds with their men and units. Forced to move rapidly from one assignment to another, unit officers are always learning their jobs rather than providing experienced performance. Just as an officer gains experience in his new post it is time to move to another. This condition produces officers who are overly concerned with their efficiency reports. Tyrannized by the doctrine of "zero defects," they are so future oriented that in their present posts they try only to avoid mistakes until they leave for a new assignment.

Finally, the frequent rotations in assignments produce an officer corps characterized by the ethos of entrepreneurial competition and careerism in which every officer must look out for himself. Such a system engenders a set of values corrosive of any concept of the military as a special calling. It encourages attitudes in which one's men are seen as instrumentalities to the advancement of one's career, thereby eroding any sense of moral or ethical obligation. There is no place left in the system for the competent officer who wishes to spend his career in a given area of expertise, foregoing the press of promotion. He *must* move through a series of assignments or he is surely passed over for promotion and, eventually, is forced to leave service. Linking promotion to retention instead of linking retention to competence and experience is a serious flaw in the system.[31]

The American officer corps today is characterized by amateurism. Placing officers with little experience in a series of unit assignments assures that large numbers of officers in critical posts will have little or no experience in their jobs. At the platoon and company level, this condition has been worsened by the shortage of officers in these ranks and by the policy of accelerating the promotion of second lieutenants, themselves inexperienced, to higher grades. Few officers are well trained for the positions they occupy, and few are allowed to remain in their positions long enough to acquire that experience.

Evidence of amateurism can be found most readily at the small-unit level, that is, at the battalion commander level and below within a division. A study of the 8th Infantry Division done in 1980 reveals that 65 percent of the battalion commanders in the division had not served with troops for either ten years or more before taking command of their battalions.[32] Indeed, one battalion commander had not been in a troop unit assignment for seventeen years prior to assuming command of his battalion. Since such men are inexperienced and are not likely to be allowed to remain with their battalions longer than twenty-four months and since most of the battalion staff and the troops themselves are also in a state of constant turnover, the officers' amateurism is not surprising.

The average assignment turnover in the army is at least 89 percent a year and probably much higher.[33] The effect on unit cohesion, training, combat-effectiveness, and the development of a professional NCO corps is massive. On balance, large numbers of officers occupy positions for which they are ill equipped, which only adds to the manifest difficulties already confronting American units.

Given the difficulties confronting the American officer, considerable problems of quality may also emerge. In the eyes of his men, the American officer leaves much to be desired. Human Readiness Report No. 5 shows how American officers are viewed by their troops.[34] When officers themselves were asked if officer leadership had been a problem in their units "during the last six months," 53.7 percent of the officers said it was a problem and 20.6 percent felt that the problem was getting worse.[35] Only 8.7 percent thought the problem was improving. When the focus is shifted to those officers who served in troop units, the perceptions of officer quality worsen. Among officers serving with troop units 59.1 percent felt that the quality of officer leadership was a problem for them and 23.1 percent that the problem was getting worse.[36] As examined from the point of view of commanders, 51.7 percent thought the quality of officer leadership in their units was a problem, 18.4 percent saw the problem as growing worse, and 19.5 percent felt the problem was at least stable.[37] The views of officers in combat units are very important since it is they who, after all, have the greatest responsibility for bringing their units to combat-readiness. Of these officers, 57.0 percent felt that the quality of officer leadership in their units was a problem in the preceding six months and 22.8 percent that the problem was increasing.[38]

The problem of officer quality is not a new one. In 1971, the Army War College completed its study on officer quality.[39] That study noted the growing emphasis on careerism within the corps as well as the tendency toward protecting one's career to become a dominant value. Also documented was the propensity of officers to make the welfare of their men secondary to the pursuit of their careers. A decade later much the same conditions persist. When field grade officers were asked, "What statement best approximates your judgment concerning general officers of today (1980): They are mostly concerned about their men; they are mostly concerned about their own career," 30.5 percent felt that their general officers were most concerned about their careers compared to 20.5 percent in 1974.[40] Viewed longitudinally, then, field grade officers increasingly see their general officers as becoming more career oriented. At the same time, only 1.4 percent of the field grade officers thought their general officers were most concerned about their men, a rate slightly less than half the 2.5 percent who felt that way in 1974.[41] It is easy to see how the average soldier may come to feel that his officers do not genuinely care for him; certainly, that is the officers' perception of their generals.

When field grade officers were asked to evaluate their peers along the same dimensions, much the same picture of the careerist officer emerged. Some 45.4 percent felt that their brother field grade officers were concerned mostly about their own careers, a number that exceeds the 44.4 percent who thought that their peers were concerned about their missions and troop welfare combined.[42] Moreover, the percentage who assessed their peers as careerists increased from the 44.8 percent who did so five years earlier. This again documents an upward trend in career orientation.

At the same time, the number of field grade officers who stated that their peers were more concerned about the welfare of their men fell from 2.2 percent in 1974 to 1.3 percent in 1979, again reflecting a decline in a critical dimension of officer leadership.[43] The field grade officers of today are the generals of tomorrow, and there is every reason to believe that future generals will share the concern for career over troop welfare. Perhaps the system has constructed certain parameters to ensure the selection of officers contingent on their ability to demonstrate certain attitudes and values.[44] Whatever the case may be, general and field grade officers are almost twenty-five times more concerned about their own career as they are about the welfare of their men.

In 1972, the Army War College Study offered the following portrait of the American Army officer. He was

the ambitious transitory commander, marginally skilled in the complexities of his duties, engulfed in producing statistical results and avoiding personal failure, too busy to talk with and listen to subordinates, and determined to submit acceptably optimistic reports which reflect faultless completion of a variety of tasks at the expense of sweat and frustration of his subordinates.[45]

The War College Study documented the transition of the officer corps away from its traditional role as warriors and gladiators to its new role as managers and entrepreneurs. Evidence available on officer attitudes in 1980 suggests that many of these characteristics remain today.

The findings of Human Readiness Report No. 5 strongly support this view.

For instance, 83.8 percent of army officers worldwide and 87.2 percent of officers at field grade rank felt that "competition is good for the Army because it keeps us sharp, eliminates dead wood, and is a good motivator."[46] The notion of an officer corps comprised of competitors as opposed to a brotherhood of peers took firm root in the American Army by 1972. Along the same lines, there is the feeling that competition reduces effectiveness and that it may well have gotten out of hand; 68.2 percent of company grade officers felt that there was "too much competition" and that many officers were "caught up in a competitive jungle." Among the field grade officers 66.6 percent also felt this way.[47] Yet, when officers were asked if they would "prefer a somewhat less need to compete," only 43.6 percent of the company grade and 37.7 percent of the field officers thought this way.[48] Although most agree that the competition among officers is excessive and often has negative results, only a minority prefers reducing this competition. It may well be that the officer corps has become so thoroughly imbued with managerial and entrepreneurial values that it knows no other way by which to evaluate itself.

The tyranny of statistics pointed to by the War College Study in 1971 also seems to be with us in the 1980s. Among the company grade and field grade officers respectively, 83.9 percent and 81.6 percent agreed that the "use of statistics leads to competition on numbers not on the issues."[49] The misuse of statistical indicators is reflected in the views of company grade officers, 79.5 percent of whom agreed that because of statistical indicators "one often cannot tell what's important due to the ambiguity of shifting priorities to compete or to waste time on non-essentials"; 72.1 percent of field grade officers also agreed.[50] In short, the emphasis on marginalities pointed out in 1971 appears constant.

Perhaps the corollary of focusing upon statistical marginalities as indicators of officer performance is that it often leads to sacrificing the truth about more important indicators as a way of protecting one's career. Thus, 72.5 percent of company grade officers agreed that "training may be sacrificed" by focusing upon less important issues; 63.3 percent of these same officers perceived that this "sacrifice" was necessary in order to stay competitive for promotion and to look good for one's superiors. Along the same lines, 78.4 percent of company grade officers felt that "the need to stay competitive caused some shading of the truth" in evaluating their unit's performance, and 65.6 percent of the field grade officers agreed. Indeed, 43.7 percent of company grade officers and 33.8 percent of field grades felt that "officers sometimes withhold information for personal advantage."[51] Thus, an analysis of the attitudes of company and field grade officers uncovers many of the same problems that the Army War College identified as plaguing the officer corps a decade ago. The emphasis on competition, career survival, use of statistical indicators to excess, shading of the truth, and the tendency to look good even at the cost of sacrificing unit training and effectiveness seem to remain characteristic of the American officer corps. In this sense, the ten years of experience since the end of the Vietnam War has had little effect on reforming the corps.

The troops' views on officer quality is an important variable in assessing the quality of an army's officers. The number of soldiers who believed "my officers care about my welfare" fell to 40 percent, a 10 percent decline over the last five years.[52] Equally important is that only 45 percent of the soldiers thought that their officers were "competent" compared to 60 percent who thought so five years before.[53] Similar data emerged from the Westbrook study in 1980. In that study, 52 percent of the soldiers interviewed believed they "cannot count on their officers to look after their interests," while another 20 percent were unsure. In addition, 37 percent believed that their officers were not concerned about them in any meaningful way, and 28 percent believed that "most officers cannot be trusted." Thirty-two percent of the soldiers did not think that their officers would be willing to suffer the same hardships and risks in battle that their men would have to undergo.[54] Finally, the 1978 CBS poll among soldiers of the Berlin Brigade found that 53 percent of the troops interviewed said they would be willing to follow their officers into battle.[55]

It could be argued that good officer leadership must be sustained by environmental supports, an argument that seems valid from the viewpoint of military history. Through some 2,000 years, successful armies with good leadership have been marked by four basic environmental or institutional supports: a code of appropriate values, an officer corps of small size, assignment stability, and a sense of the military as a special calling.[56] Over the long run, a military force without these institutional supports will not likely be able to recruit, develop, and exercise good unit leadership. As we have already seen, the American officer corps seriously lacks each of these supports, raising serious questions about its effectiveness.

Many of the systemic and institutional forces that gave rise to the battlefield failures of officer leadership during the Vietnam War have remained in evidence ten years after that war ended. These forces were set in motion before Vietnam itself by Secretary McNamara's reforms in 1960. Assignment instability, officer shortages, the officer's remoteness from his men, the soldier's perceptions of his officers as not competent or trustworthy, the managerial values, the entrepreneurial ethics, the bloated size of the corps, the transition to occupationalism, amateurism, and rampant careerism are all characteristics of self-serving business organizations, organizations that served as the model for the changes inflicted upon the military in 1960.

The evidence suggests that the critique of the officer corps made by the Army War College Study in 1971 remains valid today. To the extent that those practices hinder or foreclose the development of effective combat leadership, they still cut across and reduce the quality of officer leadership. Whenever the quality of officer leadership in the American Army is subjected to the scrutiny of soldiers and even other officers, the judgment that continually emerges is that the officer corps is of low quality, more managerial oriented than military oriented, and has failed to develop many of the skills considered important to the development of effective combat units. To the degree that the organizational problems which crippled the officer corps during the Vietnam War remain unchanged a decade later, the corps may perform as badly in the future as it did the last time it took to the field of combat.

The Soviet Officer

Soviet Army officers enter military service from several sources under various programs. The first source is the Military College. By far the largest number of officers are commissioned upon graduation from one of the country's 143 military colleges, each of which has an average enrollment of approximately 1,000. Graduates from these colleges serve in all branches of the armed forces, including the air force and navy. Programs similar to the ROTC programs conducted at American universities are a second source of officers. These programs provide training and education in military subjects to a large number of students who then receive reserve force commissions.[57] Military training is coterminous with the civilian educational curriculum, and graduation from university leads to a reserve commission. Ordinary soldiers who are promoted through the ranks represent a third source. Upon completion of their active duty, soldiers with a secondary or higher education may earn a lieutenant's commission in the reserve forces by passing a competitive examination.[58] The Soviets apparently have little difficulty retaining good officers. Moreover, they have a very large pool of potential applicants from which to select those who are allowed to remain as career officers.

The Soviet Army today has approximately 500,000 officers on active duty, or about 16 percent of total strength. This is a somewhat larger percentage than that in most Western armies, although during Vietnam the American Army figure was 17 percent.[59] Curiously, the number of officers in the Soviet Army has increased during an actual decrease in the size of the overall military structure. Its large size may be explained by the inordinate concern of the political regime for adequate political control. Large numbers of officers generally ensure this control. Moreover, as mentioned earlier, in the Soviet Army a substantial number of junior officers hold positions and perform tasks that in Western armies would normally be performed by noncommissioned officers. Nonetheless, in a traditional military force—after which the Soviet Army is patterned—the number of officers only rarely exceeds 5 percent of total strength. Thus, the size of the Soviet officer corps marks an interesting departure from officer-manning levels found in traditional European armies.

After assignment to active duty, the Soviet officer rotates through a small number of command and staff assignments. Assignments change much less frequently than in the American Army, while he is allowed to spend a longer amount of time in a given assignment. Furthermore, the Soviet officer seems to spend far less time in staff schools than his American counterpart. The reason for the less frequent assignment turnover seems to be that the Soviet Army is a traditional army with a conscript base and, therefore, does not need to compete with the civilian economy for critical manpower, at least not to the extent that the American Army does. Consequently, there is somewhat less emphasis on staff or on the need to rotate through assignments so that every officer can maintain his upward mobility and thus decrease the chances that he will leave service for employment in the civilian sector. Officers are selected to attend advanced institutes or component branch schools, but the wholesale shepherding of large numbers of officers through staff schools, which is so characteristic of the American Army, is not typical in the Soviet Army.[60] Promotion to the next higher grade up to colonel depends upon the normal military requirements, such as academic training, service experience, duty assignments, job performance, and the all-important quality of political reliability as assessed by the unit's political officers.[61]

Unlike American officers, Soviet officers may remain on active duty until they reach the statutory age of retirement, an age that varies by rank. An officer may spend as many as twenty-five years in the military never exceeding the rank of senior or even junior lieutenant. The mandatory age of retirement for a junior lieutenant, for example, is forty. Therefore, an officer would be allowed at least twenty years of active service at this rank, not counting his reserve obligations which remain after he retires. Thus, the Soviets have not adopted one of the most disruptive and corrosive practices of the American Army, the up-or-out policy which requires an officer not promoted on schedule to leave military service.

The up-or-out policy as practiced in the American Army essentially reflects managerial and entrepreneurial values operating in a postindustrial socioeconomic environment. Under its aegis, the officer is continually required to demonstrate his competence in new skills and to compete with all other officers for promotion and assignment. Such competition supposedly increases skills and permits only the best to rise to the top and eventually be selected for command and promotion to general officer. Consequently, the American Army has few officers with twenty years' experience still in the ranks of lieutenant, captain, or even major. Traditional armies such as the Soviet Army are characterized by a highly stable leadership, especially officers at the lower ranks. These officers spend their entire careers as combat unit commanders, thereby enhancing small-unit cohesion and effectiveness.[62] By contrast, modern military structures manifest a great deal of officer assignment rotation and of cutting off officers who do not come up to standard. As a result, the Soviet rate of assignment turnover for officers is much lower than that of the American Army. Unit commanders are allowed to remain with their units for much longer periods, as are staff officers.

Since the Soviet Army has not adopted an up-or-out policy, it has maintained a basic, traditional form of military organization. Accordingly, this organization would be expected to provide the same advantages to the Soviet Army at the small-unit level that it has provided to traditional armies in the past. The Soviets tend to maintain officers for long periods in command and staff positions precisely because they are competent at that level of performance, although they may not be particularly qualified for promotion to higher rank. This practice seems to mitigate the operation of the infamous "Peter principle." The Soviets have refused to link retention in service to promotion, preferring to follow the traditional model and to link it to performance. This position is exactly the opposite from that adopted by the American Army.

As a result, there is greater assignment stability within the Soviet officer corps. The Soviet officer normally commits himself to a twenty-five year career of service, and most officers remain in active service for the entire period, regardless of how rapidly they are promoted. The officer is not continually shifted from one assignment to another, nor must he live under the pressure of being terminated if he fails to make his "next" promotion on schedule. Therefore officers in command positions can increase their levels of competence and sense of identification with their troops. Another possible effect is that many officers better identify with their units if the officers have held their positions for years and are greatly experienced.

The quality of the Soviet officer is open to some debate. The Soviets seem to have particular difficulty in staffing their officer corps with individuals interested in command positions.[63] The emphasis placed upon science and technical education, an emphasis that begins during the officer's military college or university training, seems to work against the development of officers oriented toward command. The tendency instead is to produce officers who are highly specialized and technically oriented. The stress placed upon technical qualifications minimizes reliance upon judgmental qualifications, which in a totalitarian regime is a desirable result.

The bureaucratization attendant to Soviet society seems also to have penetrated the Soviet officer corps. Important here is the tendency to develop an "upward looking posture."[64] Meeting the requirements of superiors often takes precedence over tending to the problems of the troops. The introduction of "socialist competitions" among units as a training device and the increased reliance upon performance reports for promotion have reinforced this tendency.[65] As in the American Army, getting high marks on one's efficiency report often displaces the substance of the reports. Undoubtedly, one reason why the officer develops bureaucratic perspectives is that his efficiency report is prepared by his superiors in consultation with the unit's political officer.[66] Increasingly, the officer corps tends to avoid responsibility for mistakes rather than deal with them. Moreover, the Soviet officer corps tends toward goal displacement and scapegoating, and the emphasis on political loyalty in judging military competence only increases this tendency. In the eyes of the party, an officer is primarily a political rather than a military leader, and Soviet military authorities themselves stress party loyalty as the "primary characteristic" of a good officer.[67] Under these conditions, it is not surprising that officers would tend to develop bureaucratic defense mechanisms.

Soviet training doctrine also promotes bureaucratization. Unlike the American Army which places a premium upon a young officer exercising initiative and taking risks, the Soviet Army stresses conformity to existing schedules and plans.[68] At the same time, the Soviet Army has an exaggerated compulsion to meet deadlines outlined in operational plans. Soviet military journals are replete with convoluted arguments that try to resolve the tension between initiative and following plans by instilling in the officer something called "correct initiative."[69] Nonetheless, initiative for the Soviet officer is still largely reduced to following operational plans. Consequently, the officer's duty to provide initiative and judgment to his command is subordinated to the larger requirements of observing orders and meeting operational checkpoints and deadlines.

Another influence on the officer corps is the feeling of many officers that the regime does not really trust the corps itself. The constant presence of the unit political officer, the use of KGB spies within the ranks, and the influence of the political officer on the efficiency report do little to encourage the officer to develop a sense of risk, initiative, and responsibility.[70] One result of these conditions is an officer corps that remains aloof, if not deliberately remote, from its troops. With careerism and advancement viewed as the major games to play, officers tend to minimize responsibility for mistakes by conforming to regulations and operational plans.

To discern how the Soviet soldier perceives his officers, soldiers were asked, "Given the general quality of officers that you served with in your military service, how would you rate their quality as officers?" The respondents provided the following assessments: 0.9 percent said their officers were "extremely good"; 9.7 percent "good"; 56.6 percent "average"; 14.2 percent "fair"; 15.0 percent "poor"; and 1.8 percent "very poor."[71] If the numbers are collapsed into ordinal categories, the number of "bad" officers exceeds the number of "good" officers by almost three times.

Another way to gain insight into the quality of the Soviet officer is to examine the officers' opinions by rank. When the data are arranged in this manner, some interesting dimensions emerge. If the two top-quality categories are combined, only 6.8 percent of the common soldiers in the ranks thought their officers were either good or extremely good, the lowest percentage of all ranks. By contrast, 13.8 percent of noncommissioned officers saw their superiors as good or extremely good. Surprisingly, only 14.8 percent of the officers themselves assigned their brother officers to the two top categories. This may indicate an acute shortage of quality officers within the Soviet Army. When taken together, approximately one-third of the soldiers, regardless of rank, described their officers as low-quality officers compared to only 11 percent who regarded them as high quality.[72]

The data can also be examined from the perspective of those who held positions of command. Only 11.8 percent of the enlisted commanders rated their officers as good or extremely good. Equally revealing is the fact that 29.4 percent of these same commanders rated their officers as fair, poor, or very poor.

The views of the small-unit commanders were as follows: 16.6 percent regarded their brother officers as good or extremely good, while 16.7 percent described them as fair, poor, or very poor. When these data are combined with the 31 percent of officers armywide who put their peers in the lower quality categories, the fact that almost 17 percent of officer commanders also judged their peers to be of low quality suggests that substantial numbers of Soviet officers may in fact not be competent when judged in terms of their leadership ability. If some arbitrary figure is settled upon between 16 percent and 31 percent, it might well be argued that at least 20 percent of Soviet officers are regarded as less than competent by their own peers.

The most that can be said of Soviet officer quality is that it is average when it is not assessed as below average by the troops and the officers themselves. This view is confirmed by officers and unit commanders at the enlisted and officer level, a circumstance which suggests that the quality of commanders may also be low. Although the Soviet Army officer corps has improved greatly since World War II, its overall level of quality as assessed by its men and its peers is still low, and there is much room for professional growth within the corps itself.

A dimension important for assessing the Soviet officer is the degree to which officers are seen as good leaders. One element of effective leadership is the officer's ability to convince his men that he genuinely cares about their welfare and is prepared to assume at least the same risks to which they are exposed. When troops believe their officers are uncaring, as the American troops did during Vietnam, unit disintegration rapidly sets in.[73] Among soldiers in the Soviet Army, only 22.1 percent agreed that their officers shared hardships with their troops. But amazingly, 72.8 percent of the officers perceived themselves as sharing their men's burdens. At the very least, there is a wide perceptual gap on the question, although in the best of circumstances slightly more than one-fourth of all respondents in the entire sample agreed that their officers did share the burdens of the troops.

Important, too, is the tendency of the Soviet officer to distance himself from his men. Soldiers were asked if they thought their officers "went out of their way to show an interest in their men." The responses revealed that 28.3 percent of the soldiers in the ranks felt that their officers showed an interest in their men. Specifically, soldiers were asked if they thought their officers were generally "interested in their men's personal problems." Again, a relatively low rate of affirmative responses emerged; only 31.8 percent of the soldiers felt that their officers were interested. Taken together, the average Soviet soldiers in the ranks do not seem convinced that their officers care about them or take a genuine interest in them.

The Soviet officer may be deliberately creating distance between himself and his men. By sticking close to lines of authority and not overly involving himself in his men's personal problems, he seeks to minimize responsibility. In addition, the caste system continues to operate in the Soviet Army providing a degree of social control. Soldiers were asked to agree or disagree with the statement that the officer "drew too strong a line between himself and his men; he was too

distant.'' Not surprisingly, 64.7 percent of the soldiers felt that their officers
were too distant. Among NCOs who held command positions, 86.7 percent felt
that their officers were too distant, while 46.7 percent of the enlisted commanders
also agreed. If the analysis incorporates the views of those soldiers who held no
positions of command, 81.8 percent of the common soldiers also felt that their
officers were too remote from them. An even more intriguing finding emerges
when officers themselves are questioned. Fully 90 percent of the officers holding
command positions judged their brothers to be too remote from their men. The
data support the conclusion that Soviet officers are viewed as being too distant
from the men they lead; this remoteness applies to their unit commanders as
well.

When asked whether they thought their officers ''never developed close ties
with their men,'' 77.7 percent of common soldiers and 87 percent of the NCOs
agreed. The basic perception of the Soviet officer, then, is that he is too remote
from his men and does not develop personal bonds with them or, indeed, even
with his own unit commanders.

Perhaps most basic to any assessment of the Soviet officer's combat ability
is the extent to which his troops feel he would be a good leader in combat.
Specifically, soldiers were asked if they thought their officers would ''be good
men to go into combat with.'' Among the entire sample, only 19.5 percent felt
that their officers were competent in this regard versus 58.3 percent of the NCOs.
Among common soldiers, 53.4 percent agreed, a percentage slightly higher than
the 47 percent of American soldiers who felt their officers would be competent
under fire.[74] The general perception of the Soviet officer's combat abilities seems
to vary somewhat by rank, with the lower ranks having the least faith in their
officers' battlefield abilities.

Paradoxically, Soviet unit commanders have a very high opinion of their ability
to perform under fire. No less than 70 percent of the officers holding combat
positions felt they would be ''good men to go into combat with.'' By comparison,
among soldiers in the ranks, those who held no positions of authority but who
would be expected to carry the burden of fighting, only 49.9 percent thought
their officers were competent to lead them into battle. Thus, nearly half the
Soviet soldiers did not regard their officers as good combat leaders.

Another important variable is the officer's combat judgment. Specifically,
soldiers were asked if they felt their officers ''had the kind of judgment I would
trust in combat.'' Only 22.8 percent indicated that they would trust the judgment
of their officers under fire. Equally important, 27.1 percent of the enlisted commanders—the leaders who are the spine of small-unit effectiveness—said they
trusted their officers' judgment in battle, far too small a number. It reveals a
substantive lack of mutual trust and confidence within the leadership structure
of Soviet combat units. The data are confirmed by the attitudes of soldiers who
held positions of authority, 50.8 percent of whom believed they could trust
their officers' judgment. Even among officers themselves there is little to sustain
the mutual trust in each other's judgment. Only 49.5 percent of commanding

officers felt they would trust the judgment of their brother officers in battle. The Soviet officer has failed to convince his men, his subordinate leaders, and even his peers that his judgment in battle is adequate.

Along with its other shortcomings, the Soviet officer corps is heavily bureaucratized and careerist oriented. It functions within a highly bureaucratic political system and places far too much emphasis upon political loyalty and technical skill. Many Soviet officers are far more concerned with their own careers than they should be. As a result, they neglect the troops and the development of critical leadership skills. The bureaucratic corps also reflects many of the problems found in most bureaucracies—especially goal displacement, avoidance of responsibility, and a tendency toward scapegoating—including the American Army. The Soviet officer corps, however, appears to have an excessive sense of careerism. This tendency is not uncommon in any military bureaucracy, but it is magnified in the overly bureaucratic environment of the Soviet state. Corollarily, officers often appear overly ambitious and adept at escaping responsibility. At the extreme, there is even a tendency to distort reports in order to make an officer appear competent in the eyes of his superiors. Anyone familiar with the officer efficiency report system and the equipment-readiness reporting system in the American Army is aware of the significant distortion that characterizes these reports, largely in response to the need to conform to bureaucratic demands.[75]

An analysis of the Soviet officer along these dimensions confirms that he has become the armed bureaucrat. With regard to the tendency toward careerism, 72.5 percent of the soldiers agreed that their officers "seemed more concerned about their own career advancement than with their men." This tendency is buttressed by the attitudes of enlisted commanders, 76.4 percent of whom felt the same way. In addition, 51.3 percent of the soldiers described their officers as "overly ambitious at the expense of their subordinates and their unit." This propensity was supported by the responses of enlisted commanders, 92.8 percent of whom saw their officers as overly ambitious.

A basic bureaucratic characteristic is the tendency to avoid responsibility when things go wrong. As noted earlier, the Soviets maintain a large officer corps in order to maximize control and minimize mistakes. The emphasis on minimizing responsibility is high because the penalties for mistakes are high. In this environment, an ambitious officer seeks to avoid responsibility. The soldiers' responses supported this expectation; 59.3 percent of them agreed that their officers "often tried to avoid taking responsibility when things went wrong." Among enlisted commanders 86.7 percent felt similarly. Part of the strategy of escaping responsibility is scapegoating, laying the blame on someone else. When Soviet soldiers were asked about it, 48.6 percent agreed that their officers "tended to blame others for things he was supposed to do when they went wrong." This view was shared by 75 percent of enlisted commanders, who would probably react to this practice with some intensity since they are most often the scapegoats.

The officer, in an effort to place himself in the best possible light, sometimes distorts reports. In the Soviet Army, it is almost impossible not to distort reports, for there are so many that they assume an importance out of proportion to their original purpose. With so many reports, it is difficult to determine which are most important, and so they all come to be regarded as equally important. The litmus test of the bureaucratic officer concerned with his own career is the willingness to distort reports in his own favor.[76] In this regard, 26.9 percent of the respondents agreed with the statement that their officers "probably distort reports to make themselves took better." Among the enlisted commanders, 71.4 percent supported this view. If the ultimate act of bureaucratic self-protection is to distort reality in official reports, Soviet officers are seen by their subordinates as willing to do so.

The quality of officer leadership as measured through the strength and quality of interpersonal relationships between officers and men is difficult to grasp. One way to go about it is to discern what indicators other scholars have used in assessing this quality in other armies and then replicate the methodology in the analysis of the Soviet and American armies. While this is perhaps not the ideal way to proceed, it at least utilizes indicators of measurement that other scholars have agreed to be useful indicators of leadership. The measures used here are extracted from the *U.S. Army War College Study on Leadership for the 1970's* done in 1971 and replicated in my earlier research on the Soviet Army in 1980.[77] The link between the two studies is the cluster of sixteen attitudinal questions common to both. The army study attempted to measure the degree to which American soldiers perceived the presence of "the time-tested principles of leadership" among their officers.[78] The study elicited statements about leadership qualities that could be tested for agreement or disagreement among a population of soldiers. When the Soviet study was undertaken, sixteen of these same statements were incorporated into the interview instrument. The result is a combined data base that allows the comparison of Soviet and American officers in terms of how they are perceived by their subordinates along four dimensions: flexibility, initiative, careerism, and troop leadership skills. This is the first attitudinal comparison of Soviet and American officers based upon an application of the same data instrument in both armies. As such, it is an imperfect instrument. Nonetheless, it at least allows a direct comparison of how Soviet and American soldiers perceive their officers when measured through responses to a set of identical questions developed by the American Army for the express purpose of testing leadership traits.

When the data are examined along the dimension of flexibility, 80 percent of American soldiers agreed that their officers "stuck to the letter of their superiors' orders"; 87.8 percent of Soviet soldiers agreed with this statement. The data suggest that both officer corps may be suffering from an excessively high degree of inflexibility. In view of the highly bureaucratic nature of the Soviet officer corps, its perceived inflexibility is not surprising. The high rate at which American officers are perceived to be inflexible is, disturbing, however. Perhaps it may be attributed to the fact the American Army has become a large, complex bureaucratic organization.

A second dimension of leadership ability is initiative. The degree to which leaders demonstrate initiative in the eyes of their men is crucial. Neither officer corps did particularly well in this category: 74.2 percent of American soldiers agreed that their officers "would hesitate to take actions in the absence of instructions from their superiors," whereas 76.2 percent of Soviet soldiers felt this way about their officers. Compared along a second dimension, 78.5 percent of American enlisted men felt that their officers "stifled the initiative of others," whereas 68.7 percent of Soviet soldiers felt this was the case. That both officer corps should produce leaders who lack initiative is perhaps a natural consequence of their tendency to produce leaders who also lack flexibility, which in turn may be a consequence of the bureaucratization of both military organizations.

Perhaps no trait of a military leader is more devastating to cohesion and trust among his men than the extent to which troops believe their leaders are unconcerned about their men's welfare and are overly concerned with their own careers. Three indicators were used to measure the extent to which troops saw their officers as oriented more toward their own careers than toward the troops' welfare. (Table 2): "overly ambitious at the expense of his subordinates," "selfish," and "would probably distort reports." The Soviet officer demonstrated a relatively high level of career orientation in the eyes of his troops, with 74 percent of Soviet enlisted men agreeing that their officers were "overly ambitious," 86.7 percent describing them as "selfish," and, finally, 68.3 percent as likely to "distort reports to make themselves look better." These findings are consonant with the highly bureaucratic nature of the officer corps and the bureaucratic and totalitarian nature of the Soviet state.

Table 2
Comparison of Attitudinal Indicators of Careerism Perceived Among Soviet and American Officers

Indicator	Soviet Officers	American Officers
	Percent	
He was overly ambitious at the expense of his subordinates and his unit.	74.4	88.5
He was selfish.	86.7	85.7
He would probably distort reports.	68.3	88.5

One surprising finding, however, is that the American officer corps is viewed as even more careerist than its Soviet counterparts. Thus, 80.5 percent of American soldiers thought their officers were "overly ambitious," a rate 14.1 percent higher than that for the Soviet officer; 80.5 percent believed their officers would distort reports, a rate 20.2 percent higher than the Soviet figure; and 85.7 percent found them selfish, a rate comparable with the 86.7 percent for Soviet officers. These findings suggest that the bureaucratization, complexity, and the erosion of professionalism in the American Army over the last twenty years may have gone much deeper than anyone thought.

The most important element of leadership is the ability to lead men *in a combat environment*. Eight dimensions of troop leadership were used for comparison here (Table 3). As shown by the data, enlisted men had at least acceptably high opinions of Soviet officers as good troop leaders. The quality of troop leadership in the Soviet Army is, therefore, adequate to the task of combat leadership, if not to the creation of an outstanding corps of troop leaders. One area in which the Soviet officer is rated very poorly is his tendency to distance himself from his troops. Eighty percent of Soviet soldiers felt that the Soviet officer "drew too strong a line between himself and his men; that he was too distant." While the Soviet officer does not do particularly well on some indicators of troop leadership, the levels of performance are adequate. Soviet troop leadership ability at the small-unit level is acceptable in most environments.

Table 3
Comparison of Attitudinal Indicators of
Troop Leadership Perceived
Among Soviet and American Officers

Indicator	Soviet Officers	American Officers
	Percent	
Always set the example for his men	70.6	80.0
Truly knew his men and respected their capabilities	66.6	82.8
Saw to it that his men had the things needed in military life	58.9	85.7
Stood up for his men when dealing with superiors	57.2	78.5
Was willing to support his subordinates when they made mistakes	92.8	77.1
Often praised his troops for doing a good job and meant it	80.9	88.5
Was concerned about the unit's morale and did everything he could to make it high	93.1	75.8
Drew too strong a line between himself and his men; was too distant	80.0	54.2

In six of the eight indicators of troop leadership shown in Table 3, the American officer did demonstrably better than the Soviet officer. For instance, 80 percent of American soldiers thought the officer "always set the example for his men," 9.4 percent above the Soviet figure. In one indicator, seeing "that his men had the things they needed in military life," American officers were given an 85.7 positive rating versus 58.9 percent for the Soviets. In the area of soldiers believing the leaders truly cared for them, American officers did remarkably well. A total of 78.5 percent, again a rate some 20 percent higher than for the Soviet officer, felt that their officers stood up for their men when dealing with their superiors, and 77.1 percent agreed that the officer was "willing to support his subordinates when they made mistakes."

Unit cohesion is based in the trust and confidence men have in their officers and in the degree to which officers establish sincere social relationships with their men. From this perspective, the American officer did much better than his Soviet counterpart. Whereas 80 percent of Soviet enlisted men thought the officer "drew too strong a line between himself and his men; he was too distant," only 54.2 percent of American soldiers perceived their officers in this way.

Along the four dimensions of leadership tested here—flexibility, initiative, careerism, and troop leadership—the American officer corps is producing better potential troop leaders than the Soviet Army. In terms of troop leadership qualities, the American officer has developed a range of troop leadership qualities traditionally associated with cohesive military units.

One word of caution: the data discussed here are more than a decade old. Since that time, the American Army has undergone a number of traumatic organizational, structural, and value changes. Thus, more recent data, such as used earlier in this chapter, show that the American officer does less well than he did ten years ago. The earlier data at least generate some general impressions about each officer corps which can be incorporated into the larger body of available data.

Conclusions

Both the Soviet and American officer corps are large bureaucratic mechanisms that operate in larger bureaucratic environments. Accordingly, some military skills and qualities are being eroded by the imperatives of career survival and advancement within each system. Typically, both Soviet and American officers seem to have lost a great deal of flexibility and initiative, characteristics that are not highly valued in any bureaucracy. Both officer corps show high levels of careerism, and, on balance, both corps seem relatively equally affected. The key question is the degree to which larger bureaucratic values and ambience have penetrated to the troop unit level and eroded traditional leadership skills. The test of any assessment must await the battlefield. However, the performance data on the American officer during Vietnam suggest that he did not perform particularly well, largely because of the failure of small-unit leadership skills. There are signs of similar failures among Soviet officers which would likely produce similar results if that army were forced to battle. The key question is whether the Soviet officer, despite sharing many of the same failures as the American officer, can be effective on the battlefield. The evidence suggests that the Soviet officer may have at least as much difficulty performing under fire as the American officer.

While both modern superpowers maintain large armies, are technologically equipped beyond anything ever seen in history, and educate and train their officers quite intensively, both may have produced officers who will not be effective on the field of battle. In this sense, both armies have cause to mourn the passing of their traditional roots. How well American and Soviet officers will perform under fire awaits the test; how well they would perform against one another remains the most interesting question of all.

Notes

1. For example, the Israeli experience in the 1973 war on the Golan Heights saw several regular frontline units with unblemished battle records simply crack apart under the stress of combat. Modern battle is often tremendously intense and stressful as weapons have become more lethal. Under these conditions, it would seem reasonable that the requirements for group cohesion would increase.

2. See Douglas Kinnard, *The War Managers* (Hanover, N.H.: University Press of New England, 1977); Cincinnatus, *Self-Destruction* (New York: Norton Co., 1981); Ward Just, *Military Men* (New York: Alfred A. Knopf, 1970); Lieutenant-Colonel William R. Corson, "The Betrayal (New York: W. W. Norton, 1968); Lieutanant-Colonel William Hauser, *America's Army in Crisis* (Baltimore: Johns Hopkins University Press, 1973); and Richard Gabriel and Paul L. Savage, *Crisis in Command: Mismanagement in the Army* (New York: Hill and Wang, 1978).

3. Gabriel and Savage, *Crisis in Command*, Chapter 2.

4. Ibid., Chapter 1; see also Richard Gabriel, "What the Army Learned from Business," *The New York Times*, April 15, 1979, p. 34.

5. See Gabriel and Savage, *Crisis in Command*. See also Hauser, *America's Army in Crisis; Just Military Men*; and Charles Moskos, "Cohesion and Demoralization in the American Army (Vietnam)," International Sociological Association Research Committee on Armed Forces and Society, March 1973.

6. Ibid., Chapter 2.

7. Ibid., pp. 33-40.

8. Ibid., p. 63.

9. Ibid.

10. Ibid., Chapter 2.

11. Ibid., p. 63.

12. Ibid., Tables 6, 7, and 8. Indeed, only three general officers met their deaths in Vietnam, two in helicopter crashes and one by provable hostile fire.

13. This figure is calculated on the number of deaths of lieutenant-colonels recorded at the Army War College. The total number killed in all MOS specialties was fifty-five.

14. Paul L. Savage, "Patterns of Excellence, Patterns of Decay," paper presented before the New York Militia Association, October 9-11, 1981, p. 13.

15. Richard A. Gabriel and Paul L. Savage, "The Environment of Military Leadership," *Military Review* (July 1980): p. 57.

16. John Keeley, "So Many Competing Demands," *The Washington Post*, July 6, 1981, pp. 4-5.

17. Human Readiness Report No. 5 (Washington, D.C.: Office of the Deputy Chief of Staff for Personnel), (August 1979), p. 12. See also "Commissioned Officer Retention Rates," *Public Affairs* (October 9, 1980): 2.

18. Ibid.

19. "This Is Your Army, 1981," Information paper, U.S. Department of the Army, Washington, D.C., December 29, 1980, p. 10.

20. Ibid., p. 9.

21. Ibid.

22. Gabriel and Savage, "The Environment of Military Leadership," p. 59.

23. Lewis Sorley, "Turbulence at the Top: Our Peripatetic Generals," *Army* (March 1981): 14-24.

24. Ibid.

25. Ibid.

26. Ibid.

27. Ibid.

28. Letter to the Editor by Major General George S. Patton, Jr., *Army* (May 1981): 7.

29. Statement before the Senate Armed Services Committee by Richard A. Gabriel (July 17, 1979).

30. Gabriel and Savage, "The Environment of Military Leadership," p. 59.

31. Statement before Senate Armed Services Committee by Gabriel, p. 7.

32. Sorley, "Turbulence at the Top," p. 21.

33. Savage, "Patterns of Excellence, Patterns of Decay," p. 12.

34. Human Readiness Report No. 5, p. C-3.

35. Ibid.

36. Ibid.

37. Ibid.

38. Ibid.

39. "Study on Military Professionalism" (Carlisle Barracks, Penn.: U.S. Army War College, 1970).

40. Human Readiness Report No. 5, p. C-15.

41. Ibid.

42. Ibid.

43. Ibid.

44. Gabriel and Savage, *Crisis in Command*, Chapter 7. The propensity of bureaucracies to coopt those within the organization who share and demonstrate its values is virtually axiomatic in the study of large organizations. That it should emerge in the military is not surprising.

45. Study on Military Professionalism, p. iv.

46. Human Readiness Report No. 5, p. C-18.

47. Ibid.

48. Ibid.

49. Ibid.

50. Ibid.

51. Ibid.

52. John Fialka, "Can the U.S. Army Fight," *The Washington Star*, December 15, 1980, p. 12. See also Human Readiness Report No. 5, p. 12.

53. Ibid.

54. Major Stephen Westbrook "The Alienated Soldier: Legacy of Our Society," *Army* (December 1979): 20.

55. *CBS News Report*, September 15, 1979.

56. Gabriel and Savage, "The Environment of Military Leadership," p. 58.

57. Gabriel, *The New Red Legions: An Attitudinal Portrait of the Soviet Army* (Westport, Conn.: Greenwood Press, 1980), p. 80.

58. Ibid.

59. Gabriel and Savage, *Crisis in Command*, Chapter 2. See also Gabriel, *The New Red Legions*, p. 81.

60. Gabriel, *The New Red Legions*, p. 82.

61. Ibid.

62. The notion that assignment stability is crucial to combat cohesion is found in Gabriel and Savage, "The Environment of Military Leadership," p. 57.

63. An interesting examination of the stress placed on the "scientific" qualities of the Soviet officer is found in Lieutenant-Colonel William P. Baxter, "The Scientific Soviet Commander," *Army* (June 1980): 39-43.

64. Again, such problems are common in all large-scale organizations; to find it in the Soviet Army is not surprising. The term itself is taken from Robert Presthus, *The Organizational Society* (New York: Vintage Books, 1964).

65. Gabriel, *The New Red Legions*, p. 84.

66. Ibid.

67. Ibid.

68. Baxter, "The Scientific Soviet Commander," p. 40.

69. Gabriel, *The New Red Legions*, p. 85.

70. Baxter, "The Scientific Soviet Commander," p. 40.

71. Gabriel, *The New Red Legions*, p. 87.

72. Ibid.

73. Gabriel and Savage, *Crisis in Command*, Chapter 2.

74. Gabriel, *The New Red Legions*, p. 100.

75. Ibid., p. 112.

76. The tendency to sacrifice substance to "looking good" in order to qualify for promotion, the focus on the trivial, and the tyranny of statistics are all noted as major problems of the American Army in Study on Military Professionalism, p. v.

77. Gabriel, *The New Red Legions*; see also Richard Gabriel, *The Quality of Troop Leadership in Soviet and American Armies: A View from the Ranks* (Washington, D.C.: Office of the Assistant Chief of Staff for Intelligence, Foreign Intelligence Division, July 1980).

78. Gabriel, "The Quality of Troop Leadership."

5

Morale and Discipline

Discipline encompasses more than the willingness of military authorities to enforce punishment for the transgression of rules. It implies the ability of troops to internalize rules so that they are self-enforcing and help the units to hold together under stress and to perform their mission. Morale and discipline are clearly related and involve the troops' confidence that they can perform the tasks assigned to them.

Historically, armies have measured morale and discipline by keeping records on the number of AWOLs, desertions, assaults on leadership elements, drug use, alcohol abuse, crime rates, and other problems. This practice goes back to the Roman Army.[1] The exact connection between any one of these problems and the state of morale and discipline in any given unit is not known but units that are plagued with these difficulties to any great degree will not likely fight well.

This analysis examines several of these indicators to assess the quality of morale and discipline in the Soviet and American armies—specifically, rates of alcohol abuse, AWOL, assaults on officers and NCOs, desertion, drug use, crimes committed by military men against others, and rates of suicide. The basic premise of the analysis is that units manifesting clusters of these problems will not perform reliably in battle.

The analysis presented here is, of course, limited by the data available. For the Soviet Army, we have data on alcohol use, AWOL and desertion rates, assaults on leadership elements, and suicide attempts, and for the American Army we have statistics on alcohol and drug use, AWOL, desertion, and crime rates. We do not have access to much information on Soviet Army crime rates and drug use. However, with regard to drug use, among soldiers interviewed by this study, only 1.8 percent listed "to get some drugs" as a reason for troops going AWOL, the lowest of all reasons provided. This figure suggests that drug use is not a serious problem among Soviet troops.[2]

The American Army

The first consideration in any study of morale and discipline in the American Army must be the extent of drug use, for it is unquestionably extensive, penetrating all ranks to an almost debilitating degree. Research conducted by the U.S. Army Medical Center at Walter Reed Hospital suggests that drug use is a symptom of other more corrosive problems that might affect military effectiveness.[3] Moreover, when we consider drug use as it affects military units, we can see that drug use is indicative of deeper problems that confront units per se, perhaps indicating a breakdown in other more systemic values and habits that support unit cohesion and combat effectiveness.

The penalties for drug use in the army are relatively minor. A soldier caught using drugs is commonly referred to a drug rehabilitation program if he agrees to treatment, or, if he refuses treatment, he is likely to be given an administrative but honorable discharge.[4] In few cases are soldiers given less than honorable discharges for this offense. Under the present rules, the most that can happen to a soldier found using drugs is that he will receive the same honorable discharge as given to those who enter combat and return alive. As Major Larry Ingraham points out, "we delude ourselves when we believe that being kicked out of service with an honorable discharge is somehow a form of punishment. Too often, drug use is nothing more than contract evasion orchestrated by service people that change their minds about their service commitments."[5] Such a policy demonstrates that the army is not prepared to impose strong sanctions against drug use. The troops themselves believe that drug use is generally unpunished.[6] The enforcement mechanisms that do exist focus on "hard drug" users and generally ignore "soft drugs."

At the very least, the toleration of drug use within the military is an indicator of poor discipline. It is also an indicator of poor leadership. During Vietnam, drug use was alarmingly widespread, with levels reaching 28 percent and perhaps as many as 800,000 new addicts or experimenters emerging from that war.[7] There is ample evidence that open and blatant drug use was known to officers at all levels of command and staff; most did nothing to prohibit it for fear that an admission of a drug problem within their units would reflect adversely upon their own performance ratings. Unfortunately, the conditions that gave rise to the wholesale use of drugs within American units remain today and, as then, represent a clear breakdown in the quality of small-unit leadership.

Drug use clearly affects the technical performance of troops. Data presented later portray how American soldiers have been debilitated by their use of drugs.[8] At the very least, there is a tangible connection between a unit's skills and the degree of drug use.

Besides a failure of leadership, discipline, and performance, the systemic use of drugs within American military units suggests that units may be lacking in cohesion. The drug culture has basically arisen in response to a lack of cohesive ties within a unit. More than one author has pointed out that drug use in a military environment occurs largely as a way of integrating and belonging to a subgroup.[9] Drug use indicates that military groups have failed to establish strong bonds of cohesion which give the soldier a sense of belonging and participation:

the dynamics of transmission and maintenance of drug use lies in friendship. In networks of social relations, drugs and alcohol serve a critical need in military organizations in drawing people together into cohesive groups and providing a sense of stability and belonging in an unstable interpersonal environment. Were we by magic to eliminate drug and alcohol abuse from the military we would be left with the question of replacement as a means of drawing people together.[10]

Using drugs requires a certain amount of privacy, and the two-and three-man rooms now common throughout the army contribute substantially to drug use by isolating the soldier into small groups.

Given the isolation of the soldier, the limited choices of duty companions, the need to belong to a stable group, the need to kill time, the limited repertoires of skills—given all of these it should not be surprising that drugs and alcohol are integrated if not central to barracks living. What else could one do as well to provide commonalities, distinct experiences, and a sense of group belonging, solidarity, and acceptance.[11]

Because the American soldier tends to be isolated from his unit, he uses drugs. Studies of hard drug users in the military have found that only 25 percent of these abusers would be identified by their peers as individuals who "had a sense of pride or commitment" to their units.[12] The drug user bonds with at most a few other drug users.

The existence of drug abuse in the military also underscores the military system's failure to properly socialize (or resocialize) the soldier to a new set of values and habits necessary to military life. Drug use "is certainly the dominant symbol of the 'me' generation that proclaims do your own thing even if you kill yourself."[13] This ethic, widespread in the general society throughout the 1970s in particular, directly contradicts the military requirement that the soldier place the group and its imperatives before himself. In a very simple sense, drug use focuses upon individuals, legitimating what is in fact an illegal activity, and thereby sustains the primacy of the individual over the group. It also sustains the notion that individuals may do whatever they want as long as they want to do so. The concern for the group before the individual which is vital to any program of military socialization that produces effective battle units is alien to the values of the drug culture. Drug use by definition undercuts the process of military socialization when it is found in large numbers as it is in American units. In these circumstances one can question the ability of such units to successfully socialize the soldier.

The systemic use of drugs by large numbers of soldiers points to more serious problems. Specifically, drugs mean poor discipline, low morale, and generally poor command leadership. Drug use also signals poor performance, as well as the psychological and sociological isolation of the soldier from his peers, superiors, and unit. Perhaps, most importantly, as noted above, it signals the military system's failure to socialize the soldier to a set of values and habits necessary to accomplishing his military role and, thus, indicates a lack of unit cohesion. From every perspective, drug use cannot be tolerated by any army that hopes to fight well.

The extent of the drug problem in the American Army has been documented in Human Readiness Report No. 5.[14] This study found that approximately 17 percent of all army soldiers, or about 110,000 enlisted troops, used marijuana or hashish weekly, with 1 percent or about 6,500 soldiers using hard drugs—heroin, cocaine, pills, and hallucinogens—at least once a week.[15] In February 1979, an army study on alcohol abuse found that first-term soldiers accounted for 80 percent of the total problem of marijuana and hashish use and for almost 75 percent of hard drug use.[16] While marijuana and hashish use is somewhat lower in the military than for the same age, racial, and sex group in the society at large, the rate at which soldiers use hard drugs is twice as high as the rate for the same demographic group in society.[17] Finally, the army's own studies suggest that the rates of drug use for all soldiers are rising, despite the military's efforts to control them through rehabilitation programs and early discharges.

Where does the soldier learn his drug habits? One study of drug use points out that, among heroin users, only 15 percent used heroin *before* entering the military. While 75 percent of heroin users had used drugs other than non-heroin prior to active service, 85 percent of heroin users in the military acquired the habit after they entered service.[18]

In 1980, the Department of Defense commissioned a private consultant firm to do a worldwide survey of American soldiers to determine the rates of drug and alcohol abuse.[19] The survey involved 15,000 respondents. The results indicate that 29 percent of the soldiers in the army had used some type of drug within the past thirty days, and 38 percent said they had used drugs during the preceding year. The rate of drug use among officers was 5 percent, with about the same number of NCOs admitting to drug use.[20] The army's own data as reported in Human Readiness Report No. 5 support these findings; they show that 4 percent of its officers use marijuana or hashish weekly, with the rate of officer use of hard drugs higher at the company level than at the field grade level.[21] The crucial combat commanders—namely, platoon and company commanders—have the highest drug use rates among all officers. As regards hard drugs, 1 percent of all officers and 2 percent of all company commanders said they used hard drugs.[22] Human Readiness Report No. 5, the Ingraham studies, and the private consultant survey of 1980, all reveal that drug use in the American Army is endemic and cuts across all ranks.

A comparison of drug-use rates in the military and civilian society makes the drug picture in the military even more disturbing. Marion Corddry points out that among members of the same demographic group in civilian society the rate of heroin use is only .05 percent compared to 12.5 percent hard drug use in the army, with 2.6 percent admitting to the use of heroin.[23] If Corddry's data are correct, the 2.6 percent of soldiers who use heroin (and 85 percent of these become addicts while in the military; they did not bring the habit with them) represents a heroin use rate *five times higher* than that for the civilian population.

Comparisons of the use of other drugs are equally disturbing. For example, the rate of amphetamine use in the civilian population is 4 percent; it is 10 percent for the army. The use of cocaine use among civilians is 10 percent compared to 7 percent for the army. For hallucinogens, the rates are about the same, with approximately 5 percent of civilians and soldiers using the drugs within the preceding thirty days. Finally, marijuana and hashish use rates, while lower in the military, are still high, with 40 percent of the soldiers using them regularly compared to 42 percent of the civilian population.[24] On balance, drug use rates in the military tend to be equal or greater than use rates found among the civilian population, which suggests that the ability of the army to socialize its soldiers to appropriate military values, to get them to bond to their units and to enforce these new habits and values is certainly questionable. Drug use seems to be clearly eroding crucial institutions and practices within the military that have historically supported discipline, cohesion and bonding, qualities vital to effective battle units.

An important facet of drug use is, of course, its impact on the soldier's performance. The soldier who is "spaced out" on drugs may have difficulty performing at the required level of skill. The 1980 worldwide drug survey tested this hypothesis by asking soldiers to evaluate the extent to which they felt drug use caused any work impairment. The survey measured work impairment across five dimensions: self-perceived lowered performance, arriving late for work, leaving early as a consequence of drug use, absenteeism, and self-perceived general impairment. The study found the rates of job impairment to be exceedingly high.[25]

Twenty-two percent of the soldiers admitted that drug use had impaired their performance on the job along at least one of the five dimensions tested;[26] 12 percent reported overall lowered work performance; 8 percent reported leaving work early or arriving late for similar reasons; 6 percent reported absenteeism as a result of drugs; and 21 percent reported being high on drugs while actually working at their jobs.[27] This last-named figure, amazing as it is, is much lower than that found by a congressional committee in September 1981 (in excess of 40 percent).[28] Thus, the Department of Defense-commissioned study established a clear link between drug use and job performance. The affect of drug use on combat performance, however, remains unknown. In fact, the army has not made a direct study of the effects of drug use on combat performance but only of skill performance.

In Human Readiness Report No.5, when soldiers were asked to select which category of responses "best describes your use of drugs during the last six months," 10.3 percent described their use of marijuana and hashish as "frequent," 2.5 percent admitted they used hard drugs "frequently," while another 5.6 percent admitted they "sometimes" used drugs during the preceding six months.[29] When first-term and NCO soldiers were examined, the results once again indicated a serious drug-use problem. Among first-term soldiers, 14.5 percent admitted to "frequent" use of marijuana and hashish and 2.8 percent to frequent use of hard drugs. By comparison, 5.2 percent of career soldiers said they used marijuana and hashish "frequently," and 2.1 percent, many of them NCOs, admitted to "frequent" use of hard drugs.[30] While the rates of soft drug use between first-term and career soldiers are significantly different, the rates of hard drug use are almost the same. In any case, each is significantly high to suggest that drug use is a serious problem within army units.

To what extent are officers aware of the drug problem? The evidence suggests they are acutely aware of it, but most feel powerless to deal with it. Human Readiness Report No. 5 found that 73.8 percent of the officers serving in troop units and 76.7 percent of unit commanders reported that marijuana abuse was a major problem with which they had to deal.[31] Among officers worldwide, 40.7 percent perceived a hard drug problem in their units. Among officers in troop units, 30 percent felt that abuse of hard drugs such as heroin was a problem; 53.2 percent of the army's commanders and 40.7 percent of unit commanders saw hard drugs as a major problem.[32] Officers reported that their units' drug problems had increased continually over the five years during which the study was conducted.

Table 4
Impact of Soft Drug Use on Battle Performance,
as Assessed by American Army Officers and NCOs

Response	Unit Commander	Company Grade Officer	Combat-Arms Officer	Combat-Support Officer	Combat-Service Officer
			Percent		
Somewhat degraded	30.6	26.8	33	28.5	18.6
Seriously degraded	—	9.7	9.3	8.1	9.1

When officers and NCOs were asked to evaluate the impact of drug use on battle performance, the results were almost unbelievable: officers in combat-arms, combat-support; and combat-service units all agreed that drug use was impairing their units' ability to perform well (Table 4). Among the combat arms, for example, 33 percent of the officers stated that drug use "somewhat degraded." ability, while 9.3 percent answered "seriously degraded."[33] Within combat-service units, 18.6 percent of the officers thought combat ability would be "somewhat degraded" and 9.1 percent said "seriously degraded."[34]

When hard drugs were examined in the same context, the results were little different. For example, 12.3 percent of company grade officers thought hard drugs "somewhat degraded" the ability of their units to perform, while 15.7 percent felt that that ability was "seriously degraded."[35] (See Table 5.) Among combat-service officers, 9.3 percent reported their units would be "somewhat degraded" while 14.7 percent saw their units as "seriously degraded."[36]

Table 5
Impact of Hard Drug Use on Battle Performance,
as Assessed by American Army Officers and NCOs

Response	Unit Commander	Company Grade Officer	Combat- Arms Officer	Combat- Support Officer	Combat- Service Officer
			Percent		
Somewhat degraded	9.1	12.3	16.5	10.6	9.3
Seriously degraded	10.2	15.7	15.5	16.3	14.7

The American military is also troubled by alcohol abuse. When officers were asked to evaluate alcohol abuse as a problem, they placed it much higher on the list than drug abuse. Army data show that 7 percent of both career and first-term soldiers have a "serious" drinking problem, about the same rate as found in civilian society.[37] The Department of Defense drug study mentioned earlier reported that 84 percent of military personnel admitted to alcohol use in the preceding thirty days compared to 82 percent for the civilian population.[38]

The fact that civilian and military rates of alcohol use are similar does not mean, however, that such rates are tolerable in the military given the special nature of military tasks, its complex equipment, and its life-threatening aspects. It seems clear that a whole range of pathologies and habits tolerated in civilian society cannot be tolerated at the same levels within the military. Human Readiness Report No. 5 found that 79.7 percent of officers in troop units ranked alcohol abuse as a major problem. Of thirteen major problems ranked by these officers, alcohol abuse ranked fifth. Moreover, 81.7 percent of unit commanders identified alcohol abuse as a major problem and ranked the problem as their second most important problem. Armywide, 55.7 percent of the officers saw alcohol abuse as a problem and ranked it sixth.[39]

What is the effect of alcohol on the soldier's performance levels? The 1980 Department of Defense survey showed that 24 percent of the army's soldiers suffered some general work impairment as a result of alcohol use. Eleven percent admitted being drunk while on duty.[40] In all probability, the rate of impairment within military units is about the same as in the civilian workplace.

The more important question concerns the impact of alcohol abuse on unit readiness and combat performance, the army's studies show that the impact may be potentially debilitating. Among unit commanders, 29.9 percent felt that their units' ability to perform their wartime mission would be "somewhat degraded" by the levels of alcohol abuse, and 7.4 percent said "seriously degraded." The same concern emerged among company grade officers, with 32.9 percent responding "somewhat degraded" and 8.7 percent "seriously degraded." Field grade officers felt the same way: 24.0 percent answered "somewhat degraded" and 6.2 percent "seriously degraded."[42]

When examined by type of unit, the data are even more damaging. Thirty-seven percent of officers serving in combat arms units reported that their units' ability would be "somewhat degraded" as a result of alcohol abuse, and another 7.6 percent, "seriously degraded." Within the combat-support units, 32.4 percent of the officers felt their units would be "somewhat degraded," and another 8.1 percent stated "seriously degraded." In combat-service units, 25.3 percent of the officers thought their units' ability would be "somewhat degraded," and another 8.4 percent responded "seriously degraded."[42] Since alcohol abuse often tends to be associated with drug use, one can only hope that the data presented earlier on drug abuse are not cumulative. If drug users and alcohol abusers are not different groups, then the problem may be manageable; if, however, they do represent distinct groups, then the numbers of soldiers who are either using drugs or abusing alcohol fairly regularly constitute a majority of the soldiers.

The American Army has also been examined in terms of general discipline. Armywide, 54.5 percent of the officers, 69.5 percent of unit commanders, and 76.8 percent of officers in troop units reported major disciplinary problems.[43] When officers were asked if they had major problems of discipline "within the last six months," 69.5 percent of commanders armywide, 70.5 percent of combat arms officers, and 69.9 percent of officers in combat-support units answered yes. When the data are examined for trends, the number of officers who considered discipline to be a major problem increased over a five-year period.[44] In 1977, for example, 48.8 percent of all army officers identified discipline as a major problem "in the last six months"; by 1979, that figure had risen to 62.3 percent. Similarly, in 1977, 57.3 percent of all officers identified the general state of discipline as a major problem and three years later that number had risen to 69.5 percent.[45]

The army, however, officially argues that the incidence of indiscipline has declined significantly since the beginning of the all volunteer force. What has declined is the number of "reportable" incidents of indiscipline. Offenses that are subject to administrative disposition rather than judicial disposition, are not counted in the total number of disciplinary offenses. For example, if a soldier caught selling or using drugs is given an administrative discharge or enters a drug rehabilitation program, that incident of indiscipline is not included in the statistics. Hence, any statement that incidents of indiscipline have been declining over the last five years is really a mirage. In reality they have been rising.

This practice of concealing the disciplinary rate has been designated "managing" the disciplinary rate, or "papering out" the problem. In 1979, for example, the rate of honorable discharge was the lowest in American military history, despite the fact that many individuals given honorable discharges were given them in lieu of prosecution. A substantial number of offenses in the American Army are handled not by judicial action but by routine adminstrative action. As a result, official rates are inaccurate. Even the army admits that the number of reportable disciplinary incidents is down, largely through what it calls "the prudent use of the various expeditious discharge programs."[46] In the American Army, a whole range of offenses are dealt with by allowing the soldier to leave service; in other armies—and certainly in the Soviet Army—these same offenses would merit punishment. The number of disciplinary offenses dealt with by administrative action is highest among combat arms units. Indeed, the rate of administrative disposition in combat units is *twice* as high as noncombat units, which indicates that the real disciplinary rate is also probably higher than in other units.[47]

In the army, a whole range of "official" reasons for terminating a soldier from service may really be a smokescreen for dealing with disciplinary problems. The categories of offenses are often used to conceal true disciplinary offenses. For example, in the Navy an individual is normally discharged for character or behavior disorders, ineptitude, motivational problems, discreditable incidents, or unsuitability. Only 4 percent of navy discharges are the result of "expeditious discharges" for marginal performance. In sharp contrast, 23 percent of army discharges can be classified as expeditions. Moreover, another 26 percent are terminated under the training discharge program, compared with only 4 percent for the navy.[48] Thus, the army's rate of expeditious discharges is almost six times higher than that of the navy. Both the offender and the military are often aware that certain disciplinary violations are not punished or cost too much to prosecute. Hence, individuals leave the service often with their post-service benefits intact.

The ineffectiveness of the army in dealing with indiscipline can be seen by examining the problem of desertion. Between 1975 and 1976, the military classified 84,000 people as deserters—those absent without authorization for more than thirty days.[49] This figure represents an average desertion rate of over 53,000 soldiers a year. In 1980, the number of soldiers charged with desertion in the army was 12,330, a very large decline from the earlier total. But did the rate really drop? In truth, the rate of prosecution, and not the rate of desertion, declined. In 1980, of the 12,330 army deserters only six were successfully prosecuted for this offense by the military.[50] The army has apparently heeded the advice of the General Accounting Office (GAO) report of January 1977 which in noting that the cost of apprehending deserters was approaching $58 million a year, recommended that the military administratively release deserters from military service rather than apprehend and prosecute them.[51] The military saw several advantages in this approach, not the least of which was that it allowed the army to portray its disciplinary rate as declining. The facts, however, have not changed: the rate of desertion in the American Army remains relatively high.

Desertion in the army over the last four years has shown a general upward trend. In 1976, the desertion rate averaged 15.4 soldiers per 1,000; today that rate is 19.6 soldiers per 1,000,[52] and it would be even higher if the statistics did not omit those for whom an administrative solution was imposed. Judging from the available data the number of desertions may be as high as 42,000 per year in the army alone.

Yet another indicator of poor discipline in any army is the AWOL rate—the number of soldiers who are absent without leave. In the last four years the rate has remained constant, according to official statistics. In 1976 the AWOL rate was 43.6 soldiers per 1,000, compared to 41.6 per 1,000 in 1980.[53] Again it must be emphasized that these data are lower than the actual rate because they do not reflect the AWOL cases which were solved administratively. In March 1979, a GAO report dealing with the AWOL problem noted that in the year ending in June 1977 the military services had reported 608,000 AWOLs, costing the government over $1 billion.[54] The report revealed that the most serious AWOL offense, absent for more than thirty days (an offense equivalent to desertion), was the AWOL-related offense most frequently dealt with by administrative discharge, precisely to avoid a court martial. The report also pointed out that, although serious legal penalties may be imposed for being AWOL, including prison sentences, punishments were almost always substantially less. Thus, the army was again dealing with problems administratively rather than judicially and therefore, tended to distort official AWOL statistics.

According to GAO analysis, in 42 percent of the cases AWOL was dealt with by administrative action, and in most of the remaining cases it was treated as a minor offense. In fact, AWOL was seventy times more likely to be handled administratively than by court martial. Eighty percent of the AWOL soldiers went AWOL for a second time, and 65 percent three or more times.[55] Without severe punishment, it was noted that "military members can discern from the services practices that the likelihood of severe punishment is low and the chances for an administrative discharge rather high."[56] The American Army's lenient policies apparently encourage AWOL. Moreover, the troops rightly perceive that going AWOL is often the most expeditious way of getting out of military service.

High AWOL and desertion rates are unambiguous indicators of bad discipline and poor quality leadership. When soldiers go AWOL, unit morale and effectiveness are diminished, if for no other reason than that others in the unit must perform the AWOL soldier's duties. Training as units also becomes difficult when key individuals are absent, and more so when the case involves tank or gun crews. More importantly, unpunished cases of AWOL and desertion send clear signals to other soldiers that they, too, may escape the rigors of military life, if only for a while, by simply "going over the wall." Finally, the fact that officers and NCOs cooperate in the system of "papering out" or "managing" the disciplinary rate does not speak well for their sense of integrity and trust. How can soldiers be expected to trust their leaders when they see them subverting the integrity of the unit, all in defense of career and promotion?

Unit effectiveness is also affected by the rate of criminal violence within the military. The rate of crime committed by military personnel during the 1976-1980 period remained relatively constant: 6.82 crimes of violence per 1,000 soldiers in 1976 versus 6.47 per 1,000 in 1980.[57] However, since many crimes are formally ignored or processed administratively, the official data are somewhat suspect. One indication of how high the rate may be emerged in an unofficial report which observed that in 1979 over 8,875 soldiers in Germany alone—over half a division—were arrested for the single offense of selling drugs. Included in these sales was $67 million worth of heroin and cocaine.[58]

Human Readiness Report No. 5 investigated morale independently over a five-year period and found that a large number of officers thought their units suffered from serious morale problems. Among officers in troop units, 78.8 percent named morale as a major problem, ranking it the sixth most serious of a list of thirteen that they had to confront on a daily basis.[59] Among unit commanders, 67.5 percent felt morale was a major problem, and 73.2 percent of all officers armywide felt the same way.[60]

Closely related to morale is the degree of esprit de corps shown. The same survey revealed that 65.8 percent of officers in troop units, 53.6 percent of troop unit commanders, and 59.1 percent of officers armywide considered lack of esprit de corps a major problem in their unit. They ranked it as the third most important problem with which they had to deal.[61] Variables such as high rates of drug abuse, alcohol abuse, high disciplinary rates, and low esprit de corps, together with failure to punish many obvious discipline-related offenses, are likely to result in lowered morale and spirit. As a result, too, the better soldiers may be discouraged from staying in military service or performing up to their potential. One sociologist has suggested that the most competent soldiers are not staying in service beyond their first tour of duty, precisely because of the degenerating unit climate, that is, the presence of drugs, violence, and disciplinary offenses that go unpublished.[62]

Conclusions

In general, the "unit climate" of American units is not good. The data in Table 6 present the army's findings concerning the quality of unit climate as assessed by officers armywide across four variables.[63] The data reveal that officers in all types of units see serious problems of motivation, discipline, morale, and esprit de corps among their men. A majority of commanders in combat arms and combat-support units in CONUS, the Pacific, and Europe also believe the unit climate is so poor as to affect these units' ability to fight. Units marked by low motivation, low levels of morale, poor discipline, and esprit de corps are in trouble enough. When these units are hammered continuously by drug use, alcohol abuse, failure to punish crime, AWOL, and desertions, transforming such units into effective battle groups becomes a near impossibility.

The Soviet Soldier

Obtaining sufficient useful data on a totalitarian society is a formidable task. Nonetheless, by working with the information released in the official press and relying heavily upon my earlier sample survey of Soviet soldiers, an analysis of morale and discipline in Soviet units is possible.

An analysis of alcohol abuse in Soviet military units must be preceded by an understanding of the role alcohol plays in the larger Russian society. Anyone familiar with Russian life is aware that alcohol abuse represents a major and chronic problem for the overseers of Soviet society.[64] Nationally, the Russians tend to consume what we consider an excess of alcohol.

Table 6
Percentage of American Officers Armywide
Who Indicated Problems in Their Units

Unit	Motivation	Discipline	Morale	Esprit
Commanders	74.4	69.5	67.5	53.6
Officers in TO&E units	84.4	76.8	78.0	65.8
Combat arms units	83.8	78.5	76.2	58.6
Other TO&E units	80.7	69.9	78.0	65.6
CONUS-based units	71.1	58.8	72.2	59.6
Pacific-based units	75.8	65.3	72.9	59.8
European-based units	83.3	73.8	79.8	64.2
All officers armywide	73.9	62.3	73.8	60.5

As indicated in military journals, Russian soldiers at all ranks have at least the same high rates of alcohol-related problems as does the society at large. Articles in the Soviet press often complain of the soldier's eagerness to spend most of his monthly pay on vodka.[65] Moreover, his tendency to steal equipment in order to barter with the local population for alcohol is well documented.[66] Soviet military periodicals give the impression that heavy and chronic alcohol use is characteristic of Soviet military life, an impression that is confirmed by the data from my survey of Soviet soldiers. One soldier in the survey commented that, "even if you are not an alcoholic when you go into the army, you are when you come out."[67]

As reported by official sources, drunkenness in Soviet military units seems to cut across all ranks. Reports from soldiers in elite or technical units suggest that rates of alcohol use in these units are just as high as in infantry or tank units.[68] This impression is contrary to the notion received from articles in the Soviet press, which single out border guards and construction battalions as manifesting the highest rates of alcohol abuse. All Soviet units suffer to some degree from alcohol-related problems but then again so does Soviet society. As reflected by Soviet soldiers, Soviet officers, and the Soviet press, the rate of alcohol use in Soviet units may be higher than that in the society at large. It also seems evident that alcohol use is in general a reaction to the harshness of Soviet military life.

In an effort to analyze the subject of alcohol use in Soviet units, soldiers were asked whether they thought their "superior officers regarded excessive drinking as a major problem in the military." Some 66.4 percent thought their officers felt that alcohol abuse was a problem. The degree of alcohol consumption may well be affecting the ability of some soldiers and some units to perform their wartime mission.[69] For example, when soldiers were asked whether they ever heard of or saw a noncommissioned officer drunk on duty, 64.6 percent answered yes.[70] Moreover, there were no meaningful differences in the rates of NCO drunkenness among different types of units. Whether one examines infantry units, tank units, support units, or even strategic rocket units, the rate of NCO drunkenness on duty remained between 68 and 69 percent. In addition, when soldiers were asked whether they ever saw or heard of an officer drunk on duty, 55.8 percent reported they had.[71] Although the rate of officer drunkenness is below that of NCOs, it is only slightly lower. The main thrust of the evidence suggests that large numbers of Soviet soldiers will not be surprised to witness either an officer or an NCO reporting drunk on duty at some time during their two-year enlistment.

In order to discern if the level of public drinking among officers varies by type of unit, the data were arranged to test this aspect. Apparently, the type of unit is not critical in determining the rate of public drunkenness among officers. Although the overall rate of alcohol consumption by officers in all types of units is high, there is no evidence that duty with a certain type of unit compels greater drinking. For example, 46.4 percent of the soldiers in infantry units reported seeing an officer drunk on duty, compared to 41.7 percent in armored units. In artillery units, the rate was 36.6 percent and for strategic rocket forces, 69 percent. Drinking in support units among officers was 65.7 percent, which was somewhat higher on the average than for combat arms officers.[72]

But how much does the common soldier drink? It appears that Soviet soldiers drink heavily whenever they can. Of course, the availability of alcohol for the average soldier is a problem. In fact, a number of Soviet soldiers reported that they drank more in civilian life but attributed that to the fact that alcohol was much more expensive and harder to come by on a common soldier's meager salary. Still, 27.4 percent of the sample said it drank more in the military than in civilian life, a finding that runs somewhat contrary to the impression of heavy drinking among soldiers that one receives from Soviet journals.[73]

The degree to which drinking represents a serious problem in military units can be related to other dimensions of military life. When soldiers were asked about the punishment for drinking while on duty, 83.2 percent agreed that it was "severe."[74] However, soldiers also indicated that NCOs and officers, because of their own high rate of drinking, often "looked through their fingers" at the soldiers' drinking and often avoided reporting drunken soldiers because it would reflect adversely on their control of the unit.

How often are ordinary soldiers drunk while on duty? Interestingly, only 15.9 percent indicated that being drunk on duty occurred either often or very often; another 25.7 percent said it occurred seldomly; and 54.8 percent said it was a rare or uncommon occurrence.[75] This rate compares with a rate of 40 percent of American soldiers who admitted to being drunk on duty.[76] Thus, although both Soviet and American soldiers appear to drink heavily, far fewer of the Soviet soldiers admitted to being drunk on duty than did American soldiers.

How does alcohol abuse in Soviet units reflect other problems associated with morale and discipline? There is a sense in which alcohol abuse and its associated pathologies affect the ability of soldiers to perform under stress. Morale and discipline are crucially important in themselves but if Soviet units contain large numbers of soldiers who abuse alcohol then the ability of the unit to perform adequately on the basis of that variable alone becomes questionable. Reciprocally, then, in the eyes of the troops alcohol use clearly represents an important aspect of morale and discipline. It is, on the one hand, a reflection of low morale and discipline and, on the other, a cause of it. How, then, does the Soviet soldier perceive the amount of drinking that he witnesses in his unit? When soldiers were asked "if the amount of drinking in their unit affected the ability of their unit to perform its mission," 30.1 percent agreed.[77] This fact alone, that almost one-third of the soldiers thought mission ability would be affected by excessive drinking, cannot but negatively affect morale and discipline. In a sense, it becomes a self-fulfilling prophecy that begins to affect combat ability because large numbers of troops believe it does. Soviet authorities, while aware of the excessive drinking, have apparently not been successful in stopping it.

Another indicator of morale and discipline in the Soviet Army for which we have statistics is the number of soldiers who go AWOL and the ability of commanders to control the problem. In all armies throughout history, soldiers have gone absent without leave, and they will continue to do so.[78] The mere existence of AWOLs in a unit does not, therefore, suggest much about the unit. When AWOLs occur in significant numbers, however, it might be surmised that the levels of the unit discipline and morale are low. The failure of NCOs and officers to stem the tide, as is the case in the American Army, is perhaps an even clearer indication that the quality of unit morale is low, as is the unit leaders' ability to enforce discipline. The evidence suggests that the number of soldiers who go AWOL in Soviet units may constitute a considerable problem for the Soviet Army.

In view of the army's traditional and bureaucratic structure, Soviet unit leaders are concerned about high AWOL rates far beyond the usual limits, for high rates adversely affect the performance ratings of NCOs and officers. Furthermore, high AWOL rates in Soviet units are not the exact equivalent of rates in Western armies inasmuch as they occur in an environment that has almost total control of the Soviet soldier's life. The system itself places a bureaucratic premium on minimizing AWOL reports in order to minimize official responsibility, at least as much as it reflects a genuine concern for the state of unit morale and discipline. When soldiers were asked whether they thought their "superiors were concerned about the problem of soldiers going absent without leave," 69.9 percent responded yes.[79] The soldiers themselves are, therefore, aware that the AWOL problem is serious enough to merit their unit leaders' genuine concern.

Surprisingly, AWOL rates are rather high within Soviet units. Soldiers were asked, "how often did soldiers in your unit leave the base without permission to see women?" The point of the question was not to determine how much effect the desire for women had upon the AWOL rate but to unobtrusively measure how often Soviet soldiers were prepared to go AWOL in the first place. Interestingly, 46.6 percent of the respondents confirmed that soldiers left their units without permission to see women "often" or "very often." However, 24.8

percent said that soldiers "seldom" went AWOL for this reason, and another 15.9 percent said it was "rare" when they did.[80] Nonetheless, the 46.6 percent figure can be used as an approximate indicator of the AWOL rate in the Soviet Army, a rate comparable to that in the American Army. If accurate, it means that four of every ten soldiers will go AWOL at some time during their military service or at least know someone who did. As in American units, authorities tend to look the other way on AWOL, especially if the soldier is gone for only a short while and if he does not get into further difficulty. Although the punishments are harsh—85.5 percent of the soldiers said so—they are not uniformly administered so that, as in all armies, rates of punishment vary considerably from unit to unit. Nonetheless, Russia's AWOL rates are unexpectedly high for a totalitarian army.

In order to examine why Soviet soldiers go AWOL, soldiers were asked to select three reasons from a list of eight. A total of 83.2 percent mentioned "to meet women" as a reason, but even more, 85 percent, cited the reason was "to get some vodka." Another common reason, mentioned 55.7 percent, was "to escape military life for short time."[81] Not a single soldier mentioned "trying to get away from the military for good" as a reason. Hence, when Soviet soldiers go AWOL, they apparently expect to return to their units on their own. Little thought is given to attempting to escape military service for good. Yet, the fact that a substantial number of soldiers do risk severe punishment by going AWOL to "escape military life for a short time" confirms what many soldiers say— that the harsh regimen and constant organization of Soviet military life often become so oppressive that AWOL is a blatant and rational reaction to it. Soldiers simply "go over the wall" to get away from it, if only for a few hours or a few days.

If Soviet AWOL rates are as high as our data reveal, it is unreasonable to expect Soviet authorities to be continually punishing troops almost as a matter of course. Conversations with soldiers suggest that some officers ignore the fact that a soldier has gone AWOL if he gets back in time or if his comrades are able to make adequate excuses for him. In his own mind, the soldier makes the distinction between leaving for a short time and trying to get away for good. He is well aware that in most cases the second option has no real validity at all.

In an effort to obtain a more exact AWOL rate in Soviet units, soldiers were asked, "how often did soldiers in your unit go absent without leave?" It will be recalled that earlier the rate as measured by an unobtrusive indicator was 46.6 percent. Responses to the more direct question reveal similar rates: 49.5 percent of the soldiers felt that soldiers in their units went AWOL "very often" or "often"; 21.2 percent said "fairly often" and only 28.3 percent said "rarely" or "almost never."[82] When calculated by one measure, the AWOL rate is 46 percent; when calculated by another, it is 49.5 percent. It may, therefore, be said that Soviet AWOL rates are at least 40 percent, a rate close to that found in the American Army. Thus, despite the bureaucratization of the Soviet Army, its traditional mode of organization, and its use of large numbers of officers and

NCOs to maintain control, it appears that Soviet authorities have not been notably more successful in stopping or even significantly reducing AWOL rates than have American authorities, although, no doubt, for vastly different reasons.

Next, it was asked whether those who served in the military thought AWOL was a major problem: "in general, is going absent without leave a major problem in the military?" Not surprisingly, 77 percent of the soldiers at all ranks thought it was. When Soviet NCOs were asked the same question, 85.2 percent felt that AWOL was a major problem in their units. The view from the officer corps is consistent, with 78.9 percent agreeing that AWOL was a "major problem in the military."[83] To the extent that AWOL rates are a reflection of low morale and poor discipline, Soviet units may not be faring particularly well.

When enlisted commanders, including fireteam leaders, element leaders, and squad leaders—were asked about the seriousness of the AWOL problem, 88.2 percent thought it was a major problem. This is disheartening for those in the Soviet Army who wish to build strong disciplined units. Of commanding officers, 63.6 percent thought the AWOL problem had reached major proportions.[84]

To the extent that AWOL represents a reaction to the harsh tenor of Soviet military life, AWOL rates will continue to remain high as long as the quality of military life remains low. To the degree that AWOL rates reflect deep problems of morale and discipline, the incidence of AWOL suggests that these problems are found at all levels of command and in all types of units. That the problem is found throughout Soviet military history suggests further that it is a traditional problem, one that the Soviet Army has been unable to solve.

One of the more unambiguous indicators of low morale and indiscipline is the degree to which leadership elements are subject to physical assault by their own men. At the extreme is the case of the American Army in Vietnam where perhaps 1,000 officers and men were assassinated by their own troops.[85] In the Soviet Army, physical attacks on officers and NCOs appear to be an almost common feature of military life. In dozens of interviews time and again, stories were told in which NCOs and officers were the victims of assaults by soldiers who had reached the breaking point. The obvious question is why such assaults occur as frequently as they do. A number of the assaults on NCOs are the result of frustration and rage built up over the harsh tenor and regimentation of military life in general. In addition, training conditions are harsh so that it is not unreasonable that a soldier can fly into a rage and attack his perceived tormentor, namely, his NCO, warrant officers, or even his officers. This seems more valid in light of the informal caste system of exploitation to which the soldier is continually subject. Yet another reason for assaults may be related to alcohol abuse. Articles in the Soviet press attribute this kind of behavior to alcohol abuse, to drunken soldiers who release frustrations in drunken rages.

No matter how ambitious the military structure is in enforcing its rules, it cannot enforce every rule and regulation every day. At some point, it must rely upon the soldier to internalize certain norms as mechanisms for controlling group behavior. If it cannot do so, the level of troop discipline is low, although the

level of overt prosecution of violators of rules may be high. This seems to be
what is happening in Soviet units. To the degree that internalization of behavioral
norms supports good discipline, alcoholic rages, the discomforts of military life,
and the desire to escape it are all factors that contribute to assaults on leadership
elements. Judging from the number of assaults reported on officers and NCOs,
the extent of norm internalization seems low. The high rates of assault suggest
that both morale and discipline are low in many Soviet units.

When soldiers were asked, "did anyone in your unit ever physically assault
a warrant officer, NCO, or officer," the responses were surprising: 36.3 percent
of the soldiers reported witnessing assaults on warrant officers and an even higher
number, 62.8 percent, indicated they had direct knowledge of assaults on noncommissioned officers. When asked about assaults on officers, an amazingly
high 36 percent of the respondents said they had witnessed such assaults.[86] These
respondents reported direct knowledge of such assaults. When they were asked
if they had "heard stories about other units where officers had been assaulted,"
an even higher number of respondents, 57.5 percent, reported yes.[87] At the very
least, the evidence suggests that the rate of assaults on leadership elements may
be much higher than heretofore thought.

Units whose men assault their leaders often disintegrate when placed in battle.
Such units breed at least two specific problems. First, they tend to refuse to
engage in combat or they mutiny (as happened in some American units during
the Vietnam War); second, they tend to remove by violence those leadership
elements whom they regard as dangerous, a circumstance that also happened
with some frequency in Vietnam. The high rates of assault on Soviet leadership
elements suggest that in combat, when normal mechanisms of control erode and
pressures increase, Soviet leaders may well find themselves faced with troops
who refuse to engage or obey their officers. At the extreme, officers may even
face the possibility of being killed by their own men.

There is, of course, no way to prove this hypothesis short of committing Soviet
units to sustained battle. But all the elements of low morale and discipline, as
reflected in alcohol abuse, AWOL rates, and assaults on officers, appear to be
present within Soviet units. Certainly, the rates of officer assault in the Soviet
Army are far higher than anything witnessed in the American, British, West
German, French, or Canadian forces. In the West, incidents of an officer being
struck by enlisted men are quite rare.

As mentioned earlier, desertion in totalitarian armies is not the same thing as
it is in Western armies. Troops who "wander away" from their units in the
West often have some place to go and some money to get along on; they also
have some chance of success since the formal search for the soldier is normally
not undertaken until he has been missing for thirty days. In addition, the civilian
population is usually not enthusiastic about cooperating with military authorities
in turning in deserters, nor are there checks on internal movements or the om-
nipresent secret police. Important to understanding the degree of frustration
required to produce desertion in the U.S. Army, for example, is the fact that

penalties for being caught are relatively light. In many instances, they amount to only a formal reprimand or even to honorable separation from service. Few soldiers in the American Army are ever jailed for desertion. Most soldiers apparently desert as the result of the objectively minor frustrations of military life.

In the Soviet Army, none of these conditions obtains. Controls on military and civilian authorities are so strong that few soldiers who desert will remain at large for very long or will escape punishment. Soviet authorities begin searching for the AWOL soldier immediately, and he is classified as a deserter far more rapidly than in the West. Soviet authorities have a curious but effective way of determining if a soldier is a deserter or just AWOL: they find out whether the soldier took his weapon or a piece of military equipment with him. Soldiers who go AWOL pointedly leave behind any equipment that could reasonably be construed as a weapon; those who desert tend to take their weapons with them as they try to escape military life.

Soviet authorities react quite differently to a desertion than to an AWOL, and they react more quickly and more firmly. There is no doubt as to the penalties the deserter can expect. Deserters are usually placed in penal battalions where they serve up to eight months' "dead time," time that is not counted against their two-year enlistment. The Soviet press frequently mentions that the ultimate penalty for desertion is death.[88] The continual treatment in the press of the grave penalties that can be levied for desertion leads one to suspect that desertion in Soviet units may be quite high, although, interestingly, the Soviet press only rarely reports actual incidents of desertion itself.

The deserter faces such severe penalties that the act itself may well border on the irrational. The pattern of frustration and rage may be so deep that the reaction of desertion is itself an act of rage. Intriguingly, the Soviet policy on desertion may be not to give the soldier an opportunity to surrender. There are no hard sources in the military press that acknowledge this policy, but from time to time snatches of information become available which point to it. Soldiers who desert with their weapons may expect to be killed in a shootout.[89] Desertion in the Soviet Army has serious implications, not only for the soldier who deserts but also for the whole unit's morale and discipline.

Interviews with Soviet soldiers point out that desertions are a big problem for the Soviet Army and that they occur at a very high rate—certainly higher than we would have expected and close to the American rate. The soldiers also stated that officers desert, which suggests that the quality of life in the officer corps may sometimes drive officers to desperate measures. That is the thrust of Victor Belenko's testimony as to the feelings of his brother officers.[90] Even in the Soviet Air Force, conditions are at times so difficult that officers desert.

In order to press the analysis of desertion along more empirical lines, soldiers were asked about desertion in a series of questions focusing on the degree to which stories about desertion circulated among the troops. Soldiers were asked, "in general were the stories you heard about soldiers deserting very common, common, generally uncommon, rare or almost never?" A total of 23.9 percent said they had heard such stories commonly or very commonly; only 4.4 percent indicated they were uncommon; 46.9 percent answered rarely; and 22.1 percent said almost never.[91] In general, a new army recruit is probably aware that desertions occur. In a totalitarian system, the fact that he hears such stories at all may well indicate a serious problem.

In examining whether the soldiers had first-hand or direct knowledge of deserters in their units, they were asked, "when you were in the military did anyone in your unit ever desert?" In response, 49.6 percent, or about the same percentage of soldiers who indicated they had personal knowledge of soldiers going AWOL, said they had such personal knowledge.[92] This rate is much higher than anticipated and roughly approximates the American Army rate.

The level of desertion can be determined by measuring the Soviet authorities' concern about the problem. As noted earlier, the Soviet press constantly prints articles outlining the harsh penalties for desertion, although it rarely prints details of specific cases. When soldiers were asked if they thought their superiors were "concerned about the problem of desertion" in their units, 64.6 percent said yes. Soldiers were also asked if they thought "desertion was a big problem in the military"; 47.8 percent of those interviewed said it was.[93] When stratified on the basis of rank, 65.4 percent of the NCOs thought it was a major problem as did 42.1 percent of the officers.[94] If the data are only marginally correct, the problem of desertion seems as much a problem in the Soviet Army as it was in the Tsarist Army and, indeed, as it was for the Red Army in World War II. Soldiers who served in the army forty years ago indicated that desertion was a problem even then. Even if we allow for some exaggeration, it is still difficult to explain why so many soldiers under such diverse conditions consistently report the occurrence of the same phenomenon unless there is at least some truth to the tale.

Suicide, too, may sometimes be an indication of low morale. When suicide is found in a sustained pattern, it is unambiguous evidence that members of the units have been subject to severe stress for long periods. Soviet sociologists and psychologists, as well as articles in the official press, provide very little insight into suicide in Soviet society and almost no information about its occurrence in the Soviet military.[95] The evidence we have is merely impressionistic and suggests that the suicide rate for Soviet society is probably higher than that for the United States. The secrecy associated with a totalitarian system, the complete control of the press, the restrictions on travelers, the unwillingness of local inhabitants to talk, and, of course, the tendency noted by both Victor Belenko and Aleksei Myagkov to classify military suicides as training accidents considerably reduces our knowledge in this area. One thing we do know from defectors, a fact confirmed by our own interviews, is that Soviet authorities are concerned about the problem of suicide. In our study of Soviet soldiers, 47.8 percent reported that their superiors were concerned about it in their units.[96]

The surprising aspect of suicide in the Soviet Army is the degree to which the soldiers themselves see it as a not uncommon event. To discover that some officer shot himself or to learn that a new recruit took his own life does not seem to shock Soviet soldiers. Whether this is because they have heard stories about suicide before they entered the military or have witnessed it while in service is not clear. Compared to the number of stories about suicide in the American Army, the number in circulation in the Soviet Army seems excessive. Some 84.1 percent of the soldiers in Soviet units indicated that they "first heard stories about suicide in other units." When soldiers were asked directly, "how common are the stories about suicide attempts," 21.2 percent indicated they were common or very common. Another 17.7 percent indicated that such stories were uncommon, and 38.9 percent said they were rare. Only 16.8 percent of the soldiers reported they almost never heard such stories about suicide.[97] Whatever the actual incidence of suicide, there are considerable rumors about it among the troops.

In an effort to measure suicide rates, Soviet soldiers were asked, "when you were in the military did anyone in your unit ever commit suicide?" Of those interviewed, 48.7 percent reported having some direct knowledge of suicide in their units during their tour of military duty. When soldiers were asked "did anyone in your unit ever *attempt* to commit suicide," 53.1 percent answered yes.[98] These are surprisingly high figures.

An interesting difference between the incidence of suicide in Soviet and American units is its pattern of occurrence. The American soldier is most likely to commit suicide during basic training. Once in the mainstream of military life, however, suicide as a troop problem all but disappears. The pattern in Soviet military units is different. While Soviet soldiers are likely to be exposed to attempted suicide during basic training, most suicides occur after basic training is complete and the soldier has integrated into his military unit. Almost all suicide incidents reportedly occurred among troops who had been stationed with their units for some time. Some 59.3 percent of the respondents also noted that suicide occurred "after the soldier had been with his unit for a while."[99] Suicide rates among soldiers who had supposedly been integrated into their units were more than double the rates for basic training.

One of the more intriguing aspects of suicide in Soviet military units was offered by a respondent who is also a social scientist. He suggests that suicide rates in Soviet units are almost double those found in the society at large. A good guess would place the rate of suicide in Soviet military units at approximately 1.15 per 1,000, or approximately 3,000 per year. Boris M. Segal, in the only available study on the subject (and it is fifteen years old), notes that the suicide rate for draft-age males in Soviet society is 0.20 per 1,000.[100] Assuming that each analyst is correct, the figures indicate that suicide rates within the military are at least double those found in civilian society. The rates at which Soviet soldiers report suicide in their units confirm that it is occurring at far higher rates than in Soviet society at large.

Conclusion

The presence of such major indicators of low morale and poor discipline as alcohol abuse, AWOL, assaults on officers, desertion, and suicide indicates that

Soviet military units may be suffering from serious morale and discipline problems. It may be surmised that such units may not perform well on the battlefield.

While the state of morale and discipline in American and Soviet units is important, the ultimate concern of this analysis is to fit these findings into a larger formula to assess the degree to which Soviet and American units can be expected to perform adequately under fire. Central to this concern, of course, is the degree to which units reflecting problems of morale and discipline can sustain cohesion in battle. It is to this question that this study now turns.

Notes

1. They are still used to measure morale and discipline in the Israeli Army today. See Reuven Gal, "Characteristics of Heroism," paper delivered at the Canadian Leadership Symposium, Royal Roads Military College, Victoria, British Columbia (June 5, 1981).

2. Gabriel, *The New Red Legions: An Attitudinal Portrait of the Soviet Army* (Westport, Conn.: Greenwood Press, 1980), p. 161.

3. Larry Ingraham, *The Boys in the Barracks* (Washington, D.C.: Walter Reed Army Institute of Research, 1978), Chapter 3.

4. Ingraham, "Anatomy of an Elephant: The Shoeleather Epidemiology of Drug Use in the US Army," paper presented at Counterpush Training Workshop, Ramstein, Germany (March 21, 1980), p. 14.

5. Ibid.

6. Ibid.

7. These are commonly cited figures which seem to emerge at various academic and military panels and, in general, are assumed to be accurate at least by their proponents. While I can find no hard data to support them, their unchallenged use may speak somewhat to their general accuracy.

8. Human Readiness Report No. 5 (Washington, D.C.: Office of the Deputy Chief of Staff for Personnel, August 1979) addressed a whole section regarding the impact of drugs on combat ability.

9. The clearest statements and arguments to this effect are found in the various works by Ingraham cited throughout this study.

10. Ingraham et al., "Anatomy of an Elephant," pp. 14-15.

11. Ibid., p. 10.

12. Ibid., p. 13.

13. Ibid., p. 14.

14. Human Readiness Report No. 5, p. 19.

15. Ibid.

16. Ibid.

17. Ibid.

18. Ingraham, "The Anatomy of an Elephant," p. 14.

19. "The Worldwide Survey of Non-medical Drug Use and Alcohol Use Among Military Personnel, 1980," done by Burt Associates Inc., Bethesda, Maryland. Cited in detail in *Army Times*, December 15, 1980.

20. Ibid., p. 4.

21. Human Readiness Report No. 5, p. 19.

22. Ibid.

23. Marion Corddry, "War in Europe: The Enemy Is Troop Drug Use," *Army* (January 1979), p. 36.

24. "Worldwide Survey of Non-medical Drug Use," p. 4.

25. Ibid., p. 5.

26. Ibid.

27. Ibid.

28. As reported by an ABC News Report of September 21, 1981, congressional hearings produced the figure of 42 percent of the soldiers who admitted using drugs while on duty.

29. Human Readiness Report No. 5, p. F-13.

30. Ibid.

31. Ibid., p. F-26.

32. Ibid.

33. Ibid., p. F-24.

34. Ibid.

35. Ibid.

36. Ibid.

37. Human Readiness Report No. 5, p. 19.

38. "Worldwide Survey of Non-medical Drug Use," p. 4.

39. Human Readiness Report No. 5, p. 5.

40. Worldwide Survey of Non-medical Drug Use," p. 4.

41. Human Readiness Report No. 5, p. F-24.

42. Ibid.

43. Ibid, p. 5.; see also p. D-28.

44. Ibid., p. D-26.

45. Ibid.

46. Ibid., p. 10.

47. Ibid.

48. GAO Report, "Active Duty Manpower Problems Must Be Solved," (November 1979), p. 8.

49. GAO Report, "Millions Spent to Apprehend Military Deserters as unqualified for Retention" (January 31, 1977), p. 1.

50. *The Washington Star*, December 18, 1980, p. 6.

51. GAO Report, "Millions Spent," pp. 13-21.

52. "This Is Your Army, 1981," Information paper, U.S. Department of the Army, Washington, D.C., December 29, 1980, p. 3.

53. Ibid.

54. GAO Report, "Awol in the Military" (March 30, 1979), p. 1.

55. Ibid, pp. ii-iii.

56. Ibid., p. ii.

57. "This Is Your Army, 1981," p. 3.

58. *The Washington Post*, August 23, 1980, p. 9.

59. Human Readiness Report No. 5, p. 5.

60. Ibid., p. D-24.

61. Ibid., p. 5.

62. Charles Moskos, "Saving the All-Volunteer Force," *The Public Interest*, No. 61 (Fall 1980): 77-78.

63. Human Readiness Report No. 5, p. D-28.

64. Gabriel, *The New Red Legions*, p. 153.

65. For more information on alcohol abuse as a problem in Soviet society, see Walter D. Connor, *Deviance in Soviet Society* (New York: Columbia University Press, 1972), Chapter 4; see also *New York Times*, February 11, 1974, p. 11, for an interesting piece on alcohol use by Soviet youth.

66. Gabriel, *The New Red Legions*, p. 153.

67. Ibid.

68. Ibid., p. 158.

69. For more information on the effect of alcohol on the combat ability of Soviet soldiers, see Victor Belenko's testimony in the *New York Times*, January 13, 1974, p. 1, and September 10, 1974, p. 24. Finally, Aleksei Myagkov, *Inside the KGB: An Exposé by an Officer of the Third Directorate* (London: Foreign Affairs Publishing Co., 1977).

70. Gabriel, *The New Red Legions*, p. 155.

71. Ibid.

72. Ibid.

73. "Awash in a Sea of Vodka: Drunkenness in Russia," *Horizon* (Winter 1976): 3.

74. Gabriel, *The New Red Legions*, p. 156.

75. Ibid., p. 157.

76. "Worldwide Survey of Non-medical Drug Use," p. 4.

77. Gabriel, *The New Red Legions*, p. 157.

78. It has been a common problem in all armies since time immemorial, so much so that much fun is made about it. For example, during World War I, to go AWOL in the British Army was "to take French leave." Not to be outdone, the French regarded a soldier who had gone AWOL as one who had "been given an English pass."

79. Gabriel., *The New Red Legions*, p. 160.

80. Ibid.

81. Ibid., p. 161.

82. Ibid., p. 162.

83. Ibid., p. 163.

84. Ibid.

85. See Richard A. Gabriel and Paul L. Savage, *Crisis in Command: Mismanagement in the Army* (New York: Hill and Wang, 1978), Chapter 2.

86. Gabriel, *The New Red Legions*, p. 167.

87. Ibid.

88. For a list of punishments available to Soviet military authorities to deal with desertion, see *Bloknot agitatora* (May 1972): p. 2.

89. *Los Angeles Times*, March 24, 1972, p. 4.

90. Belenko, *New York Times*, January 13, 1974, p. 1.

91. Gabriel, *The New Red Legions*, p. 172.

92. Ibid., p. 173.

93. Ibid., p. 175.

94. Ibid.

95. One of the more thorough, if outdated, works on suicide in the Soviet Union is found in Jacques Choron, "Concerning Suicide in Soviet Russia," *Bulletin of Suicidology* (December 1968): 31-36.

96. Myagkov, *Inside the KGB*, p. 108, notes the tendency to classify suicides in the

military as training accidents. As to its magnitude, see Gabriel, *The New Red Legions*, p. 177.

97. Ibid., p. 178.
98. Ibid.
99. Ibid., p. 179.
100. Boris M. Segal, "The Incidence of Suicide in the Soviet Union," *Radio Liberty Dispatch* (February 2, 1977).

6

Unit Cohesion

Many comparisons have been made between the Soviet and American armies, but little attention is ever paid to the quality of the troops or to the theoretical conceptions that underpin the training doctrines of each army. This gap in our knowledge must be bridged, for it will help us determine how each army will seek to build cohesion in its battle units.

With regard to the doctrinal basis of training in each army, it is often over-looked that each army proceeds from a very different set of ideas as to what makes men fight, what bonds them together, and what techniques are required to keep battle units cohesive and effective under fire. Apparently, there is no study that systematically compares Soviet and American models of combat cohesion and that attempts to evaluate each model in terms of existing historical and sociological findings relating to the cases of cohesion. This chapter attempts to correct this omission.

No army can be considered effective unless it can rely upon its units to cohere under the terrifying stress of combat. Moreover, no army can expect to develop highly cohesive units unless it first develops theoretical doctrines that support the development and application of specific techniques designed to build cohesion. Thus, it may be assumed that training doctrines in the Soviet and American armies are existing reflections of what is necessary to keep units together in combat and to assure their effectiveness in performing their missions. The extent to which these doctrines and techniques contribute to cohesive units is, of course, a central question for analysts. What is intriguing is that Soviet and American models of military cohesion are radically different, as are their training techniques.

The Soviet Model

The Soviet model of military cohesion is based on the proposition that ideological conviction is the soldier's most important motivation to fight. The Soviet training literature often refers to ideological conviction as "the decisive motivational force behind all soldiers' actions and deeds."[1] Soviet doctrine posits a central role for ideology in the development of other military skills. Thus, "The leading role in the structure of moral-combat traits belongs to the ideological component, which defines the orientation and content of other components. Its foundation is comprised of the political consciousness and communist conviction of the soldier.''[2] No less an authority than Marshall A. A. Grechko subordinated the acquisition of military skills to ideological convictions when he said ''the first and foremost requirement of officers is to be ideologically convinced. . .and an active champion of party policy.''[3] Other high-level officers and official military periodicals continually reflect the same view.[4] In the Soviet view, then, there can be no motivation in any military unit that is not firmly rooted in the soldier's ideological conviction and consciousness. According to Grechko, ''the ideological approach and political maturity are the foundations of all other traits which a true soldier requires.''[5]

Ideological conviction is also the core element that produces cohesion within the military unit. The effectiveness of military units is repeatedly attributed to ideological conviction and consciousness.[6] Thus, ''the training process in our Army is inseparably linked to the indoctrination process.''[7] With regard to units, the Soviets distinguish very clearly between ''collectives'' and ''corporations.'' Collectives are effective military units precisely because the goals of the group are not confined to the group per se but serve a higher ''socially significant motive.''[8] Corporations, on the other hand, have ''goals which arise only out of intragroup needs and interests.''[9] Accordingly, the distinguishing characteristic of an effective cohesive military group is the presence of its ''socially significant motives,'' or, in other words, ideology and ideological conviction. Without appropriate ideological consciousness, groups become ''parochial'' and ineffective as military units.[10]

The stress upon ideology as a factor in military motivation and cohesion is a logical extension of the totalitarian and ideological character of the Soviet system itself.[11] As Marxists, the Soviets maintain that *all* social institutions, including military units, reflect the underlying forces of economic production and distribution. Accordingly, the socialist nature of the civilian society is projected into the military insofar as ideology is affirmed to be the basic raison d'etre of the regime and constitutes the guiding principles of the social order. The Soviets would argue that in all spheres of life they have created a new ''socialist man'' motivated by an understanding and conviction of the ideology of Marxist-Leninism. This motivation is central to the personality of ''socialist man'' and is demonstrated in all aspects of social, economic, political, and military life. Soviet man, therefore, fights for noble, historically inevitable ideals—ideals that are ''socially significant'' and that transcend values generated only by intragroup activity and group interests.[12]

The Soviets affirm that without proper ideological conviction military effectiveness is not possible. Corollarily, they imply that with proper ideological conviction and consciousness, these factors in themselves will motivate the individual soldier and produce cohesion in the military collective.[13] The Soviets are not naive enough to turn their training camps into indoctrination centers on these grounds. Soviet doctrine notes that other elements are needed along with indoctrination. Such elements fall into three categories: (1) *professional military traits*, by which the Soviets mean the acquisition of a high level of proficiency in terms of equipment, weapons systems, tactics, and general military expertise; (2) *psychological traits*, the ability to withstand the stress of modern warfare often achieved by making training conditions extremely harsh and realistic; and (3) *physical traits*, physical development and the ability to withstand hardship.[14] But motivation and cohesion are never purely technical qualities acquired by training. They are primarily "moral-combat" qualities, and they result from "the ideological component, which defines the orientation and content of the other components. The foundation is comprised of the political consciousness and communist conviction of the soldier."[15] Thus, the techniques of military expertise in themselves will produce neither motivation nor cohesion in military units. Such techniques are tangential to ideological conviction and consciousness.

So intent are the Soviets in their belief that ideological consciousness is vital to military effectiveness and unit cohesion that thay are openly fearful of any kind of attachments within military units that may result from forces other than ideological ones. There is the fear that the development of attachments and emotions toward one's fellow soldiers on grounds other than "socially significant motives" will tend to produce a negative sense of "combat comradeship" that generates loyalties beyond the control of the regime.[16] Official Soviet military periodicals note that there is a potential danger in the formation of "microcollectives"—a code name for groups that tend to form around some basis other than ideology. Such groups represent an "incorrect interpretation of comradeship" that "tends toward ... supporting a narrow circle of people."[17] It is feared that attachments to the microcollective will set up competition for the loyalty of the troops and erode their ideological convictions. Inasmuch as Soviet doctrine links effectiveness to conviction, any erosion within a military group of its "socially significant motives" is logically to be viewed with alarm. Such primary groups are seen as corrosive of the basic element contributing to cohesion and effectiveness, and rigorous efforts are made to break up such groups "as an essential condition for binding collectives on a healthy basis."[18]

If it is assumed that ideology is the basic motivating force for the Soviet soldier and that ideological conviction is the cement holding military units together in combat; and if it is further assumed that ideology has its source in the basic organization of the social order to which the Soviet soldier is exposed both within and outside the military, what role does that imply for the leader of the military group? What is the function of the military leader in the Soviet model?

Not surprisingly, the first function of the leader in Soviet military doctrine is to be a model of ideological conviction himself and to take steps to instill and strengthen this conviction in his troops. Leaders are also to be alert for the negative effects of attachments that may arise from nonideological causes.[19] As Grechko observes, "the first and foremost requirement of officers is to be ideologically convinced ... and active champions of party policy."[20] Indeed, *Red*

Star in an editorial went so far as to say that "constant political work is the paramount task of commanders."[21] If the premises of the Soviet model concerning the preeminent role of ideology in military cohesion and effectiveness are accepted, then the role of the military leader is quite logical.

Some appreciation of the military leader's role in Soviet military theory can be obtained by examining a revealing article entitled "The Ways and Means of Instilling High Moral-Combat Traits in Soviet Soldiers."[22] The authors address the tasks upon which a military leader must concentrate to instill cohesion and effectiveness in his unit. They emphasize ideological indoctrination, with the leader given the task of conducting indoctrination sessions through dissemination of revolutionary labor and combat traditions and unmasking the aggressive essence of imperialism.[23] But the article is most revealing for what it omits. It provides no treatment of or guidelines for the officer or NCO to follow in order to build attachments to and within the unit which are not based upon ideology. In short, the role of the military leader is "to construct the indoctrinational process and to supervise the activities of subordinates."[24]

In another Soviet training publication, the same view of the military leader's role is offered:

The duty of commanders and political workers is to maintain positive mental states in men and collectives during combat, instill confidence in victory in one's subordinates, firmly control troops, ably encourage combat eagerness, correctly place Party and Komsomol activities, and inform one's subordinates on the development of events.[25]

There are no injunctions, so profuse in American leadership manuals, to take the initiative, assume responsibility, care for the welfare of the troops, bear hardships with the troops, expose oneself to risk, and generally convince the troops that their leader understands their fears and cares about them. Such roles for the Soviet military leader are made unnecessary by the prior assumption that only ideology generates motivational forces. The employment of these other roles rests on the assumption that military groups generate their own sense of attachment among their members as a result of their own experiences and reactions, and not as a result of larger "socially significant motives" and ideological forces. Given the Soviet rejection of such bourgeois doctrines,[26] the sphere of leadership activity for the Soviet military leader is much more limited than that of his American counterpart.

Indeed, it is difficult to escape the impression that leadership in the Soviet model consists of a largely *technical* task focusing upon the scientific[27] application of those techniques designed to stimulate ideological conviction among the soldiery. Accordingly, the stress on the officer's political role and his responsibility to closely coordinate with political officers is readily understandable. The Soviet model admits of few tasks beyond that of ideological stimulation that the military leader can perform to contribute to cohesion and motivation. This reliance upon ideology to motivate the soldier and generate cohesion in battle is strong and, perhaps, even a bit naive. In any event, it does considerably reduce the role and responsibilities of the small-unit leader.

The reduced role for leadership elements in contributing to military motivation and cohesion, or at least confining that role largely to indoctrination, is consistent with the ideological and totalitarian nature of the Soviet social order. Specifically, any motivation generated by attachments formed to informal groups (primary groups in military units under stress) is correctly regarded as potentially corrosive of the regime's control. This is true in the military and in the society at large. Totalitarian regimes are driven by their own dynamics to become "totalist" in their desire to control all aspects of individual life. Moreover, since the raison d'etre of the regime is premised upon its possession and pursuit of a sacred ideology, any group that does not reflect the proper ideological motivation is perceived as "parochial" and must be dealt with.[28]

Soviet military doctrine clearly reflects this view when it defines a collective as "an organized group of people who are part of a society and united by common goals and joint socially useful activity."[29] Any group that arises only out of intragroup needs and interests is to be regarded with suspicion precisely because such groups lack the necessary ideological justification in terms of socially significant goals that transcend the group's specific interest. The notion that men might forge attachments to each other, especially in military groups, that have no ideological component is denounced as "parochial" and "bourgeois." There can be no question of motivation, cohesion, or effectiveness within military groups arising in this manner:

Courage, bravery, and heroism can be displayed by soldiers on a mass scale, can become a standard for behavior in combat *only* if they are linked with the noble ideals, with the conviction that the purpose of the army and its war aims correspond to the interests of the people, the genuine interests of the country.[30]

One also surmises from the foregoing that ideology serves as the critical bridge in establishing a motivational connection between the military environment and the larger society—indeed, perhaps even with the forces of history itself. There is, then, no such thing in the Soviet view as a unit motivated or held together by forces that are purely internally generated by the unit. As a result, there is no need for the leader to assume responsibility for generating the kinds of nonideological attachments that produce cohesion. Motivation and cohesion result from elements external to the group, namely, ideology and political consciousness.

In summary, the Soviet model of military cohesion is based squarely on the proposition that the Soviet social order has created a new "socialist man" who is motivated by an understanding and appreciation of the elements of Marxist-Leninist ideology. This basic motivating force of human behavior is the same for individuals in civilian and military roles. Cohesion of military units results from the unit's collective understanding and consciousness of the high ideals and noble goals of Communist ideology. To be sure, Soviet training requires technical proficiency in military skills but is quick to affirm that such skills per se are ineffective without proper ideological motivation. In this environment, the role of the military leader is to become an example of ideological motivation and to maintain that conviction on the part of his troops as the basic generator of motivation, cohesion, and combat-effectiveness. Given the premises of Soviet doctrine, there is naturally a deep suspicion of any type of informal group which may form within military units. Such groups (which, as we shall see, are viewed as fundamental to American notions of cohesion) are regarded as potential "islands of resistance,"[31] negativism, and parochialism, and as being of bourgeois origin. Because such groups are not perceived as contributing to cohesion, the leader is not required to develop close attachments with them. In these circumstances, leadership becomes almost a technical task; almost a science rather than an art.

The American Model

While the American model of military cohesion is decidedly different from the Soviet model, it, too, is a reflection of the society that supports it. In the American case, the theoretical supports for military cohesion are marked by an absence of deep concern for ideology. In a society so heavily dependent on pluralism and economic "free enterprise," this condition is hardly surprising. Lacking the cohesive force of ideology, American military thought has had to establish combat cohesion through other elements.[32]

The American military has adopted the work of A. H. Maslow as its theoretical foundation for explaining cohesion and motivation in military units.[33] Individuals, Maslow maintains, are fundamentally motivated by two generic types of needs: physical needs and learned needs.[34] Physical needs include such obvious conditions of survival as food, water, shelter, and the elimination of waste.[35] More important to any notion of what makes men under stress remain together and remain effective is the concept of learned needs. Learned needs include the following: the need to feel safe, the need for social acceptance and belonging, the need for esteem, and the need for self-fulfillment.[36] Learned needs are the result of the individual's total life-experiences in a society. The individual soldier brings to the military an already developed set of learned needs; these needs are accepted as given when the soldier enters the military environment.[37]

A basic question may be raised at this point. Even assuming a relative homogeneity of learned needs, it is clear that the manner in which any given individual may stress one need over another will vary widely within the population. Which needs, then, take precedence? The question appears unanswerable in that the soldier is taken into the unit with his needs and preferences already formed by his prior social experiences. In short, the military must work with the soldier as it finds him.[38]

Motivation in a military environment is accomplished by recognizing individual learned needs and assuring an "alignment of personal and unit goals."[39]

The basic assumption, of course, is that the individual soldier can be made to see that he can achieve his individual needs by fulfilling unit functions. Once this connection between organizational and individual goals is established for the soldier, motivation will result.[40] Once again one can raise a question as to what happens when the individual is placed in a situation, say extreme combat stress, where he begins to perceive that his learned personal needs (safety) clearly are divergent from the unit's goals (continue the attack). If the premises of the model hold, unit disintegration would be expected to result. The point is that divergencies between unit goals and individual goals expressed in terms of fulfilling learned needs lead logically to some degree of discohesion.

If individual motivation results from an identity of group and personal goals, what is the role of the group in stimulating motivation and cohesion? In American military doctrine, the group is perceived in mechanistic or instrumental terms. Thus, "group norms vary from individual needs only in that they are a collection of the individuals in the groups."[41] The group can never have an existence or value apart from its contribution to meeting individual needs. There is no question of any "organic" or "corporative" nature of the group.[42] It is only an instrumentality for meeting individual needs.

Since the group is primarily an instrumentality for satisfying individual needs in terms of stimulating motivation and cohesion, the military utilizes the analogy of a contract to explain the relationship between the individual soldier and the larger unit of which he is a part: "...under the terms of the informal contract, both the organization and the soldier depend upon each other for the satisfaction of their expectations, and each must meet the terms of the contract according to what the other expects."[43] It is emphasized that the group has no value beyond its instrumental value, and the loyalty to the group is based on instrumental calculations, namely, the extent to which the group meets individual needs. Loyalty to the group will result, and motivation and cohesion will be generated only as long as the group fulfills its part of the informal contract and continues to meet individual needs through group activity.

What are the linkages between the military unit and the larger social order? In the first place, a primary linkage is posited insofar as the individual soldier's value system is formed in the society as a result of personal experiences.[44] It must be expected that wider societal values will penetrate the military and will be reflected in the relations between the individual and the military unit.[45] Furthermore, whatever values and attitudes the individual acquires in the wider social arena are functions of his basic need requirements. Accordingly, the same "need profile" which motivates a person in civilian life is expected to motivate him in military life. *There is no requirement to develop purely military values and attitudes; civilian mechanisms of motivation are simply transposed into the military environment.* Finally, a primary linkage with the larger social order is established in the *process* of motivation, namely, dovetailing self-interests to the organization in an entrepreneurial fashion. The motivational process is the same in civilian life as in military life. There is no expectation that self-interest will be foregone for higher group interests. There is only the imperative that individual interests will be best served by observing group norms. In this sense, the dominant entrepreneurial ethic of the larger American society is linked with the anticipated behavior of military groups precisely on the grounds that the process of motivation is the same for both.

There is no assumed ideological link, as in the Soviet Union, for the very obvious reason that there is no formal ideological code in American society. The decentralization of American life and the logic of free enterprise combine to produce an ethos of the entrepreneur which, in terms of the strategies needed to obtain self-interest, comprise a linkage with group activity in a military environment.[46] There is no coherent belief in an ideology which is transposed into military life; there is only the belief that the entrepreneurial process will remain the same motivating force for the soldier in a military unit as for the individual in the society at large.

This conception of the group in military life is very important, for it suggests there is no need for a socialization mechanism to create new values, destroy old ones, or establish and transmit values and goals that are deemed specifically appropriate to military service. In short, the motivational process and values appropriate to civilian life are seen to be equally appropriate in the military environment. There is, therefore, nothing in the military experience per se that requires the individual's resocialization to it.[47]

Given the foregoing model of cohesion, what is the role of the leader? American doctrine, although not always consistent with its theoretical underpinnings, posits a vigorous and straightforward role for the leader in generating individual motivation and unit cohesion. Leadership in the American model is seen as situational; the application of leadership techniques depends very much upon the circumstances surrounding any decision.[48] It differs in this respect from the Soviet model in which leadership is seen to be more a matter of applying scientific principles in a planned manner. Leadership in the American view is not a science so much as it is a judgmental art. Probably most importantly, the American model of leadership requires that the military leader be directly responsible for everything his unit does or fails to do, including, of course, the responsibility for motivation and combat cohesion.[49] While there is the recognized need for management, a bow to the more diffuse conditions that may well affect motivation or cohesion, the American model notes that there are few requirements for management at the small-unit level.[50] Here leadership is the key element in keeping units effective.

Equally compelling are the American model's injunctions for the individual leader to demonstrate personal courage, dependability, integrity, a sense of justice and fairness in dealing with his men, unselfishness, initiative, and risk, and to share equal hardships with his men. The American officer is to do all these things conspicuously. Finally, the American leader must "set the example" and always look after the men and their welfare as a sure means of motivating troops and building unit cohesion.[51]

The American model seems to incorporate within it a basic contradiction, at least from the theoretical point of view. Consider the heavy responsibilities placed upon the unit leader which are summed up most succintly in the dictum, "a commander is responsible for everything his unit does or fails to do." The idea that the leader must establish a bond with his men may be good military practice, but it is not one that can be logically deduced from the major theoretical assumptions made by the American model. Indeed, in light of the major theoretical assumptions made by the American model about what keeps a unit together under stress, namely, the convergence of individual and organizational goals, the injunction for officers to be courageous, honorable, set the example, share the risks, and so on, really makes little sense. All that would make sense in these circumstances would be for the leader to *manage* his resources in the attainment of organizational goals; the troops would become means to that end.[52] In short, the leadership techniques that the American model requires of its combat leaders are designed to establish a type of relationship between leader and men that is far deeper than one based upon mutual functionality. A bond requiring such things as honor, integrity, courage, and mutual respect involves things that have very little to do with the assumption of meeting individual goals through the mechanism of the group. Such things only make sense if the group itself, one's peers, and one's leaders are valued as something more than instrumentalities. They make sense only if the intragroup relationships are of corporative rather than an entrepreneurial nature.[53]

Accordingly, there appears to be a basic contradiction between the theory's postulates as to why men cohere under stress, that is, the entrepreneurial utility of the group, and the role of the leader which is to apply techniques that are effective only if the group is seen to have some independent meaning. The practice of leadership requires that the group be more than the sum of its parts, while the theory of leadership requires that the group be only a mechanism of individual entrepreneurialism.

The Models Compared

Several points of convergence and divergence are evident within the models. While both the Soviet and American models posit a link between effectiveness and cohesion of military units and their respective social orders, the nature of that linkage is radically different in each case. For the Soviets, ideological conviction forms the vital military-societal bridge, its operation being essentially the same in both environments. In American military thought, the linkage is provided by an assumed similarity of process, a similarity in the ways in which individual needs are met in both environments. In both military and civilian societies, individuals obtain personal goals through entrepreneurial calculations in which groups remain instruments. Both models accept the soldier as he is, as products of the total social experiences in their respective societies. The result of such experiences is very different: for the Soviet soldier, the result is a collectivist attitude, while for the American, the result is an individualistic entrepreneurial orientation. Neither model sees any need to provide either additional or different mechanisms of motivation in the military environment than are present in the civilian environment.

The models converge in assuming that there is no need for the military unit to establish a socialization mechanism that would serve to establish new values specifically appropriate to military life. Neither sees military life as being *sui generis* or even sufficiently different from civilian life to require an alteration in the value patterns that produce motivation and cohesion. Both models affirm that prior motivating forces are equally applicable to the military tasks of cohesion and motivation as they are to civilian tasks.

The role of leadership in generating cohesion and motivation is more consistent in the Soviet model. If it is assumed that the total nature of ideology is a motivating force, the Soviets make the first task of leadership the setting of ideological example and the continued stimulation of ideological conviction and consciousness.[54] In the American view, a whole range of leadership responsibilities and techniques is required of the leader which very clearly imply that the group is more than an instrumentality for meeting learned needs.[55] The leadership doctrines of the U.S. military require values and actions on the part of the leadership and the led that cannot be directly implied by the premises of the model. Implicit in the U.S. view of leadership is the premise that the military group must assume a corporative identity if some leadership tasks are to make any sense, while such a corporative identity stands in contradiction to the original proposition that groups have only instrumental or entrepreneurial value.

Finally, the Soviets regard leadership and its applications as far less situational and far more a scientific task than the U.S. model. Whenever the Soviet military leader stimulates ideological consciousness, he is doing so in accordance with the laws and dictates of history which, curiously, is also perceived as scientific in the Marxist lexicon.[56] U.S. military thought is quite clear in affirming that the "principles of leadership" make sense only in a subjective sense and that there is nothing immutable or necessary about any of them. In the end, leadership in the American model is an art acquired through exposure and experience.[57]

The fact that both models demonstrate certain points of similarity and difference does not lend much insight into which model is most likely to produce troops of higher quality. It seems that if we are going to try to assess the theoretical postulates that underlie Soviet and American training doctrines, some external standard of measurement is required. It may well be asked what factors social scientists have already identified as contributing to unit cohesion under battle stress? If these factors can be located, then it will be possible to assess each model against this standard with a view toward trying to make some judgments about the quality and combat-effectiveness of the troops produced under the imperatives of each system.

Cohesion and Disintegration: A Traditional View

Social scientists have always been interested in the problems associated with war, and, as a result, a considerable archive of research findings exists. Specifically, several major research efforts have focused on the problem of cohesion in military units subjected to combat stress. While these works have at times proceeded from different perspectives, they are unusual in that they have reached essentially the same conclusion about what factors are responsible for generating and maintaining unit cohesion. Such unanimity is relatively rare in the social sciences.

Probably the most definitive, if not the earliest, work in the area is the famous Shills and Janowitz study of the German Army.[58] Through a series of in-depth interviews, these two scholars tried to locate the factors which contributed to unit cohesion in the German Army in World War II. In brief, they found that German units held together under extremely severe combat stress, largely because of loyalties generated and sustained by primary groups. German soldiers, their NCOs, and their officers comprised a supporting web of strongly personal relationships generated by the experiences of combat stress itself. Soldiers came to feel a responsibility to their peers and superiors that was born of mutual risk, hardship, and the feeling that their superiors truly cared for their welfare and were prepared to expose themselves to the same risks as the troops. In this process, the primary group—the social unit of strongest attitudinal attachment—was the foremost generator of mutually supporting relationships. The group per se became more than the sum of its parts, and attachment to it was truly corporative—as indeed it was for the men who comprised it. Personal relationships to each other and to the group were rooted in something stronger than entrepreneurial utility.

Equally interesting was the finding that the German soldier was not motivated by ideological concerns except to a very small degree. This finding is surprising in view of the pervasive notion that the Nazi regime was continually exposing the troops to propaganda. Actually, Paul Hausser estimates that no more than 9 percent of all training time was spent in ideological indoctrination.[59] This is not to say that some linkages did not exist with the larger society, for clearly they did. However, the findings suggest that the notion that soldiers can be continually motivated by ideology while subject to combat stress is open to serious question. Indeed, one of the findings of all the major works on combat cohesion is that ideology plays only a minimal role.

The findings of the Shills and Janowitz study were anticipated by the earlier findings of S.L.A. Marshall in his work *Men Against Fire*.[60] Marshall studied the American Army in World War II and concluded that combat cohesion and motivation were generated by personal attachments to peers within combat units. In any case, the grand ideals for which World War II was supposedly fought appeared to have no impact on combat motivation at all. Samuel Stouffer's more comprehensive study of the American soldier in that same war, *The American Soldier*, produced the same findings.[61] More recently, John Keegan, in his *Face of Battle*, undertook a detailed study of why men remain together in battle despite terrible stress.[62] In his study of three famous English battles, Agincourt, Waterloo, and the Somme, he found a distinct absence of ideological motives contributing to cohesion. Rather, he found cohesion to spring from the mutual hardship, risk, and suffering that all involved—officers, NCOs, and common soldiers—shared. The small unit became the focus of intensely personal, almost "priestlike" attachments for which the most conspicuous acts of bravery were performed.[63] Alan Lloyd in his book *War in the Trenches* came to the same conclusion about British forces in World War 1.[64] Samuel Rolbant, in *The Israeli Soldier*, also found that military cohesion and motivation were rooted in small-unit, intensely personal attachments;[65] furthermore, he specifically noted that ideology—the supposed Masada Complex of the Jews—played almost no part in motivating the Israeli soldier.[66] Indeed, his surveys revealed an eerie absence of any generalized hatred for the Arab enemy among Israeli troops.[67] Yet, their fighting ability and courage in battle remained unquestioned by any serious observer.

Past research into the cohesion of military units demonstrates that the force of ideology, primary in the Soviet model, and of entrepreneurial utility, central to the American model, do not appear to be major motivating forces in developing and maintaining unit cohesion in combat. Furthermore, these findings appear to be valid crossculturally in the British, German, American, and Israeli armies. In addition, they appear to hold transhistorically in all kinds of battles, regardless of technology and the killing power of weaponry. In the end, the evidence suggests that cohesion is a function of strong personal loyalties to small groups developed through and sustained by a feeling that *all* participants are united by similar hardship, risk, fear, and the understanding that their leaders will endure similar conditions. When these conditions are not present, as has been suggested was the case among American troops in Vietnam, then no amount of technical military expertise or ideological feeling can produce effective cohesive military units.[68] Men appear to be willing to die for their fellow soldiers, and not for grandiose ideals or military systems.

Evaluating American and Soviet Models of Cohesion

If the traditional model of cohesion is correct in locating factors contributing to the ability of military units to withstand combat stress, then a comparison of Soviet and American models of cohesion raises some serious questions about the ability of both doctrines to produce truly effective units. There are enough differences in both models to suggest that training doctrines based upon them may not produce troops that can be expected to demonstrate high levels of cohesion in combat. The military effectiveness of such units is, therefore, subject to some doubt.

The Soviet model shows four important points of divergence from the traditional model. First, and of great importance, is the Soviet emphasis on ideology and larger social forces to produce motivation and cohesion. If past research on cohesion demonstrates anything, it is that ideology does not seem to be an important element in generating cohesion. Still, Soviet military theory stresses that without ideology unit effectiveness is impossible, and it reserves for ideology the central role in motivation, cohesion, and effectiveness.[69] The stress on ideology leads to a second important divergence, the tendency to view leadership as a largely technical task and to limit the role of the leader proportionately. Here the leader must take every opportunity to instill ideological consciousness in his troops and to ensure their expertise in military skills.[70] The assumption is, however, that one leader is as good as another as long as ideology remains present. The leader has no role in stimulating personal attachments or relationships; leadership is impersonal bordering upon the scientific.

Third, as a logical consequence of the stress on ideology, the Soviets reject the notion that military cohesion can result from loyalties generated within the group as a consequence of group experiences. This view is rejected as bourgeois.[71] Accordingly, the major finding of previous research—that the primary group is a generator of attachments among peers and superiors producing cohesion—is viewed in Soviet theory as virtually subversive. No group can possibly have independent value if it does not demonstrate higher "socially significant motives," namely, ideology.[72] Finally, Soviet thinkers on the subject of cohesion literally practice what they preach by taking active steps to break down the "negative" loyalties that seem to develop within "microcollectives." If Soviet military journals can be believed, the Soviets make an overt and deliberate effort to erode the kinds of personal attachments to the primary group that previous research has found to be so important to developing and sustaining unit cohesion. Such a practice is perfectly consistent with Soviet theory but necessarily raises some serious questions about the effectiveness of an army in which primary group attachments have been systematically weakened, if not destroyed.

The American model demonstrates three points of divergence from previous findings on cohesion. First, American theory does not posit a corporative role for the military group. Instead, American theory argues that the group is purely an instrumentality that is never greater than the sum of its parts. Loyalty to it is based upon a mutuality of convergent interests. There is never any question that the individual should be willing to sacrifice individual needs to the larger needs of the group; there is only the affirmation that individual needs can best be satisfied through the group. The corporative nature of the group and what that implies in terms of a willingness to subordinate individual needs to it (which emerges as a premise of the traditional model of cohesion) is rejected by American doctrine.

A second point of divergence concerns the civilian-military linkage as a motivating force in military units. American doctrine suggests that the forces of motivation in the civilian society are adequate to the military environment. Certainly, such forces are not primarily ideological. They are, however, founded on the assumption that the same process of need satisfaction based upon the attainment of individual needs in an entrepreneurial fashion applicable to civilian life will motivate soldiers in the military. Again, the emphasis is upon perceiving the group as an instrumentality to be utilized in an entrepreneurial way. There is no notion that relationships within the group can be premised on anything other than mutual utility or that the group has any kind of corporative value in itself. The logical of this position, if pressed, is that nothing in the nature of military groups or their components is worth dying for, since death is by definition always an "uneconomic" choice.

Finally, American doctrine logically affirms that there is no need for military units to develop mechanisms for socializing new soldiers to the military group. The need for new values in the military environment would presuppose that there was something about military life per se that required new means of motivation. But, as has been noted, the dominant assumption is that the mechanisms of motivation extant in civilian life are equally appropriate to the military environment. Accordingly, there is no need to develop mechanisms for socializing the soldier to the primary group; one can truly socialize to corporative entities only, not to entrepreneurial instrumentalities.

Although both the Soviet and American doctrines diverge from the traditional model at important points, the American position is somewhat closer to the traditional model—at least in terms of how the doctrine is practiced. American leadership manuals demand responsibilities and practices of its leaders that come very close to the things required of the leader in the traditional model.[73] Indeed, there are only marginal differences between the two. Therefore, while the model of cohesion in American military theory is very different from the traditional model, the actual implementation of the doctrine seems at points to ignore the theory and to include within it many of the practices that only make sense relative to the traditional model. The same cannot be said for the Soviets who appear to be convinced of the validity of their approach and to implement it with considerable vigor.[74] In the end, it may be that what really counts is training practice rather than theoretical doctrine.

The reasons why Soviet and American doctrine diverge from the traditional model of military cohesion are clear enough. In the Soviet case, the totalitarian nature of a regime which manifests an ideology claiming to be scientific cannot permit attachments to small groups to develop, for they become potential "islands of resistance" to the regime. Totalitarian regimes are totalist and seek to penetrate all aspects of social life, including military life. Moreover, to admit that cohesion may be a function of personal attachments undercuts the ideological claim of the regime to explain *all* aspects of society and history. It also implies that men may be motivated by things other than the "underlying forces of production and distribution." Accordingly, Soviet military doctrine regarding cohesion must necessarily diverge from the traditional model.

In the American case, the reasons for divergence are somewhat more complex. Any nation forged in free enterprise, emphasizing the pursuit of individual self-interest as the highest goal, stressing laissez-faire, Social Darwinist, and Madisonian notions of economics, social life, and politics is hard pressed to evolve *any* standards upon which all can agree.[75] Loyalty which cannot be directed to common ends is directed to a commonality of means, namely, the pursuit of individual needs as the highest goal. The *process* of pursuit becomes the central value of society. In the military, any doctrine which suggested there was a higher goal than the individual and that the individual ought to sacrifice the pursuit of his interests to it would stand in stark contradiction to major social values. Hence, the American Army has adopted an entrepreneurial notion of how to motivate soldiers and to produce unit cohesion. Whatever its faults, this perspective has the virtue of being consistent with the values of the larger American society.[76]

Both the American and Soviet models of unit cohesion diverge enough to raise serious questions about the effectiveness of the soldiers and military units produced by the training doctrines supported by each model. The problem is more than theoretical; its potential implications for the performance of both Soviet and American units in battle are serious indeed. It is hard to escape the impression that American and Soviet military theorists have come to believe that the nature of modern military conflict is so qualitatively different from past conflicts that a greater reliance must be placed upon either ideology, in the Soviet case, or systems management, in the American case. The belief seems prevalent that the acquisition of military skills and technological expertise when welded to a larger system of supply, mobilization, and economic production designed to place technologies at the service of the soldier will combine to produce effective, cohesive, and ultimately victorious units on the battlefield. This may prove to be the case. However, if the lessons of past wars are any guide, neither technology nor military expertise appears to have had much effect on the level of cohesion demonstrated by military units in combat. Moreover, the evidence presented earlier is sufficient to raise serious questions about the cohesiveness of American and Soviet units, even if we grant that each army's theories of cohesion are valid. There is, then, serious reason to question whether *either* Soviet or American units will reveal themselves to be effective under fire.

Cohesion in the American Army

In assessing the degree of cohesion of the American Army, the Vietnam experience provides a case study for examining the performance of combat units modeled on the theory of cohesion outlined above. The analyst has an unprecedented opportunity to examine how well those units did in battle. Many of the reasons for the poor performance of these units are related to the faulty doctrine of cohesion used by the American Army.

The argument has already been made that the collapse of small-unit cohesion in Vietnam can be traced to several institutional and systemic practices within the army. These practices, in turn, can be traced directly to an erroneous doctrine of what is required to produce effective, cohesive battle units. Examples of these systemic practices include the use of the DEROS system, failure to use unit rotation, rapid personnel turnover among small-unit leaders, too large an officer corps, failure of the corps to bear its fair share of hardship and death, shorter tours for officers in combat than for troops, institutionalization of the up-or-out system, failure to establish a proper code of ethics, and rampant careerism. All of these practices characterized the American effort in Vietnam and still characterize the American Army today.[77] It might be argued that the performance levels of American units in Vietnam are likely to be repeated as long as these conditions remain.

There is little evidence that suggests the army has reexamined closely its doctrine of cohesion or that it has dismantled or corrected any of the major policies that produced such disastrous results at the small-unit level. Indeed, all of the major practices mentioned above remain in force today. With the single exception of a reduction in the size of the officer corps from 17 percent of total strength to 11 percent, none of the conditions that contributed so much to the discohesion of American units has been eliminated. The American Army has been unable to rid itself of systemic practices which cut directly across its ability to build reliable cohesive units. In addition, the erroneous doctrine of cohesion which has given rise to so many of these practices remains unchanged and generally unchallenged from within the army's training establishment.

What of the army today? It has been ten years since the Vietnam War ended, and it seems a fair question to inquire about the army's present levels of cohesion. The available evidence suggests that the levels today may, in fact, be considerably below those found in Soviet units and, perhaps, even below those evident during the Vietnam War. In 1979, Human Readiness Study No. 5, a study of sixty battalions, found a direct relationship between "command climate" as measured by soldier, NCO, and officer perceptions of their unit's abilities and the actual performance of their units.[78] The study found what military historians have always known: a direct relationship between the extent of interpersonal ties of leaders and men, unit cohesion, and the ability of a unit to perform well. As a consequence, the army developed a mechanism to measure what it called "unit climate" in order to quantify anticipated unit performance. It developed four basic indicators of unit climate: morale, motivation, esprit de corps, and discipline.[79] An analysis of each of these indicators over a five-year period, based on the army's own data, indicates that the quality of unit climate, and thus their corollaries, unit cohesion and unit performance, have been in a steady state of decline.

With regard to morale as a specific indicator of unit climate, the data revealed a consistent decline over the last few years. Commonly, only 25 percent of first-term soldiers reported that their unit morale was either high or very high, a figure that compares with the 35 percent figure of 1975.[80] This decline is also reflected in the perceptions of career soldiers. The number of career soldiers who rated their unit morale as high declined from 40 percent in 1976 to less than 30 percent in 1979.[81] Based on the opinions of the soldiers themselves, then, unit morale is low and has been declining for several years.

When we examine motivation, the second indicator, similar results emerge. The degree to which soldiers perceive their units as being well motivated has declined steadily. At present, about 65 percent of first-term soldiers indicated that soldiers in their units "worked hard to get things done"; in 1975 the rate was 70 percent, a slight but significant decline. Career soldiers indicated a similar trend, down from 75 percent in 1975 to 65 percent at present.[82] This decline among all soldiers was evident armywide and appeared most severe among troops stationed in Europe, precisely among units that were supposed to be the most battleworthy and most prepared to fight. The generally low state of motivation is confirmed by the high number of unit commanders in both combat arms units and TO&E units who thought that the motivation of their men was a problem. Fully 74.4 percent of unit commanders throughout the army saw motivation as a major problem among their men. The numbers are even more damaging when assessed by type of unit. Whereas 84.4 percent of officers in TO&E units agreed that motivation was a major problem, 83.8 percent of the officers in combat arms units also assessed troop motivation as a major problem.[83] The data are consistent, demonstrating that both troops and officers believe that motivation among units is generally low and declining.

A similar problem emerges with regard to esprit de corps. This indicator has declined generally, especially among first-term soldiers stationed in Europe. Thus, 53.6 percent of unit commanders felt that esprit was a problem with which they had to deal, as did 58.6 percent of the officers in combat units.[84] When soldiers in the ranks were asked directly if their fellow soldiers were proud to be members of their units, the data demonstrated a very low rate of attachment. When soldiers were asked, "are the soldiers in your unit or organization proud to be members of your unit," only 36.2 percent of the first-term soldiers armywide and 40.1 percent of career soldiers agreed this was the case.[85] Among all enlisted soldiers armywide, 37.9 percent agreed that "soldiers in their units were proud to be members of their units."[86] Once again, the data pertaining to a key indicator of unit climate and cohesion suggest that levels of cohesion may be somewhat less than what may be required for effective combat performance.

Soldiers' perceptions of the quality of unit discipline revealed essentially the same findings. Among the troops themselves, 20 percent believed that military control and discipline within their units were too loose.[87] Thus, this statistic bears out our earlier analysis of unit discipline. With regard to officer perceptions of the state of unit discipline, 69.5 percent of the unit commanders armywide and a staggering number of combat arms unit commanders, 78.5 percent, believed discipline to be a major problem.[88] Whether measured by our earlier analysis or by the perceptions of the men and officers within units, the evidence is consistent in pointing out the poor quality of unit discipline throughout American military units.

"Quality NCOs"—that is, those whom the army defines as not being substance abusers or disciplinary problems themselves—saw the state of unit discipline as very low. Almost 60 percent of them said that their units would not do a good job if forced to do battle.[89] Many officers also perceived that the indicators of unit climate had declined over the preceding four years. The percentage of officers and commanders serving in troop units who stated that motivation, discipline, and morale were major problems in their units increased steadily after 1976. About 15 percent more officers believed they had worse problems in these areas in 1979 than they had in 1976.[90]

The army study on unit climate concluded that "most available indicators imply that unit climate although generally improving during the first years of the all volunteer force has been gradually worsening during the past two years. This trend is consistent with declining motivation, morale, and discipline and has been accompanied by junior enlisted and NCO perceptions of decreasing unit readiness."[91] The evidence marshaled by the army's studies implies a clear relationship between unit cohesion and unit ability to perform in battle.[92] Furthermore, as measured by the four indicators used by the study, it may be concluded that the level of cohesion of American units is generally low and even declining. This does not augur well for the ability of such units to perform under fire.

If one assembles data from other studies to test dimensions of cohesion identified earlier in the analysis of U.S. units, it appears that cohesion levels in American units may be at an unacceptably low level. For example, only 40 percent of the soldiers in 1980 believed that officers cared about their welfare, a decline from 50 percent in 1976. In addition, only 40 percent thought their officers could be relied upon to protect their welfare.[93] Along similar lines, 45 percent of the soldiers believed their officers were competent, down from 60 percent four years earlier.[94] Thus, along two crucial dimensions—the degree to which soldiers see their officers as genuinely concerned about them and the degree to which they see them as competent—over the last few years the American soldier has viewed his officers as neither caring nor competent. At the very least, these two indicators are declining.

With regard to another crucial indicator, the trust soldiers are willing to place in their leaders, American units may also be lacking in this vital dimension of cohesion. The Westbrook study revealed that 52 percent of the troops believed they could not count on their leaders (officers and NCOs) to "look out for their soldiers' interests," and another 20 percent were unsure whether they could count on them.[95] In addition, 37 percent of the soldiers believed that their officers were not concerned with them, and 15 percent were unsure. Finally, 28 percent of the troops said their leaders could not be trusted, and 23 percent were uncertain whether they could.[96]

Another aspect of cohesion that deserves attention is the degree to which American soldiers feel isolated from their comrades. Cohesion requires a strong identification of the soldier with his primary group, namely, the platoon or squad comprised of his peers.[97] The high rates of drug abuse in American units indicate a lack of cohesiveness in many military units. Several studies demonstrate that drug use is an indicator of peer isolation. In 1979, the Human Readiness Study published its findings on the relationship between drug use and the social climate in units. Specifically it concluded that the general climate of military life at the troop level promotes a reduction to the lowest common denominator of group life bordering on deviancy as the norm. This sets the stage for drug use. Soldiers who are isolated, unstimulated, non-aggressive in seeking sensible alternatives, and anti-authority minded develop group solidarity in part through common use of drugs.[98]

In short, the isolation attendant to drug users is spreading through many units in which drug use is high. The Ingraham study cited earlier produced similar findings and Edward K. Jeffer, in examining the isolation of soldiers as related to drug use found that "substance abuse is not simply an alien and malignant growth in what otherwise would be the Army's healthy enlisted population but a necessary element filling a vacuum derived from needs for group membership and individual identity."[99] In short, drug use is endemic in American units not because the troops are drawn from the lower strata of American society "but because social conditions in the army itself are fostering it." Only 15 percent of hard drug users had prior hard drug experience with the remaining 85 percent acquiring the habit in the military.[100] Apparently the isolation of the American soldier from his peers as an independent condition of military life is affecting unit cohesion. From this perspective, drug use is a symptom of the lack of unit cohesion rather than a cause.

In measuring the American soldiers' opinions of their leaders' effectiveness in battle, again a generally low level of the indicators of cohesion was found. For example, in Westbrook's study 43 percent of the soldiers felt they were "accomplishing nothing as soldiers" and another 19 percent did not know if they were.[101] Moreover, the isolated and aimless soldier is not willing to place his trust in his leaders or his unit. Only 44 percent believed that their units "would make every effort to reach them if they were cut off in battle," and 31 percent were not sure. Taken together, at least 75 percent of American battle troops were at least unsure they could rely on their units in battle.[102] Finally, 32 percent of the soldiers surveyed did not believe their leaders would "in battle be willing to go through every thing that they make their men go through," and 21 percent were not certain. If the data are combined, upwards of 53 percent of American soldiers did not believe their leadership elements would be willing to assume the same hardships, burdens, and risks to which they would be subject in combat.[103]

The army's policies proved deficient in producing cohesive units during ten years of war in Vietnam. Since very little has been done to change these policies, it comes as no surprise that in using independent indicators one still finds low levels of cohesion within American units today. Indeed, the levels are generally no higher today than they were during the Vietnam War and might be considerably lower than they were a decade ago.

There is a strong relationship between the way soldiers assess the quality of their officers and NCOs and the manner in which they are likely to behave under fire.[104] With regard to officers, Human Readiness Report No. 5 asked soldiers to rank the quality of their officers along a five-point scale from "very high" to "very low." Interestingly, about 20 percent of the officers were assigned to each category. Thus, 20 percent of the officers were judged as "very high" quality, 20 percent as "high," and another 20 percent as "average." In the lower quality ranges, 20 percent were judged as "low" and another 20 percent as "very low."[105] Let us recall data on the quality of Soviet officers: Soviet soldiers ranked only 0.9 percent of their officers as "extremely good" and 9.7 percent as "good." Fully 56.6 percent of the officers were described as "average," 14.2 percent were "fair," 15.2 percent "poor," and 1.8 percent "very poor."[106] If the data are collapsed into three categories—good, medium, and low quality—the American officer does somewhat better in the eyes of his men than does the Soviet officer. For example, only 10.6 percent of Soviet troops rated their officers as "good" compared to approximately 40 percent for American troops. In the medium range, 56.5 percent of Soviet officers were deemed to be of medium quality compared to only 20 percent for American officers. However, when we look at the lower end of the quality scale, 31.2 percent of Soviet officers were judged to be poor compared to almost 40 percent for American officers. Thus, the number of good quality officers as perceived by the troops themselves was far higher in the American Army than in the Soviet Army. At the same time, a significantly higher number of officers were judged of poor quality in the American Army. On balance, however, the American officer was generally regarded as a better leader than his Soviet counterpart at least in the eyes of his men.

The quality of leadership in American units was the problem most often selected by officers and men in the Human Readiness Report. Moreover, the problem of quality leadership was more acute in the combat arms than in other units.[107] Almost 60 percent of officer commanders in combat arms units, as well as 40 percent of commanders of other units, thought the problem of leadership to be of critical importance at the junior NCO level. With regard to unit commanders and officers in other units, 85 percent assessed junior NCO leadership quality as the most prevalent problem within their units, and many said that the problem was getting worse. By comparison, 70 percent cited the low quality of senior NCO leadership and 60 percent the low quality of officer leadership as a current serious problem.[108] Hence, leadership quality seems to be a problem at all levels and in all types of units, with the problem being worst of all in the combat units.[109]

By objective standards, the quality of small-unit leadership at both the officer and NCO level remains a significant problem for the American Army. Certainly, there is no evidence that the quality of leadership is so much better relative to Soviet units as to compensate for the problems faced by American units. The quality of American unit leadership, while better than Soviet units, is insufficient to make a significant difference in battlefield performance.

In the end, of course, the true test of leadership quality and unit cohesion awaits the battlefield. The researcher can only deal with the perceptions of soldiers in peacetime garrisons. Yet, the fact that over the last five years officers and

NCOs alike, commanders in all types of units, and officers in combat arms units have singled out leadership quality as the most difficult problem suggests that the army may not have the level of cohesion adequate to the test of battle.

Cohesion in the Soviet Army

It is difficult to measure cohesion in the Soviet Army, given the obvious limitations on data collection. In addition, except for the limited incursions into East Germany in 1953, Poland in 1956, Hungary in 1957, Czechoslovakia in 1968, and most recently Afghanistan in 1982—all actions in which Soviet forces held strong tactical and strategic advantages and met only limited resistance— the Soviet Army has been inactive since 1945. Thus, there is little in the way of combat case studies that can be used to assess the cohesion of Soviet units. This analysis, therefore, uses the Soviet doctrine of cohesion outlined earlier as a yardstick and tries to determine how well it works. The focus of the analysis is upon the constituent elements of that doctrine and therefore rests on ideology, motivation, leadership, and the degree to which the institutional practices of the army itself tend to develop and sustain interpersonal ties between leaders and their men.

The Soviets believe that unit cohesion is strongly rooted in ideological conviction and indoctrination. Accordingly, Soviet units may be examined from the vantage point of how their leaders and soldiers perceive ideology as an effective motivator. To the extent that they see ideology as an effective force, it might be surmised that Soviet doctrine is correct and that its application to military units is generally effective. The Soviet Army's stress on ideology is evident in the requirement that all soldiers spend considerable time each week engaged in political indoctrination classes. When Soviet soldiers were asked to estimate how much time each week they spent in such classes, the estimates varied from as much as twenty hours a week to as little as five. The average time was 8.6 hours per week, or almost a full training day spent on attending political classes and ideological indoctrination sessions. This figure demonstrates how important ideology is to the military authorities.[110]

What do the soldiers think of ideology and their classes in political subjects? Do they feel that these classes stimulate and sustain a belief in ideology, and, more importantly, do they feel they contribute to motivating the soldier and making him perform well in battle? Soldiers were asked, "among the soldiers that you knew do you think that these kinds of classes are important in making a soldier want to be a good soldier?" Only 20.4 percent thought that political and indoctrination classes were important to making a soldier want to be a good soldier. The majority, 75.2 percent, thought that political and ideological classes either did not contribute to a soldier's motivation or were irrelevant.[111] The common soldier clearly regards classes in political subjects and ideological training as essentially a waste of time. Certainly, there is no evidence that they contribute very highly to any sense of motivation or unit cohesion.

It is valuable to assess the importance of ideology to the Soviet soldier as an independent factor given its central importance in Soviet doctrine. The soldier may regard political classes and ideology as not motivating but nonetheless still important to a soldier's ability and will to fight. Respondents were asked, "on a scale from one to ten in which one is the least important and ten the most important, how important is the soldier's belief in Marxism-Leninism in motivating him to fight well?" The responses were arranged along a semantic differential scale that allowed fairly precise measurements. If the data are separated into three categories—High (8-10), Medium (4-7), and Low (0-3)—the evidence shows that most soldiers do not regard ideology as an important combat-motivating force. Only 8 percent ranked ideology in the High category as a motivator, 13.2 percent put it in the Medium category, and 75.1 percent placed it in the Low category; 3.7 percent did not respond.[112] The data indicate the stark unimportance with which most Soviet soldiers regard ideology as a motivating force in their behavior. The mean score for the entire sample was only 2.6 points.

In order to provide another independent test of the value of ideology as a combat motivator, soldiers were asked, "in your opinion, how important do you think that a belief in an ideology—Marxism-Leninism—is in motivating a soldier to fight well? Do you think it is the most important factor, a very important factor, not very important at all, or almost totally unimportant?" If we use this question as an independent test, only 8.8 percent of Soviet soldiers thought ideology was "the most important" factor, while 9.7 percent said it was "very important." At the same time, 16.8 percent answered "not very important," and 62.8 percent said "almost totally unimportant." If we collapse the last two categories, 79.6 percent of the Soviet soldiers interviewed stated that ideology was not an important force "in making a soldier fight well."[113]

But even if the troops themselves are not convinced of the value of ideology, leadership elements could feel quite differently. Let us focus first on those men who held command positions—enlisted commanders. Of these, 27.8 percent regarded ideology as either "the most important" or a "very important" factor in motivating their men to fight well. At the other extreme, 11.1 percent said "not very important," and 61 percent "almost totally unimportant." Small-unit enlisted commanders, therefore, have very little faith in the value of ideology in preparing troops to fight well.[114] Much the same picture emerged when commanding officers were interviewed. Only 16.7 percent of these commanders believed ideology to be a "very important" factor, and none believed it was the "most important" element. At the other end of the spectrum, 66.7 percent considered it an "almost totally unimportant" element. Finally, of those soldiers who held neither command nor supervisory positions, only 19.3 percent felt that ideology was either the "most important" or a "very important" factor; 17.5 percent answered not very important at all, and 63.2 percent "almost totally unimportant."[115] Taken together, the data indicate that the soldiers and their unit commanders, especially small-unit leaders, do not believe that ideology is an important factor in making the Soviet soldier fight well. This was the finding, despite the fact that ideology holds a central position in official Soviet doctrine regarding the generation of cohesion in battle units. It may well be that Soviet doctrine is mistaken. As to the training practices that result from that doctrine, it may be questioned whether cohesion and motivation are being instilled in Soviet soldiers as a result of doctrinal implementation.

If ideology is not an important motivating factor for the Soviet soldier, what is? The answers the Soviet soldiers gave to the question of what makes a soldier fight well shed some light on the failure of Soviet doctrine to deal with factors other than ideology. For example, 44.2 percent of the soldiers said that the most important motivational factor for them was "not wanting to appear as a coward in front of one's friends."[116] As in other armies, it appears that the feelings soldiers develop for one another, their ties with their comrades, and their sense of belonging to a unit are more important than ideology. As S.L.A. Marshall has written, "when one's values are measured as being a man among men one would rather die than to lose that value placed upon one's self."[117] Other responses include 20.4 percent of the soldiers who felt that "close ties to one's comrades in the unit" were important to making them fight well.[118] The evidence suggests that the forces motivating the Soviet soldier are no different from those that have motivated soldiers throughout history. They are forces generated internally by the group to which the soldier belongs, and, in the Soviet case, they appear to have little or no relationship to ideology. Paradoxically, Soviet doctrine makes no allowance for such internally generated ties. Indeed, as mentioned earlier, the Soviets often take steps to disrupt such ties among soldiers on the grounds that they constitute an "incorrect basis for military groups."[119] Soviet doctrine may not only be incorrect in a theoretical sense as a major mechanism for motivating its training but may actually be disrupting other mechanisms that contribute to motivation. At the very least, Soviet doctrine ignores potentially important elements in motivating the soldier.

Soviet soldiers mentioned other motivations for fighting well: 16.8 percent cited the "support of one's friends back home," and 10.6 percent identified ideology. Somewhat surprisingly, only 4.4 percent thought that "feeling that one's officers and NCOs care about you" was an important motivator.[120] This response may reflect the soldier's feeling that his NCOs and officers do not apparently care about him.

If the data are arranged by rank, we find that for the common soldier with no leadership responsibilities, the desire "not to appear a coward" is the most frequently chosen motivating response; 47.4 percent selected it as their first choice. Among common soldiers, ideology was the least chosen response, with only 14 percent selecting it. The same holds true for noncommissioned officers, 41.1 percent of whom felt that "not wanting to appear a coward" was their major motivating force in fighting well; 31 percent of the NCOs also thought that "close ties to one's comrades in the unit" was a major motivating force. Again, ideology placed last on the list of possible motivators. For Soviet officers, only 10.5 percent felt that caring for their men was necessary to motivate the soldier. Most, 42.1 percent, felt that not wanting to appear a coward or that homefront support (26.3 percent) was more important.[121] Thus, neither the NCO nor officer corps appeared to believe that leaders had to demonstrate their care or concern to their soldiers in order to motivate them to fight well. That they should also not be concerned about developing strong motivational ties with their units is, therefore, not surprising, especially in light of the Soviet emphasis on ideology. This emphasis on ideology as the primary mechanism for developing unit cohesion is not supported by the attitudes of the soldiers themselves, however. The men see a number of other factors as far more important.

A difficulty in trying to assess the cohesiveness of Soviet units is how to operationalize the definition of unit cohesion and specify its empirical indicators. By focusing upon the degree to which strong interpersonal ties are perceived to exist among peers and between subordinates and superiors, we can use several valid indicators. Most basic are indicators that measure the soldiers' attachment to their fellow soldiers and their units. Soviet soldiers were asked, "how close to your fellow soldiers did you feel when you were in the military?" Only 5.3 percent said "very close," 14.2 percent answered "close," and 29.2 percent, moderately close. At the other end of the scale, 18.3 percent felt they were "not close at all," and, somewhat surprisingly, 31 percent said they "felt few bonds with their peers." Thus, a total of 49.3 percent said they had established few or no close ties with their peers. [122]

Among soldiers who held command positions, none said they felt "very close" ties with their fellow soldiers, but 41.2 percent responded that they had established "close" ties. In comparison, 8.3 percent of the officers holding command positions felt they had established "very close" ties with their men. However, the officers established close ties with their men at only one-fifth the rate for enlisted commanders. From another perspective, 35.3 percent of the enlisted commanders said they had failed to establish close ties with their men or "were not close at all" or "felt few bonds with them." Among the commanding officers, 41.6 percent had much the same response.[123]

Also important to cohesion is the degree to which soldiers develop feelings of pride in their units. Soviet soldiers were asked, "how strongly did you develop feelings of pride and affection for your military unit?" Only 1.8 percent answered "very strong" feelings, and 4.4 percent said "strong." Another 8 percent said they had "moderate" feelings of pride, 24.8 percent said "not very strong," and 22.1 percent replied that "unit pride did not concern me very much." The most damaging statistic, however, is the 37.2 percent who indicate they had developed "no feelings of unit pride at all."[124]

The same analysis can be applied to leadership elements. When enlisted commanders were asked about their feelings of unit pride and affection, only 5.9 percent answered "very strong" or "strong" while 58.8 percent said that "unit pride did not concern me very much" or that they had "no feelings of pride at all." Among the commanding officers, 25 percent said "strong" or "very strong," but 41.7 percent said either that they had established no pride at all or that unit pride did not concern them very much.[125]

Yet another indicator of strong personal attachments within units is the degree to which leadership elements are seen by their men as having established strong personal ties with them. When Soviet soldiers were asked whether their officers had "developed strong personal ties with their men," 49.5 percent replied that their officers had never developed such attachments. Moreover, 31.8 percent indicated that their NCOs had never established strong attachments to their men either. Only 44 percent of the soldiers felt that their officers "encouraged strong ties with their military units," and only 18.6 percent thought that their NCOs did so.[126]

Another component of cohesion is the degree to which soldiers perceive the quality of leadership that they must follow. Five basic dimensions of leadership can be identified: fairness, personal concern of officers for their men, knowledge of one's men and their limitations, competence, and willingness to share hardship and risk.[127] To the extent that an officer or NCO possesses these qualities of leadership, he is likely to be able to engender the trust of his men in his judgment. In an attempt to assess the quality of fairness, Soviet soldiers were asked, "how often do more experienced soldiers treat new recruits unfairly?" In all, 37.2 percent answered "very often" and 31.9 percent "often."[128] The fact that 69.1 percent of the soldiers felt that new soldiers were often treated unfairly by older soldiers indicates that existing practices may not be sustaining strong interpersonal ties. Indeed, 76.1 percent of the soldiers agreed that this unfair treatment had a decidedly negative effect on morale.[129]

If soldiers see their officers as being aware of this unfair treatment and unwilling to do anything about it, their ties to their leaders weaken. When asked, "are officers aware of the unfair treatment that soldiers receive from other soldiers," 84.1 percent said that their officers knew and did nothing to stop it. These perceptions of unfair treatment extended to the NCOs as well. When soldiers were asked, "how often do sergeants treat troops unfairly," 23.9 percent said "very often" and 32.7 percent "often."[130]

The degree to which soldiers feel they can go to their officers for help when they are treated unfairly is an accurate measure of how soldiers see the fairness of their officers. When asked, "in general, do soldiers feel they can go to their officers or sergeants with complaints about being treated unfairly," 33.6 percent said they could and 63.7 percent said they could not.[131] In a number of open-ended interviews with Soviet soldiers, many said that while one could technically approach a superior about being treated unfairly, it would be pointless to do so since most superiors were already aware of the unfair treatment of the troops. Furthermore, such a complaint would probably bring greater hardship on the soldier who complained.

Another dimension of cohesion is the degree to which leadership elements are believed to demonstrate personal and genuine concern for their men. Soldiers were asked if they felt their officers and NCOs "went out of their way to show an interest in their men." Some 28.3 percent felt this was the case. The perceptions of the NCO fared worse, with only 15.9 percent believing that their

NCO showed an interest in their men. When asked if their leaders "were genuinely interested in their men's personal problems," 31.8 percent of the soldiers thought their officers were, but only 15 percent felt their NCOs cared about them. A related question asked whether leaders "listened with genuine sympathy to the problems of the troops." In this regard, 21.3 percent of the soldiers felt their officers listened to them, but, again, only 13.3 percent thought their NCOs did.[132]

Still another aspect of the ability of leaders to form personal ties was explored when the soldiers were asked if their leaders "treated people in an impersonal manner; like cogs in a machine." Here 63.7 percent agreed, while 44.3 percent felt that NCOs also did so.[133] Directly tied to this element is the degree to which troops see their officers as more concerned about their own advancement than about the welfare of their men. When soldiers were asked if their leaders "were more concerned about their men than their own advancement," only 11.5 percent agreed. Moreover, only 8.9 percent of the NCOs were thought to be concerned about their men.[134]

Another aspect of the failure of leaders to show enough concern for their men can be seen in the degree to which soldiers perceived their leaders as being available to deal with the problems of their men. A total of 29.2 percent felt that their officers were generally available to their men "to deal with their problems," while 26.6 percent felt their NCOs were.[135] These data reinforce the idea that Soviet small-unit leaders are not developing strong personal attachments.

There is a pervasive fear among soldiers that every officer and NCO must work to overcome, the fear that soldiers will be treated as mere means to obtaining military objectives with virtually no concern for their safety. It is imperative that small-unit leaders convince their men that they know their abilities and are prepared to respect their limitations. Soldiers must also be convinced that their leaders will stand up for them when they believe they are in danger of being misused. Accordingly, a critical element of leadership in small units is the ability of officers and NCOs to convince their men that they will protect them from higher authorities when there is good reason to do so.

In order to assess this aspect of cohesion, soldiers were asked if their leaders "truly knew their men and respected their capabilities." Some 29.2 percent of the soldiers thought that their officers did, while only 17.7 percent felt the NCOs did.[136] In a related question, Soviet soldiers were asked if their officers and NCOs "stood up for their men when dealing with their superiors." In response, 26.5 percent said their officers could be relied upon to do so, while only 18.5 percent trusted their NCOs to do likewise. Along the same lines, only 16.8 percent of the soldiers thought their officers were "willing to support subordinates when they make mistakes," and 12.4 percent felt their NCOs would do so.[137]

The effective leader is able to convince his men that he is willing to expose himself to at least the same burdens they bear and the same risks. How well do Soviet small-unit leaders measure up by this standard? Soldiers were asked to assess whether their leaders "always set the example for their men." Only 23.9

percent thought that their officers did, and a mere 16 percent felt their NCOs were good exemplars.[138] Most small-unit leaders are not seen by their men as good role models.

Soldiers must also believe that their leaders will share hardships with them. This is important in peacetime and even more so in combat. Soldiers follow those who demonstrate they are prepared to risk the same burden of death to which their men are exposed and often kill those who fail to do so. Soviet leaders at the small-unit level apparently have not convinced their men that they will share their hardships. Only 22.1 percent of the troops believed their officers shared hardships with their troops, while 38.9 percent thought their NCOs do.[139]

A final dimension of leadership as it contributes to unit cohesion deals with the trust soldiers have in their leaders under fire. Units made up of soldiers who see their leaders as ineffective, untrustworthy, and incompetent in battle are unlikely to remain cohesive. When Soviet soldiers were asked if their leaders would be good men to go into combat with, only 19.5 percent felt their officers would be competent in this regard. Noncommissioned officers, those crucial links between the soldiers and officers, scored even lower, with a meagre 15 percent of their men believing they would be good leaders in combat.[140]

Conclusions

In terms of what we know from military history, military sociology, and military psychology about the cohesion of men in battle, Soviet military units appear deficient in some important qualities. Substantial deficiencies appear for all elements of cohesion examined. In addition, various studies show the Soviet small-unit leader to be inflexible, to avoid responsibility, and to have failed to establish strong ties with his men. Furthermore, the Soviet soldier has few strong attachments to his leaders, his units, or even his peers. Thus, many of the elements of cohesion that have historically marked the successful combat units are starkly absent from Soviet units—as they are from American units.

As long as the Soviets continue to stress ideology and the Americans entre-preneurial utility as the basis for military cohesion, it will be very difficult for leaders in either army to develop the strong personal attachments characteristic of cohesive battle units. In this sense, the very doctrines that underpin each army's training practices are working at cross-purposes with developing unit cohesion. Under these circumstances, regardless of their advanced technical equipment, both armies will remain subject to fragmentation under the stress of battle.

Notes

1. Colonel A. M. Danchenko and Colonel I. F. Vydrin, eds., *Military Pedagogy: A Soviet View* (Moscow: Voyenizdat, 1973), p. 280.

2. Ibid.

3. *Krasnaya zevezda*, March 24, 1972, pp. 1-3.

4. For example, Colonel General M. Tankayev, the commanding general of the

Northern Group of Forces, is quoted as having said that "The Soviet officer is above all a political indoctrinator," *Kommunist vooruzhennykh sil*, No. 14, July 1972, pp. 36-42; also, *Red Star* in an editorial of March 27, 1973, states that "constant political work among servicemen is the paramount task of commanders."

5. A. A. Grechko, *On Guard for Peace and the Building of Communism*, p. 65 (quoted in Danchenko and Vydrin, *Military Pedagogy*, p. 280.

6. For a good treatment of the stated relationship between ideology and combat-effectiveness in Soviet thought, see Herbert Goldhamer, *The Soviet Soldier* (New York: Crane, Russak and Co.), pp. 206-208. An article in *Kommunist vooruzhennykh sil* of July 1972, No. 14, pp. 36-42, stated that "the training process in our army is inseparably linked to the indoctrination process."

7. Ibid.

8. Y. V. V. Shlyag, A. D. Goltchkin, and K. K. Platonov, eds., *Military Psychology: A Soviet View* (Moscow: Voyenizdat, 1972), p. 280.

9. Ibid.

10. This is precisely the critique of Western military doctrine that is made by Soviet theorists. See "Contemporary Bourgeois Military Pedagogy and Its Reactionary Essence," in Danchenko: and Vydrin, *Military Pedagogy*, pp. 348-62.

11. *Military Psychology*, p. 283.

12. Ibid., p. 280.

13. Ibid. The argument quotes A. S. Makarenko to the effect that "collectivist relations are not simply mutual aid within the group, but rather the essential joint serving of a goal beyond the limit of the given group." Makarenko, "Mysl," *Personality and Labor* (Moscow, 1965), p. 119.

14. *Military Pedagogy*, pp. 278-83.

15. Ibid., p. 280.

16. Goldhamer, *The Soviet Soldier*, p. 194.

17. *Krasnaya zvezda*, August 13, 1971, pp. 2-3.

18. Ibid.

19. *Military Psychology*, pp. 306-307.

20. Grechko, On Guard for Peace; *Krasnaya zvezda*, March 24, 1972, pp. 1-3.

21. *Krasnaya zvezda*, March 27, 1973, p. 1.

22. "The Ways and Means of Instilling High Moral-Combat Traits in Soviet Soldiers," in *Military Pedagogy*, pp. 283-88.

23. Ibid., p. 284.

24. Ibid., p. 288.

25. *Military Psychology: A Soviet View*, p. 211.

26. For the case against Western doctrine, see "Contemporary Bourgeois Military Pedagogy and Its Reactionary Essence," in *Military Pedagogy*, pp. 348-62.

27. Perhaps more than any other military establishment in the world, the Soviet Army constantly undertakes research efforts and attempts to apply their findings. This orientation seems to result from the ideological bent of Soviet theorists to demonstrate the "scientific" character of Marxism.

28. Goldhamer, *The Soviet Soldier*, pp. 194-95.

29. *Military Psychology*, p. 280.

30. *Marxism-Leninism on War and Army: A Soviet View* (Moscow: Progress Publishers, 1973), p. 274.

31. I have taken this phrase from Carl J. Friedrich and Zbigniew K. Brzezinski, *Totalitarian Dictatorship and Autocracy* (New York: Frederick Praeger Publishers, 1966).

32. The basic text and training manual utilized in the Advanced Officers Course in the U.S. Army is FM 22-100, *Military Leadership*. I wish to express my thanks to Colonel H. C. Van Meter, director of the U.S. Army Infantry School at Fort Benning, Georgia, for providing me with the manuals and course outlines utilized in the army's advanced officer course in military leadership.

33. *Military Leadership*, p. 7-1.

34. Ibid., pp. 7-2, 7-3.

35. Ibid.

36. Ibid., p. 7-4.

37. Ibid., p. 8-3.

38. Ibid., p. 8-6.

39. Ibid.

40. Ibid.

41. *Military Leadership*, p. 7-4.

42. For more detail on the important distinction between "corporative" and "entre- preneurial" groups, see Richard A. Gabriel, "Acquiring New Values in Military Bur- eaucracies: A Preliminary Model," in Paul L. Savage and Richard A. Gabriel, eds., *Managers and Gladiators,* (Boston, Hawk Press, 1979). See also, *Crisis in Command*: *Mismanagement in the Army* (New York: Hill and Wang, 1978), Chapter 6.

43. *Military Leadership*, p. 8-2.

44. Ibid., pp. 6-1, 6-2.

45. Ibid. This view permeates all of Chapters 6 and 7. In addition, it might well be pointed out that the argument that the army could not produce good soldiers in the Vietnam conflict because of the penetration of anti-authority values attendant to the larger social order is a common one. For a critique of this view, see Gabriel and Savage, "Cohesion and Disintegration in the American Army: An Alternative Perspective," *Armed Forces and Society* 2, No. 3 (May 1976): 340-76.

46. Gabriel and Savage, *Crisis in Command*, Chapter 1.

47. Anyone who has spent any time in the military, especially in combat, is likely to question the suggestion that military life and civilian life are motivational equivalents.

48. *Military Leadership*, p. 1-2. The notion that military leadership requires a good deal of judgment and experience is a premise constantly reaffirmed in American Army manuals.

49. Ibid., p. 8-6.

50. Ibid., p. 1-3.

51. Ibid., Chapter 2 lists and discusses fourteen traits of military leadership.

52. For a detailed exposition of this argument, see Colonel Donald B. Vought and Captain John C. Binkley, "Army Leadership: A Long Range Perspective," in Gabriel and Savage, *Military Bureaucracy in Transition*, pp. 1-39.

53. Richard A. Gabriel, "Acquiring New Values in Military Bureaucracies."

54. Grechko, *On Guard for Peace.*

55. *Military Leadership*, Chapter 2.

56. *Military Pedagogy*, Chapter 14.

57. Indeed, FM 22-100 stresses that a good leader gives his subordinates the op- portunity to take the initiative and exercise responsibility as the only way young leaders

can gain the experience necessary to good leadership. Indeed, the failure to provide such opportunities is considered a failure of leadership. *Military Leadership*, pp. 2-10, 2-11.

58. Edward A. Shills and Morris Janowitz, "Cohesion and Disintegration in the German Wehrmacht in World War II," *Public Opinion Quarterly* 12 (1948). This work remains the seminal and definitive study to this day.

59. Paul Hausser, *Soldaten wie Andere Auch-Der Weg Der Waffen SS* [Soldiers as Others: The Way of the Waffen SS] (Osnabrueck: Munin Verlag, 1969), p. 89.

60. S.L.A. Marshall, *Men Against Fire* (New York: William Morrow, 1947).

61. Samuel Stouffer, et al., *The American Soldier* (Princeton, N.J.: Princeton University Press, 1949).

62. John Keegan, *The Face of Battle* (New York: Viking Press, 1976).

63. Comments by John Keegan at the Inter-University Seminar for Armed Forces and Society Annual Conference in Chicago in October 1977.

64. Alan Lloyd, *War in the Trenches* (New York: D. McKay and Co., 1976).

65. Samuel Rolbant, *The Israeli Soldier: Profile of an Army* (London: A.S. Barnes and Co., Inc., 1970).

66. Ibid., pp. 235-42.

67. Ibid., pp. 248-88.

68. This argument is made extensively in Gabriel and Savage, *Crisis in Command*. In effect, a technologically and technically superior American force in Vietnam was fought to a draw by an army far less well equipped. The authors suggest that the lack of American unit cohesion and leadership was a major contributing factor in this situation.

69. *Military Pedagogy*, p. 282.

70. A.A. Grechko, *On Guard for Peace*, in Danchenko and Vydrin, *Military Pedagogy*, p. 280.

71. *Marxism-Leninism on War and Army*, p. 272.

72. *Military Psychology*, p. 280.

73. *Military Leadership*, Chapter 2.

74. For an analysis of the Soviet Army with regard to its morale and discipline and how these are undermined by Soviet efforts to erode personal attachments to military groups, see Richard A. Gabriel, "The Morale of the Soviet Army," *Military Review* 23, No. 10 (October 1978): 27-39; and Richard A. Gabriel, "Combat Cohesion in Soviet and American Military Units," *Parameters* 8, No. 4 (December 1978): 16-27.

75. This argument can be found in complete form in Richard A. Gabriel and Paul L. Savage, "Law in America: A Profession in Search of Direction," *The Catholic Lawyer* 22, No. 2 (Spring 1976): 87-100.

76. For a more complete treatment of this point, see Richard A. Gabriel, *To Serve with Honor: A Treatise on Military Ethics and the Way of the Soldier* (Westport, Conn.:Greenwood Press, 1982), Chapter 1.

77. Gabriel and Savage, *Crisis in Command*, Chapter 8. See also Gabriel and Savage, "The Environment of Military Leadership," *Military Review* (July 1980): 55-59.

78. Human Readiness Report No. 5 (Washington, D.C.: Office of the Deputy Chief of Staff for Personnel, August 1979), p. 14. This conclusion is also consistent with the findings of the Israeli Army done by Colonel Reuven Gal, "Characteristics of Heroism," paper delivered at the Canadian Leadership Symposium, Royal Roads Military College, Victoria, British Columbia (June 5, 1981).

79. Human Readiness Report No. 5, p. D-28; see also p. 14.

80. Ibid.

81. Ibid.

82. Ibid.

83. Ibid., p. D-28.

84. Ibid.

85. Ibid., p. D-7.

86. Ibid.

87. Ibid., p. 15.

88. Ibid., p. D-28.

89. Ibid., p. 16.

90. Ibid.

91. Ibid.

92. See note 78 above.

93. *Washington Star*, December 15, 1980, p. 2.

94. Ibid.

95. Major Stephen Westbrook, "The Alienated Soldier: Legacy of Our Society"*Army* (December 1979), p. 20.

96. Ibid.

97. Shills and Janowitz, "Cohesion and Disentegration in the German Wehrmach."

98. Marion Corddry, "War in Europe: The Enemy Is Troop Drug Use," *Army* (January 1979): 36.

99. Lieutenant-Colonel Edward K. Jeffer, "The Word Is Quality, Not Quantity," *Army* (February 1981): 16.

100. Larry H. Ingraham, "Drugs, Morale, and the Facts of Barracks Living in the American Army," paper presented at the Anglo-American Psychiatry Symposium, Plymouth, England, October 1978, p. 12.

101. Westbrook, "The Alienated Soldier," p. 20.

102. Ibid.

103. Ibid.

104. Human Readiness Report No. 5, 1979.

105. Human Readiness Report No. 5, p. 11.

106. Gabriel, *The New Red Legions: An Attitudinal Portrait of the Soviet Army* (Westport, Conn.: Greenwood Press, 1980), p. 88.

107. Human Readiness Report No. 5, p. C-2.

108. Ibid.

109. Ibid.

110. Gabriel, *The New Red Legions*, p. 190.

111. Ibid.

112. Ibid.

113. Ibid., p. 113.

114. Ibid.

115. Ibid., p. 192.

116. Ibid., p. 193.

117. Marshall, *Men Against Fire*, p. 97.

118. Gabriel, *The New Red Legions*, p. 194.

119. *Marxism-Leninism on War and Army*, p. 274.

120. Gabriel, *The New Red Legions*, p. 194.

121. Ibid.

122. Ibid., p. 197.

123. Ibid., p. 198.
124. Ibid.
125. Ibid., p. 199.
126. Ibid., p. 200.
127. Ibid., p. 201.
128. Ibid.
129. Ibid.
130. Ibid.
131. Ibid., p. 202.
132. Ibid., p. 203.
133. Ibid.
134. Ibid.
135. Ibid.
136. Ibid., p. 204.
137. Ibid., p. 205.
138. Ibid., p. 206.
139. Ibid.
140. Ibid., p. 201.

7

Combat Ability

Assessing a soldier's combat ability and performance is perhaps the most difficult and risky task in any analysis of armies. Evidence we have from history and psychology, however, suggests that certain dimensions have the greatest effect on combat performance. This chapter examines two of these analytical dimensions. The first encompasses soldiers' perceptions of their own abilities and officers' perceptions of the abilities of their men. The expectations that men have of themselves, their comrades, and their superiors are crucial to battle performance. Units with low expectations are likely to live up to such expectations when the shooting starts. The same is true of the way officers and NCOs see their men.

The second analytical dimension involves the soldiers' demonstrated level of technical skill. While history shows us that good leadership, high levels of cohesion, dedication, and a willingness to endure hardship are more important than technical skills, assuredly low technical proficiency works against battle effectiveness. Thus, armies may be assessed as to their expected levels of combat performance against the standard of how well they succeed in giving their soldiers and units the necessary military skills. These skills should be examined in relation to the degree to which they are instituted within an ambience of group cohesion so that individual soldiers will see that their skills are related to the performance of their units. Success in battle hinges on maintaining technical proficiency and a sense of unit identity.[1]

The American Army

As shown in the previous chapters, American troops are characterized by low motivation, low mental abilities, and low morale. At the same time, the army as an institution has developed practices, habits, and values which in themselves contribute to poor training. Even if a recruit enters the army with high motivation, adequate mental skills, and proper habits, it is problematical whether the American Army, with its institutional problems, can transform him into a good soldier. Certainly, the high turnover rate of many units combined with the soldier's

tendency to be isolated from his peers, to live off-post, and to use drugs seems
to have disturbed the American military environment. This environment alone
would make it difficult for any recruit to develop into a good combat soldier.
Quite apart from the other difficulties that already afflict the army, there is strong
evidence that both training and performance remain at an unacceptably low level.

The army's basic training program is inadequate. Since the introduction of
the AVF, in an effort to respond to budget priorities, the training time has been
increasingly cut. As a result, more and more training tasks are being shifted to
the unit commanders. For example, at present basic training for the average
recruit lasts only seven weeks.[2] Even after the attack on Pearl Harbor, when the
army found itself critically short of manpower and rushed training in order to
field an army as rapidly as possible, recruits were still given a minimum of eight
weeks of basic training.[3] The military studied the effects of its basic training
program in 1943 and raised the requirement from eight weeks to seventeen weeks,
because it found that troops needed at least that amount once they reached the
front.[4] By the World War II standard, today's American soldier receives *less
than half* the basic training than his World War II counterpart did some forty
years ago. The Pentagon wants to return to at least the eight-week period, a
change that is not expected to occur before October 1983.[5] Even if the change
is made, for the foreseeable future the training period of the American soldier
will remain at a level far below that of World War II and considerably below
that of the Soviet Army.[6]

The amount of training the American soldier receives even after he has reached
his unit is far below that given the Soviet soldier, or, for that matter, any of
America's major Western allies. A study completed by the army's TRADOC
command in 1972 and updated in 1978 demonstrated that the armies of Australia,
Canada, Great Britain, France, and West Germany get approximately *four times
as much* training as the American soldier. With regard to complex weapons
systems training, the amount of training given Allied soldiers is even more than
four times that in the American Army.

Table 7
Daily Schedule of the American Soldier

Activity	Hour	Time Elapsed
Reveille	0545	5 minutes
Morning formation	0600	10 minutes
Physical training (PT) daily dozen and 20-minute run	0600-0700	60 minutes
Personal hygiene/chow	0700-0745	45 minutes
Second morning formation	0745-0800	15 minutes
Training and work details	0800-1145	3 hours-45 minutes
Lunch	1145-1230	45 minutes
Training and equipment maintenance	1230-1645	4 hours-15 minutes
End of day formation	1645	10 minutes

Table 7 provides a "typical" daily schedule for a member of an American mechanized infantry company. While theoretically almost eight hours are spent daily in training, in fact much of that training does not occur. In the first place, little of what passes for training is in the field; far more of it takes place in classrooms. Second, lectures on such compulsory subjects as racial relations, alcohol and drug abuse, and other subjects come out of time allotted for training and are credited as training time. Third, field training is even further limited by budget constraints which severely limit the amount of ammunition that can be expended. It is not unusual for American companies to run out of funds for field training long before the year is out. Finally, the fact that the American soldier has no further military responsibilities once the "workday" has ended at 1645, that he may leave the post at anytime after this, and that many of the soldiers live off-post further reduces the time available for his training.

Not only has the amount of time spent on training decreased, but also the quality of training has declined sharply. The quality of discipline in training, for example, has been considerably lessened since 1973. In August 1979, TRA-DOC introduced a series of what it called "constructive training techniques" and began to dismantle most of the disciplinary aspects normally associated with basic training. The army now required that the troops call their drill sergeants by that title and prohibited sergeants from calling their troops anything but "soldier." At the same time, the requirement for short haircuts was done away with, as were other rules dealing with long hair, mustaches, beards, talking in the mess hall, and other aspects that sustained the traditional ambience of basic training. In the words of TRADOC's directive, "non-productive stress created by verbal or physical abuse" was to be no longer tolerated. The army also formally abandoned the traditional doctrine that a recruit might have to be "torn down and built up," a notion that has been fundamental to the resocialization of civilian recruits to the military way almost from time immemorial.

According to the new doctrine, the training emphasis was to be placed upon "self-discipline" among the troops as opposed to "enforced collective discipline," and new emphasis was to be placed upon creating a "positive climate" among leaders so that troops would respond favorably to them.[8] In short, the stress was not upon discipline, but upon the soldier's rights and privileges. Much of the background ambience of military training which has historically involved the soldier's resocialization through discipline, isolation, and, sometimes, collective punishments in order to create a sense of unit identity has now been abandoned. As a result, in survey after survey, basic training has been shown to be "too soft" and unchallenging.[9] A young training officer summed up these changes when he said of his troops, "they will lay down their arms costing the lives of you and me; the so called professionals who trained them prepared them for nothing."[10]

General Don Starry, former commander of TRADOC, has pointed out that, within the American soldier's seven-week training period, the *rate* of his training has been so severely slowed down to accommodate those soldiers with low mental skill levels that many soldiers leave basic training without having been taught the basic skills needed for survival.[11] Hence, not only does the soldier not have sufficient time to train, but also the pace of training has slowed considerably. As General Starry has stated almost all MOS soldiers are graduating from their training courses with less than adequate training. Using the example of the basic infantryman, General Starry has observed that the army has identified seventy basic skills crucial to the infantryman's performance and survival on the battlefield. With regard to the rate at which soldiers can learn these skills in the short training period allowed, General Starry says: "I can only give him forty nine of these skills, a little over half the critical skills, before the soldier leaves basic training. If he has to fight he really needs all seventy of these critical skills."[12] In Starry's view then, both the amount of time available to train the American soldier and the pace of that training often produce substantial numbers of inadequately trained soldiers.

This conclusion applies even more to the learning skills crews need to handle high-powered weapons systems such as tanks, artillery vehicles, and armored personnel carriers. These units must train together for long periods if they are to be able to fight well as a team. Because of short training periods and rapid unit turnover, in some instances between 30 and 40 percent of the men in a given crew are likely to be little more than half-trained beginners.[13] Whether one focuses upon the individual infantryman or on soldiers trained for crew-served weapons systems, many American soldiers are not being given adequate training.

Other factors contribute to the poor quality of training. The fact that the rate of personnel turnover is so high makes it almost impossible for soldiers to train effectively. When units are in turbulence, especially crew-served units, it becomes very difficult to forge effective battle units because the unit cannot train as a unit but must constantly integrate untrained members into its midst, replacing the more experienced soldiers who have left. General Starry has pointed out that the rotation rate of soldiers in American units is about "two times too high" in order to train troops effectively in the field.[14]

Poor training is often the result of army policy which systematically feeds inexperienced officers into training units.[15] At one training post, an official study team noted that many of the officers were first assignment new lieutenants who had no prior experience as troop leaders.[16] Training units are often commanded and directed by officers who have neither combat nor prior troop-leading experience. Along the same lines, an interesting phenomenon occurred during the initial years of the AVF. In an effort to boost enlistments, the army systematically stripped its combat units of its best NCOs, many of them battle experienced, and assigned them to recruiting duty. Thus, it reduced the opportunity for the soldier to be trained or led by experienced NCOs. In addition, many of the NCOs left behind were, by definition, of low quality, a condition that characterizes the NCO corps today. The findings of the Army Training Study that the levels of crew training after being assigned to a unit were "essentially flat" indicate that many sergeants assigned to training units "do not demonstrate the technical knowledge to accomplish their jobs and train their subordinates to a high standard of performance."[17] The army's own studies reveal that in many cases the quality of NCO in the training program, whether in schools or once the soldier has been assigned to his unit, remains so low as to preclude effective troop training.

In 1978, the army undertook a two-year study to analyze the quality of its troop training. It surveyed at random a sample of the entire army at all levels at a cost of some $282,000 and produced a general summary of the weaknesses of the American training system. The conclusions of the report were cited in the Pivoratto Report to the Congress on July 20, 1979.[18] According to the army's own findings:

There is no coherent overall training system known in practice throughout the Army today. Further, the high turnover and changes in duty position mitigate against achieving the high training readiness required to execute the mission of the United States Army which is national defense. Therefore, there is considerable evidence that when measured against the standards necessary to win outnumbered many units are not conducting satisfactory training.[19]

This assessment supports the findings of other armywide studies with regard to training. When officers were asked whether they were satisfied with unit training, only 40.6 percent of the company grade officers and 56.4 percent of the field grade officers said they were.[20] The data point inextricably to the conclusion that the American soldier is receiving training that is inadequate in both quality and amount. In addition, when the evidence is examined, it becomes even clearer that the American soldier is most likely not to perform well in combat.

The effectiveness of the American soldier's combat training can be analyzed in three ways. The first way is to examine the soldiers' performance on skill-qualifying tests. In 1980, the army introduced a method of quantifying training results to provide some measure of the proficiency of its training program. The SQT or Skill Qualification Test is a soldier's "report card." The grades on individual SQTs are used to evaluate training effectiveness and to decide who qualifies for promotion. Until very recently (1980), a soldier had to achieve a skill qualification level of 80 percent in order to qualify for promotion. That level has since been reduced to 60 percent.[21] The tests have also been changed in the last three years to emphasize fewer written questions and more "hands-on training" or practical application of skills. This reduction is a bow in the direction of the low-quality soldier. The SQT, administered to all troops at different times throughout the army, is the army's prime measurement of a soldier's performance level.

In 1979, data made available to the Congress revealed the armywide results of the SQT scores. An incredibly large number of soldiers could not pass even rudimentary tests in performing their own jobs.

For example, consider the following statistics:[22]

Type of Soldier	Number Tested	Percent Who Failed
Artillery crewman	1,574	86
Nuclear weapons maintenance specialist	385	90
Tank and artillery repairman	371	98
Hawk surface-to-air missile specialist	1,095	82
Cannon fire direction specialist	2,794	86
Ammunitions specialist	1,547	81
Traffic management specialist	1,122	74
Tracked vehicle maintenance repairman	3,022	89

Additional data demonstrate that 77 percent of the army's computer programmers failed their skill-qualifying test. Moreover, 94 percent of the field artillery target acquisition specialists did not pass, leaving only 6 percent armywide to qualify for promotion; and 91 percent of the aviation maintenance personnel and 83 percent of the transportation personnel failed. Sixty-nine percent of those soldiers working in communications could not pass nor could 49 percent of the combat engineers and 75 percent of food service operations personnel.[23]

The Army Training Study of 1980 tested thousands of soldiers in all sixteen army divisions in the United States, Europe, and Korea for their ability to perform their jobs. Among a sample of 1,288 M-60 tank crewmen, 28 percent of the gunners tested in the United States and 21 percent of the gunners in Germany "did not know where to aim when using battle sights."[24] The field performance of these crews averaged 40 to 50 percent *below* the level of skill required to meet combat-readiness standards.[25] In one sample of fifty-two crews tested, *all* members of the tank crews failed the gunnery test.[26] With regard to crew-served weapons, tests on the Red Eye missile found that a very high percentage of Red Eye gunners were drawn from the lowest mental categories. The study concluded that for reasons of combat-effectiveness the army should eliminate Category 3B personnel from the Red Eye program because they are usually not able to hit the targets.[27] A worldwide assessment of the army units using the Red Eye missile found that 100 percent of the units were plagued by serious problems and that many units were judged to be "non-combat effective."[28] From the perspective of crew-served weapons requiring the mastery of some technology, a basic conclusion of the Army Training Study is that the intelligence levels of some crews may be too low to operate the weapons systems well enough to meet the army's own standards of combat-ready performance.

Additional tests undertaken by the Army Training Study found that in a study of 666 tank repairmen, the chances that a tank repairman would correctly find and diagnose a repair problem were only between 15 and 33 percent. The chances were greater than three out of four that he would misdiagnose the problem, even assuming that he was able to find the problem to begin with. If he found the problem, the chances that he could successfully repair it correctly fell between

33 and 58 percent.[29] Thus, the chances that the soldier could repair the problem were only slightly better than half. Such findings make it very clear that the American soldier is not well trained to handle complex weaponry.

The Army Training Study concluded that a large number of crew-manning weapons systems were inadequately staffed by soldiers whose intelligence levels were far too low for them to perform well. But the major thrust of the study was to analyze the training environment as a whole. Its conclusion was shocking; "Analysis across all respondents indicates one overriding conclusion: there has been little perceived change in the training environment since 1971 and that environment is still seen as hostile to the conduct of good training."[30] As measured by two separate indicators—the Army Training Study and the Skill Qualifying Tests—the soldiers tested showed a glaring lack of technical skill performance.

A final indicator of a soldier's fighting ability is his performance in field exercises. Two important exercises undertaken by American soldiers in Europe every year are the Canadian Cup tank competition and the Boeselager combat vehicle competition using armored personnel carriers. The NATO alliance regards both as excellent tests of the ability of units to fight and maneuver. The Canadian Cup is an international tank competition which tests the ability of tank crews to fire and maneuver. In 1977, U.S. tank crews placed last in NATO's most prestigious tank gunnery competition. American crews were beaten by Canadian, West German, Belgian, British, and Dutch crews.[31] In 1979, after two years of trying to recruit and train an elite tank crew (a procedure which, by the way, is against the rules), the American team did somewhat better and placed fourth out of five teams beaten again by the West Germans, Belgians, and the English. During the 1979 contest, it took West German crews an average of 2.3 seconds to identify targets, while it took American crews twice as long.[32] Even now, most Europeans consider American crews to be below standard.

In the Boeselager armored cavalry competition, American and NATO units maneuver against one another in an effort to test how well each unit can conduct its various missions. In the 1980 competition, the American crews were beaten by six West German crews, two from Canada, and one from the Netherlands. Even on training ranges, when matched against NATO allies the performance of American units is not very good.

After the failures in the tank and armored personnel carrier competitions, an army assessment found that the majority of its tank gunners and vehicle commanders ranked only in the upper 40-percent range of intelligence, a point noted by the Army Training Study as well.[33] A survey of 1,288 tank gunners revealed that many of the gunners and vehicle commanders rapidly forgot what they had learned in training and that additional field training in Europe did not significantly improve their ability to perform up to standard.[34] The Army Training Study also showed that tank crew proficiency among American units in Europe was 40 percent *lower* than combat requirements and 50 percent lower than combat requirements among units based in the United States.[35] In short, the actual performance of American troops on training ranges, coupled with their low performance as measured by the SQT, makes the American soldier's ability to perform in battle dubious.

If combat ability is measured by the quality of training and the ability of the soldier to perform his technical skills in a training environment, then the American is inferior compared to both the Soviet soldier and his NATO allies. When compared to the soldier in Vietnam, Korea, and World War II, he does poorly. It is hard to believe that the low performance levels demonstrated so glaringly in a number of studies and competitions could possibly have afflicted earlier American armies; at least there is no evidence that it did so.

The soldier's ability to perform well in battle depends heavily on how well the larger military organization performs its role. The organization deploys the soldier to battle, equips him for it, sustains him in it, and evacuates him as a casualty from the battle area. When the shortcomings of the American soldier are placed in the larger organizational context, the question of how well he is likely to perform under realistic battle conditions can be assessed. A number of official studies as well as outside "think-tank" reports suggest that the failure of the larger military organization to support the soldier adequately further diminishes the soldier's ability to perform in battle.

Perhaps the most powerful examination of the American soldier's battle ability was undertaken in October 1978 during "Nifty Nugget." This exercise was the first governmentwide war mobilization exercise carried out after World War II. It involved over 1,000 military officers and high-level civilian officials, and lasted a month. Its scenario was to test the ability of the U.S. Army and other major military arms to respond to a simulated sudden attack by heavily armored conventional units mounted by the Warsaw Pact nations in Central Europe. The object was to test the ability of the United States to mount and logistically sustain a large military ground force in the European theater long enough to credibly defend itself until larger mobilization could be undertaken. "Nifty Nugget" was generated as a result of the failures of the yet still secret "Mobex 76" exercises that revealed severe shortcomings in the American military's ability to accomplish its assigned mission.[36]

An analysis of what happened during "Nifty Nugget" raises serious questions about the American Army's ability to carry out its mission in Central Europe. In the first place, the exercise revealed considerable shortages in combat power; most combat elements of two of the army's sixteen regular divisions ceased to exist even before the mock battle was joined. These divisions, along with a large number of reserve units, were "cannibalized," split apart and reassigned to other units, in an attempt to fill the holes in those units already deployed on the battlefield. As a consequence, about 400,000 men were deployed to Europe, but most were jammed into existing battle units in order to take up the losses resulting from heavy casualties.[37] Very little in the way of a coordinated defense was possible.

Another shortcoming that emerged was that the conflict envisioned by the scenario called for somewhere between 200,000 and 500,000 more troops than the army could deliver. The existing capacity to transport these soldiers to Europe along with their tanks and field equipment was overwhelmed.[38] The exercise showed that while it was possible for the famous "aluminum bridge" to move nearly 400,000 soldiers to Europe in about a week and a half, it was impossible to move them with their equipment. Consequently, the army that arrived was deployed without equipment.[39]

"Nifty Nugget" demonstrated severe shortages in ammunition and other spare parts. While there was, for example, a plentiful supply of 120mm tank ammunition for the new XM-1 tank (not then deployed), there were not enough smaller rounds required by the M-60 tanks, which comprise the greatest number of tanks now deployed in the American Army.[40] Serious shortages of rifle, mortar, and artillery ammunition also existed. On balance, the army's ability to move enough shells, missiles, fuel, food, spare parts, and other basic equipment was totally inadequate relative to its combat requirements.

A considerable failure emerged in the army's inability to deal with its own casualties. The army's active and reserve components are short about 3,500 doctors, to say nothing of medics, nurses, operating room specialists, and other personnel needed to care for wounded soldiers.[41] Hence, half the doctors required to treat battle casualties in Europe would not be available, nor would there be sufficient hospital space even at the theater level to deal with anticipated casualties. To offset this problem, the army has developed plans to fly the more seriously wounded battle casualties to the United States for treatment. However, postponement of their treatment and the amount of time required to move them across the Atlantic would result in approximately 20,000 more casualty deaths than would have occurred had they been treated at the theater level.[42] Moreover, men who might have been treated and returned to the front also wound up in stateside hospitals. In short, "Nifty Nugget" pointed up the army's failure to sustain its troops in battle with adequate supplies of ammunition, equipment, supplies, weapons, and even medical care.

"Nifty Nugget" also demonstrated that the army's ability to mobilize and deploy for a sudden attack in Europe short of nuclear war was extremely limited. The ability to provide adequate numbers of men and equipment to deal with such an attack is in serious doubt. As one officer pointed out, "this was one war we could have lost."[43] None of the army mobilization stations tested during the exercise could support the mobilization of reserve component units. "Nifty Nugget," therefore, made clear that the failures of "Mobex 76" two years earlier had remained uncorrected.

In 1980, the army undertook yet another analysis of its own combat capacity. This study was done in September 1980 during the annual evaluation of the army's "readiness posture." While readiness data are normally classified, the condition of the army's strength was leaked to the press. In a published report, the army acknowledged that six of its ten combat divisions stationed in the United States were not ready to fight.[44] The army admitted that these divisions were deficient in personnel, equipment, and training and were not combat-ready. Two of these noncombat-ready divisions, the 101st Air Assault Division and the 24th Infantry Division, Mechanized, were earmarked for use in the Rapid Deployment Force. Whatever shortcomings had been pointed up by "Nifty Nugget" in 1978 had not, by the army's own standards of measurement, been corrected by 1980.

In October 1980, former Secretary of Defense Melvin R. Laird, working as the American Enterprise Institute's director of Defense Policy Studies, produced a report entitled "The Problem of Military Readiness." The report suggests that American conventional forces have neither adequate numbers nor equipment to meet anticipated Soviet challenges in the 1980s.[45] The report measured American preparedness against four criteria: *force structure*, the number and types of major units; *modernization*, the rate at which equipment can be replaced in the inventory; *sustainability*, the ability to conduct long and sufficiently intense operations; and *readiness*, the ability of the force to perform its mission well. The report concluded that "our force structure is too small, our modernization programs are inadequate, and our active duty operations have severe readiness and sustainability problems."[46] With regard to the problem of sustainability, the American Enterprise Institute report noted that during a full-scale Soviet attack against Europe, "our Army ground forces could not sustain the battle for thirty days. Before that time—twenty-five days at the maximum—they would run critically short of tanks, armored personnel carriers, artillery shells, tank rounds, mortar rounds and bullets in addition to a lack of qualified personnel." The report also stated that only 62 percent of American fighting forces were "substantially or marginally" combat-ready.[47] Therefore, the Laird Study again verified that the problems which surfaced in the 1978 "Nifty Nugget" exercise were still very much in evidence as of October 1980.

In 1981, the army undertook yet another simulated wartime mobilization exercise similar to "Nifty Nugget," although smaller in scope. This time the scenario did not envision general mobilization to respond to sudden Soviet aggression. Rather, it envisioned a response to a gradual escalation of tensions. Thus, the exercise gave the army the opportunity to display its ability to deploy under the most ideal conditions. "Proud Spirit 81" again revealed, however, that the same problems uncovered by "Nifty Nugget" continued to plague the army. "Proud Spirit" revealed that a shortfall of approximately 1 million tons of ammunition and other military equipment that was supposed to be available in reserve stocks in Europe was not there.[48] The shortages were so massive that they went far beyond the army's ability to make them up. During the exercise, it was also noted that a shortage of 350,000 trained soldiers to fill units leaving the United States occurred, demonstrating that the army could not bring its frontline units in Germany up to authorized strength.[49] As the exercise went on, ammunition supplies improved only marginally over 1978 levels but remained far short of requirements. The only optimistic note was that, for the first time, there was an adequate amount of rifle ammunition. "Proud Spirit 81" showed that it now took *longer* to deploy tank units to Europe than it had during "Nifty Nugget" almost three years earlier. The shortage in rifles was so acute that the army considered ordering them from factories in South Korea.[50] Huge gaps in the reserve system showed up as they had in 1978, leaving the army some 350,000 men short of its required mobilized strength. In a word, what "Proud Spirit 81" did was to confirm the serious conditions uncovered in "Mobex 76," again in "Nifty Nugget" 78 and again in 1980. By 1983, most of those conditions were still with us and some had even gotten worse.

When the American soldier, already afflicted by a range of serious problems, is placed in the larger organizational context of the army, the evidence suggests that he cannot be expected to perform well in battle. From the perspective of overall organizational readiness and the ability to mobilize, that is, the military structure's ability to deploy the soldier, equip him for battle, sustain him in it, and evacuate him from it, the army's own exercises indicate that the soldier is severely hampered by the failures of the larger organization of which he is a part. In time of war, that structure is more likely to exacerbate the difficulties in training, skill acquisition, and cohesion which already afflict the soldier in his units. When fit into the larger organizational context, the American soldier will not likely acquit himself well on the battlefield against an enemy of even moderate military power and tenacity.

One of the more important indicators of how well the soldier would perform in battle lies in the troops' perceptions of themselves as to how they expect to perform in battle, as well as how they are perceived by their officers and NCOs. The men who serve in the units are, in a sense, in the best position to judge how well a unit can fight. In the Soviet Army, as we shall see, many of those judgments are favorable; unfortunately, the same cannot be said for the American Army.

The worldwide sample of military personnel reported in 1979 allows this indicator to be analyzed. It will be recalled that in many American units drug use and alcohol abuse are systemic. Certainly, these problems occur at much higher rates than we would expect to find in a combat-ready army. In a questionnaire utilizing these indicators, officers in combat arms units at all rank levels were asked what effect they thought substance abuse would have on their units' ability to perform their wartime mission. It turns out that 21.9 percent of the commanding officers felt that the ability of their units to perform their mission would be "seriously degraded" as a result of substance abuse by their soldiers. When the focus is switched to company grade officers, 34.1 percent felt their unit readiness for war would be "seriously degraded," while 27.6 percent of the field grade officers felt the same way.[51] Most damaging are the perceptions of officers serving in combat arms, combat-support, and combat-service units. Among officers in combat arms units, 32.4 percent said their unit's ability to perform its wartime mission would be "seriously degraded" as a result of troops taking drugs or abusing alcohol. With regard to officers in combat-support units, 32.5 percent felt their units would be "seriously degraded," and 32.2 percent of combat-service unit officers agreed.[52] If the number of officers who felt that the performance of their units would be "somewhat degraded" as a consequence of drug and alcohol abuse is added to those above, the number of officers who feel that drug and alcohol abuse is affecting the ability of their units to fight well approaches 60 percent.

Important, too, are the perceptions of NCOs. The army, understanding that a large number of NCOs are themselves unqualified, made every effort to select what it called "quality NCOs" to assess unit readiness. NCOs were asked, "how ready is your unit for combat?" Those who stated that their units could be ready for battle "in a week or less"—the best possible response provided—comprised 53 percent of the quality NCOs armywide. Forty-seven percent indicated that their units could not be ready by this standard. Perhaps more important is the fact that the 53 percent who said their units could be ready within a week represent a decline of 10 percentage points from the number who answered similarly when the question was asked in 1975. In 1975, 62.5 percent of the quality NCOs throughout the army felt their units could be ready for war within a week.[53] Thus, NCO perceptions of unit readiness have been steadily declining over the last four years.

The number of NCOs in combat arms units who perceive that their units are ready for combat has also declined. In 1979, 60.6 percent of combat arms NCOs thought their units could be ready for battle within a week, a decline of 9.3 percent since 1974.[54] In combat-support units, 57.7 percent of the NCOs in 1975 thought their units could be ready within a week; by 1979, that number had dropped to 48.2 percent.[55] In an objective sense, the number of NCOs who feel their units and men are prepared to go into battle within a week's time is much lower than we would normally expect to find in a combat-ready army. More importantly, the levels at which unit readiness is perceived as adequate have declined over the last five years. The average decline is well over 10 percent.

Of substantial importance is the way soldiers see themselves in terms of unit readiness and how well their units would perform in battle. When soldiers were asked, "how ready is your unit for combat," 60.4 percent agreed that their units could be ready to deploy within a week. This figure is down from the 66.9 percent who felt likewise in 1975.[56] Once again there is a perception armywide among enlisted men that the ability of their units and peers to perform their mission is declining. When the focus is shifted to soldiers in combat arms units, 67.8 percent felt their units could be ready to fight within a week, down from the 74.1 percent who felt similarly four years earlier. With regard to senior enlisted soldiers in the combat arms, 59.4 percent assessed their units as able to deploy within a week, down from the 70.1 percent who felt that way in 1975.[57] Even combat arms units thought that American units were not as well prepared to deploy as they were in 1975.

When soldiers were asked how well they thought they would do in battle, the responses were remarkably candid—and depressing. Soldiers were asked to agree with the statement "if my unit were to go into combat, it would do a good job."

Only 43.8 percent of the enlisted soldiers armywide thought this was the case, down from the 52 percent who thought so four years earlier.[58] The enlisted soldier's perception of his own ability to perform in battle is much lower than we would expect. Moreover, that perception has been declining. When junior enlisted men serving in the combat arms were asked the same question, 47.1 percent thought their units would do a good job in combat, down from the 50.1 percent who felt likewise four years before. Among senior enlisted men, 58.0 percent felt their units would perform well, but this too is down from the 68.3 percent who felt similarly four years earlier.[59] Thus, members of combat arms units—the units that must endure the burden of battle—believe that they will not perform particularly well. On average, less than half the troops expect their units to perform well if forced to fight.

The Soviet Soldier

The Soviet soldier spends far more time in actual training than his American counterpart. Theoretically, the Soviet soldier spends a full twenty-four hour day within the confines of the military post, and with the exception of a pass every month or two, he lives in that military environment every day. The Soviet soldier's training conditions are very much like those of traditional Western armies prior to World War II. Penned in his garrison, the Soviet soldier is subject to a heavy training schedule. He spends most of his time either in the field or preparing for it by maintaining his equipment. Table 8 presents a complete schedule of an average training day in the Soviet Army.[60] The number of hours allotted for daily training is the same in winter and summer, and intense instruction throughout the year leaves the soldier very little free time. At least six hours of each training day are devoted exclusively to scheduled instruction. Most of the remaining time is used for political classes, maintenance of clothing and equipment, and personal needs. The training schedule for Saturday is technically two to four hours shorter than the normal training day, but it usually runs just as long.[61] The shorter training day on Saturday ostensibly allows the soldier time for the cleaning and inspection of equipment. Soldiers are also required to participate in organized athletics and cultural activities, and even to donate their labor on the weekends, all of which reduces truly free time to a minimum. The training schedule reveals that some areas ostensibly used for free time are actually completely filled. For example, although allotted as free time, the care and maintenance of personal equipment are required military tasks. The same is true with regard to the time set aside for self-study. It appears as free time but must be spent studying military and political periodicals and certainly does not extend to the prerogative of reading magazines or not reading at all. Most of this time is spent in political study, ideological classes, or political indoctrination. Even the official "free time" for ninety minutes each day is normally taken up with official or quasi-official duties on most training days. The Lenin Room, the Soviet equivalent of the company game room, is avoided, for it is here that NCOs and officers often find troops to do spot details. There is little in the way

Table 8
Daily Schedule of the Soviet Soldier

Activity	Hour	Time Elapsed
Reveille	6:00- 6:05	5 minutes
Cleanup	6:10- 6:30	20 minutes
Personal hygiene	6:30- 6:50	20 minutes
Political information or inspection	6:50- 7:20	30 minutes
Breakfast	7:25- 7:55	30 minutes
Training	8:00-14:00	6 hours
Lunch	14:00-14:40	40 minutes
Afternoon rest	14:40-15:10	30 minutes
Care of personal equipment	15:10-15:30	20 minutes
Political education		
(Monday and Thursday)	15:30-18:30	3 hours
Equipment maintenance		
(Tuesday and Friday)		
Organized sports		
(Wednesday and Saturday)		
Self-study	18:30-19:40	70 minutes
Supper	19:40-20:10	30 minutes
Free time	20:10-21:40	90 minutes
Evening walk and rollcall	21:40-21:55	15 minutes
Taps	22:00	

of entertainment in Soviet military garrisons, and post exchange facilities are poorly stocked and extremely expensive.

In order to measure the quality of Soviet military training as perceived by the troops, soldiers were asked, "on a scale from one to ten in which one is the worst and ten is the best, how would you rate the military training you received?" The mean score for the entire sample at all ranks and positions was 5.2, which may be regarded as fairly high since it reflects training in all types of units at all rank levels.[62] The assessments of training quality varied somewhat by type of unit, but overall Soviet troops apparently believed the quality of their training to be generally good, with only a few seeing it as inadequate. When the scale was divided into a series of interval categories (Low: 1-3; Medium: 4-7; High: 8-10), 24.8 percent of the soldiers felt that their training fell in the lowest quality range, 47.8 percent in the medium range, and 23.1 in the high.[63] The data suggest that at least three-quarters of the troops regarded the quality of their training as at least adequate. If the 5.2 mean score is used as a balance point, then most soldiers regarded the quality of military training as generally good.

If the perceptions of unit training are stratified by rank, some interesting trends emerge. The officers tended to feel that military training was generally good with a mean score of 5.8, slightly above that for the sample as a whole. The score for the NCOs, 6.7, was considerably above the sample mean and the highest of all ranks. But common soldiers themselves, the men who must actually do the fighting, assessed the quality of their training as lowest of all with a score of 4.8.[64]

One area crucial in assessing Soviet military units is the viewpoint of unit commanders on the quality of troop training. Commanding officers and enlisted commanders are in the best positions to assess training quality accurately because they bear direct responsibility for preparing their men and units for battle. They must also take the initiative and develop the confidence of the soldiers in the training process in order to make their units effective. Accordingly, the views of these commanders must be given somewhat more weight. Among enlisted commanders, the mean score assessing the quality of training was 5.6, indicating that in their view the training was moderate to good in quality. Officers in command positions scored the quality of training at 6.8, considerably above the norm.[65] It will be recalled that American NCOs and officers generally did not score the quality of training in their units quite as high. The level at which unit commanders assessed the quality of training is high enough to warrant the conclusion that Soviet training is probably doing an adequate job in transmitting military skills, although the Soviets are not doing an excellent job. It is unlikely that Soviet soldiers are deficient in the techniques of military operations.

When the quality of training is examined by type of unit, the results are remarkably consistent. For those soldiers serving in infantry units, the average score assessing the quality of training was 5.2. Interestingly, infantrymen had the lowest scores of all combat units. Tankers, for example, rated unit training at 6.3, artillery units at 6.5, and strategic rocket units at 6.2.[66] The data suggest that there are few perceived deficiencies in the inculcation of military technique regardless of type of unit.

Since the quality of Soviet training is generally good, at least equal to or in most instances superior to that received by American troops, the question of combat-effectiveness still remains. The question can be addressed directly by asking Soviet soldiers just how they felt their units would perform under fire. If we recall what Soviet soldiers have revealed so far about their motivation, it may be that Soviet soldiers will not have a high opinion of their ability to fight or of their units' ability to perform well. On the other hand, it is possible that despite all the shortcomings of Soviet units as seen by the troops, the soldier makes very little connection between these shortcomings and performance in combat. The soldiery may regard battlefield performance as having to do with factors other than those they encounter in peacetime. In any case, it is important to ascertain just how well the Soviet soldier believes he will do under fire.

Soviet soldiers were asked, "in your opinion, how well do you think your unit will fight in actual combat?" In all 8.8 percent felt their units would fight "very well," while 36.6 percent thought "fairly well"; 33.6 percent said "moderately well." On the other side of the scale, 14.2 percent thought their units would fight "poorly" and 1.8 percent "very poorly."[67] If the data are combined, 45.1 percent felt their units would fight "very well" or "fairly well," while

33.6 percent said they would perform "moderately well." Only 16 percent felt that their units would perform either "poorly" or "very poorly." The perceptions of unit combat-effectiveness by Soviet soldiers themselves are at least acceptably high and much higher than those found in the American Army.

If the data are arranged by rank, the impression emerges that Soviet units would perform very well. Among common soldiers, 40.4 percent ranked the expected performance of their units in the two top categories, with 26.3 percent placing them in the lowest categories. Among NCOs, 57.7 percent ranked their units in the two top categories, with only 3.8 percent placing them in the lowest. Not a single NCO thought his unit would do "very poorly" in battle. Finally, among officers 55 percent felt their units would perform "very well" or "fairly well," with only 10 percent believing they would do "poorly" or "very poorly."[68] No officer thought his unit would perform very poorly. Even though troops do not generally have high regard for NCOs and officers, most continue to assess the ability of their units to perform in battle very highly. Soviet leaders have a generally higher regard for the ability of their units to endure in battle than do American officers and NCOs.

Unit commanders also believe that their units will perform well on the battlefield. Among enlisted commanders, 43.7 percent felt that their units would perform in the two top categories, with only 6.2 percent expecting them to do "poorly." Not a single unit commander at the enlisted level expected his men to perform "very poorly." Similar patterns emerged on the part of officers in command positions. Fully 58.4 percent believed that their units would perform "very well" or "fairly well" under fire, while not a single commanding officer assessed his men as performing either "poorly" or "very poorly."[69] Soviet commanders, therefore, judge their men much more favorably in this regard than do American commanders.

In order to ascertain what types of Soviet units might perform best in battle, the data are stratified by type of unit. Among soldiers in infantry units, 39.3 percent would perform in the two top categories, compared to only 10.7 percent who placed them in the two lowest categories. A surprising 76.9 percent of soldiers in tank units thought their units would perform well, compared to 15.4 percent who thought they would perform poorly. Not a single soldier thought his tank unit would perform "very poorly." Among artillery units, 54.6 percent placed their units in the top two categories, and 45.5 percent said their units would perform "moderately well." No soldiers thought their units would perform in the two lowest categories. The same pattern emerges in the strategic rocket forces where 50 percent of the soldiers expected their units to do "very well" or "fairly well" under fire; 31.8 percent thought they would do "moderately well" and 18.2 percent, "poorly." Again, not a single strategic rocketman felt his unit would do "very poorly."[70] The data, therefore, support the conclusion that Soviet soldiers appear to have great confidence in their ability to perform in battle. Probably more importantly, only a small number—usually considerably less than 10 percent—felt their units would not do well. By comparison, the expected performance levels of the American soldier are far lower.

In general, then, Soviet soldiers and their leaders expect their units to perform well in battle. When this perception is measured directly by another scale, the same findings emerge. Soldiers were asked, "on a scale of one to ten in which one is the worst and ten is the best, how well do you think your unit would do in actual combat?" Most Soviet soldiers said their units would fight well. If the data are again arranged into three categories, 24.4 percent of the soldiers felt their units would perform "less than moderately well" under fire, 56.6 percent expected them to do at least "moderately well," and 18.6 percent indicated their units would perform "very well" or "extremely well." Taken together, 75.2 percent of the soldiers expected that they would perform at least acceptably well and, perhaps, even better. When the semantic differential scale is cross-corollated by rank, generally favorable feelings emerge among all ranks as to the ability of their units to perform in battle. For the common soldier, the mean score was 4.6; for the NCOs, 6.3; and for officers, 6.2. The same findings of positive performance are evident when the data are arranged by type of unit.[71] Most units rated their ability to fight as generally moderate to excellent.

The feeling of Soviet soldiers that their units would perform well was undoubtedly buttressed by the regime's propaganda and the tendency of Soviet training doctrine to rely heavily upon prearranged plans. Nonetheless, the evidence regarding perceptions of the quality of Soviet training and anticipated battlefield performance shows that soldiers at all rank levels see their units as adequately trained and prepared to undertake their combat missions. This is not surprising in view of the enormous amount of time spent in training exercises and the regime's almost total control over the soldier's military life. The Soviet emphasis on quality training and combat skills undoubtedly has had a positive effect, and there is no doubt that the soldier regards himself as being well skilled in the application of military technique. In this sense, very little has changed; the Soviet Army has always stressed the application of fixed technique and the provision of masses of equipment. If there is a weak point in the Soviet Army, it is in the development of the social and psychological bonds that contribute so strongly to cohesion.

Conclusions

With the limitations of the available data in mind, it still seems possible to draw some tentative conclusions about the Soviet and American soldier.

The Soviet level of skill acquisition may be considerably higher than that of the American soldier. Because the Soviet Army draws from all social strata for its recruits, it does not have the great number of unintelligent soldiers who seem to plague the American Army. Consequently, it does not have the continual problem of trying to teach mentally marginal recruits sophisticated battle skills. In addition, the level of military skill as measured by various indicators of performance also seems higher in the Soviet Army than in the American Army. The failure rates among Soviet soldiers are much lower. The problem becomes more acute for the American Army when it is recalled that the American soldier has far less time to train than the Soviet soldier. Even when the ability to learn skills within one's unit is compared, American soldiers apparently have far greater difficulty acquiring adequate levels of skill even after they have been assigned to their units for long periods.

The Soviet soldier benefits from extended daily training time. Both the quantity and quality of his training time are much greater than for the American soldier. Moreover, Soviet training is more difficult and realistic. For the American soldier, the training doctrine is based on the notion that good soldiers must endure conditions in peace that are even more difficult that those they encounter in war. The Soviets' extended training time and its arduousness are further supported by the general ambience of Soviet military life which restricts and disciplines soldiers in a very traditional way. This in turn sustains a range of other social institutions which imbue the soldier with a sense that the military is very different from civilian society. This ambience is highly supportive of training and skill acquisition.

With regard to the troops' notions about their ability to perform in battle, the Soviets tend to have greater confidence in themselves than the American troops. The number of Soviet soldiers who expected their units to perform badly in battle was considerably below that in the American Army. Most of their leaders, whether officers or NCOs, commanding officers or enlisted commanders, perceived that their units would perform well in combat. In contrast, the general perception of American officers and NCOs was that their units would not do well.

The Soviet training system is able to field the better soldier. To be sure, the Soviets have many advantages to begin with. Relying upon a systematic draft, they do not have to labor under many of the difficulties confronting the American all volunteer force. Their doctrines place great stress on continuous training as well as realism, even to the sacrifice of initiative, daring, and flexibility. As a result, the soldier receives a high level of basic military skills. The Soviets also maintain stable leadership elements within units and thus do not have to endure the continual disruptions forced by personnel turnover among officers and NCOs which is so characteristic of the American Army. Thus, from a range of perspectives, the Soviet Army has certain systemic advantages that contribute more to the development of adequately trained soldiers than do the structure and organization of the American Army.

Of course, the crucial element in battle is cohesion. As pointed out earlier, Soviet units reflect fairly low levels of unit cohesion and can be expected to do so in battle. However, levels of cohesion are probably as low in American units and will probably affect American units to the same extent or even more than they affect Soviet units. Perhaps both armies will field soldiers who are only marginally better than their predecessors or, when compared with other armies of the past, even less able to field good fighting men. The judgment must, of course, await the final test of battle.

Notes

1. A combination of the perceptions of troop ability by their leaders and demonstrated technical skill are two of the three elements used by the Israeli Army to evaluate the combat performance of their units, clearly with great success.

2. John Fialka, "Army Views Manpower Situation As Possible Crisis," *The Washington Star*, March 31, 1980, p. 2.

3. Ibid.

4. Ibid.

5. John Fialka, "Social Upheaval Changes Shape of Enlisted Ranks in the Army," *The Washington Star*, December 18, 1980, p. 10.

6. For an analysis of training in the Soviet Army, see Richard A. Gabriel, *The New Red Legions: An Attitudinal Portrait of the Soviet Army* (Westport, Conn.: Greenwood Press, 1980), Chapter 7.

7. "Beard Blasts All-Vol Army," *Army Times*, May 19, 1980, p-6.

8. Fialka, *Washington Star*, (Dec. 18, 1980), p-9.

9. Ibid.

10. Ibid., p. 10.

11. Fialka, "Army Views Manpower Situation As Possible Crisis," p. 4.

12. Ibid.

13. Ibid.

14. John Fialka, "A Question of Quality," *Army* (June 1980): 31.

15. Fialka, "Army Views Manpower Situation as Possible Crisis," p. 3.

16. Ibid.

17. Fialka, "A Question of Quality," p. 31.

18. So named after the staffer, Michael Pivoratto, who prepared the private report for Cong. Robin Beard. No formal printed copies available.

19. Ibid., p. 1.

20. Human Readiness Report No. 5 (Washington, D.C.: Office of the Deputy Chief of Staff for Personnel, August 1979), p. C-18.

21. Fialka, "A Question of Quality," p. 31.

22. Ibid.

23. "Beard Blast All-Vol Army," p. 6.

24. Fialka, "A Question of Quality," p. 31.

25. Fialka, "GI Proficiency at Low Level, New Study Says," *The Washington Star*, February 3, 1980, p. 3. Data cited from the Army Readiness Study.

26. Ibid.

27. Ibid.

28. Ibid.

29. Ibid.

30. Fialka, "A Question of Quality," p. 31.

31. Fialka, "U.S. Posts Dismal Record in NATO Competitions," *The Washington Star*, December 18, 1980, pp. 4-5.

32. Ibid.

33. Ibid.

34. Ibid.

35. Ibid.

36. See John Fialka, "U.S. Again Fails Test of Ability to Mobilize," *The Washington Star*, December 21, 1980, p. 4.

37. John Fialka, "The War Game: A Mobilization Snafu," *The Washington Star* November 2, 1979, p. 2.

38. Ibid. See by the same author, "Pentagon Logistics Bridge Fails, *Washington Star* November 3, 1979, p. 4.

39. Ibid.

40. Ibid.

41. Beard Staff Study, 1981, p. 4. See also Paul L. Smith, "Medical Units Unready for War," *Army Times*, June 30, 1980, p. 3.

42. Fialka, "The War Game," p. 8.

43. Ibid.

44. "Defense Affirms Readiness Lag," *Army Times*, September 29, 1980, p. 4. See also "6 of 10 Divisions in U.S. Aren't Ready, But That's Not Unusual, Pentagon Says," *Army Times*, October 10, 1980, p-5.

45. Report cited and abstracted in Tom Philpott, "U.S. Combat Capability Given Low Marks," *Army Times*, October 6, 1980, p. 2.

46. Ibid., p. 7.

47. Ibid.

48. John Fialka, "The Pentagon's Exercise "Proud Spirit"": Little Cause for Pride," *Parameters* 11, No. 1 (March 1981): 38.

49. Ibid.

50. Fialka, "The War Game," p. 9.

51. Human Readiness Report No. 5, p. F-34.

52. Ibid.

53. Ibid. p. D-21.

54. Ibid.

55. Ibid.

56. Ibid., p. D-18.

57. Ibid.

58. Ibid., p. D-19.

59. Ibid.

60. Gabriel, *The New Red Legions*, p. 61.

61. Ibid.

62. Ibid., p. 221.

63. Ibid.

64. Ibid., p. 222.

65. Ibid.

66. Ibid., p. 223.

67. Ibid., p. 216.

68. Ibid.

69. Ibid.

70. Ibid., p. 217.

71. Ibid., p. 219.

8

Conclusions: Graphic Comparisons

Because this is a comparative work, this concluding chapter attempts a straightforward comparison of those items of analysis that are most relevant to the ability of the Soviet and American soldier to stand in battle and fight well.

The conclusions of this work are presented in simplified graph form in order to facilitate the reader's understanding. The data in these charts seek to evaluate the "comparative degree of advantage" which each army and its soldiers have over its adversary, relative to a series of sixty characteristics deemed important to military effectiveness. Since both armies are likely to reflect some undesirable characteristics or to possess desired traits to an insufficient degree, a U-model plot is used instead of the usual straight line. Thus, qualities that are present in an army but not sufficiently so to measure at least zero, the midpoint on the scale, are measured as weaknesses instead of strengths. The U-model scale allows a comparison of important qualities by noting whether they are strengths or weaknesses and by measuring the comparative degree of advantage or disadvantage each quality may portray over another. Using different types of bar graph lines extending along the U-scale makes it possible to gain an impression of the degree of comparative advantage that one army may demonstrate over the other relative to a given characteristic.

It might be objected that such comparisons are not scientific; clearly, they are not. Yet they are based on reasonable judgments rooted as strongly as possible in the available empirical evidence. Military analysts and intelligence officers make these kinds of judgments all the time on precisely the kind of data presented here—and often with far fewer data. Even so, any assessment of any given characteristic is open to debate as a consequence of more extensive analysis. Overall, however, the portrait of the strengths and weaknesses of the Soviet and American soldier presented in this book and in the accompanying charts is accurate.

Figure 1

Comparative Degree Of Advantage

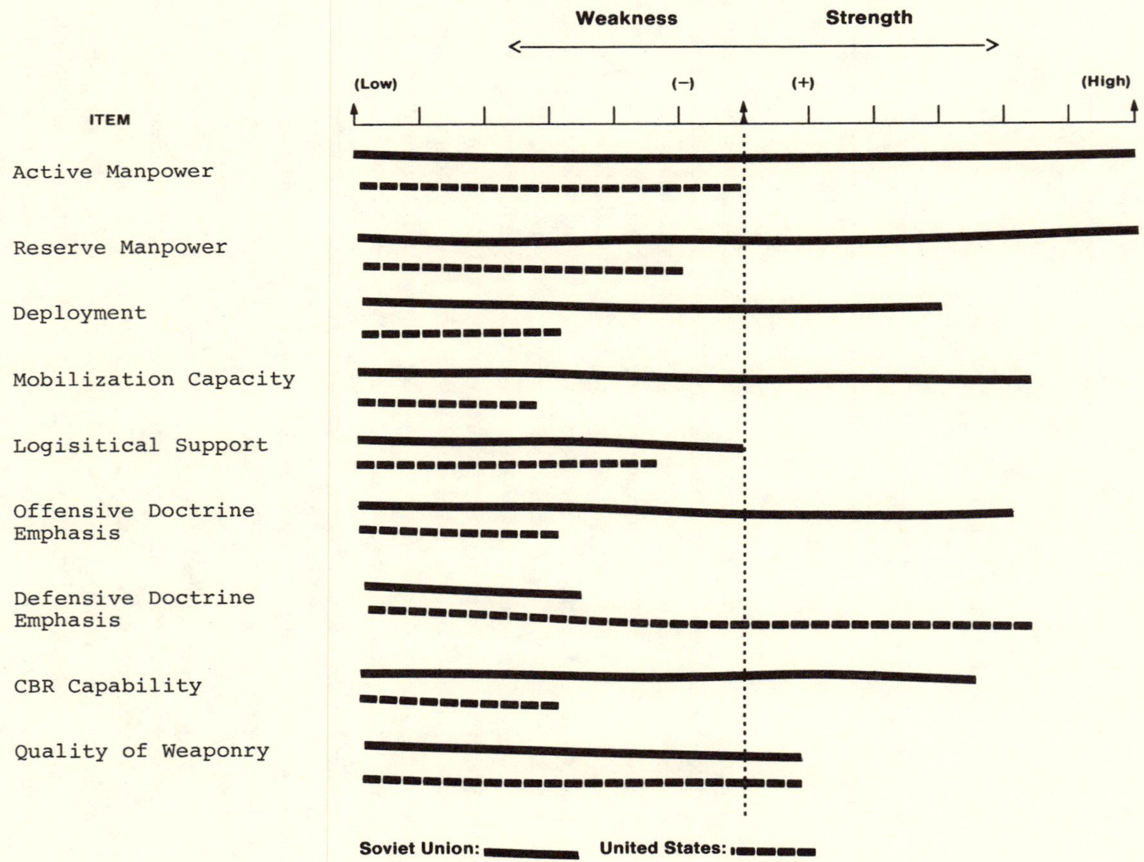

ITEM

Active Manpower

Reserve Manpower

Deployment

Mobilization Capacity

Logisitical Support

Offensive Doctrine Emphasis

Defensive Doctrine Emphasis

CBR Capability

Quality of Weaponry

Weakness — Strength

(Low) (−) (+) (High)

Soviet Union: ▬▬▬   United States: ▬ ▬ ▬

184

Figure 2
Comparative Degree Of Advantage

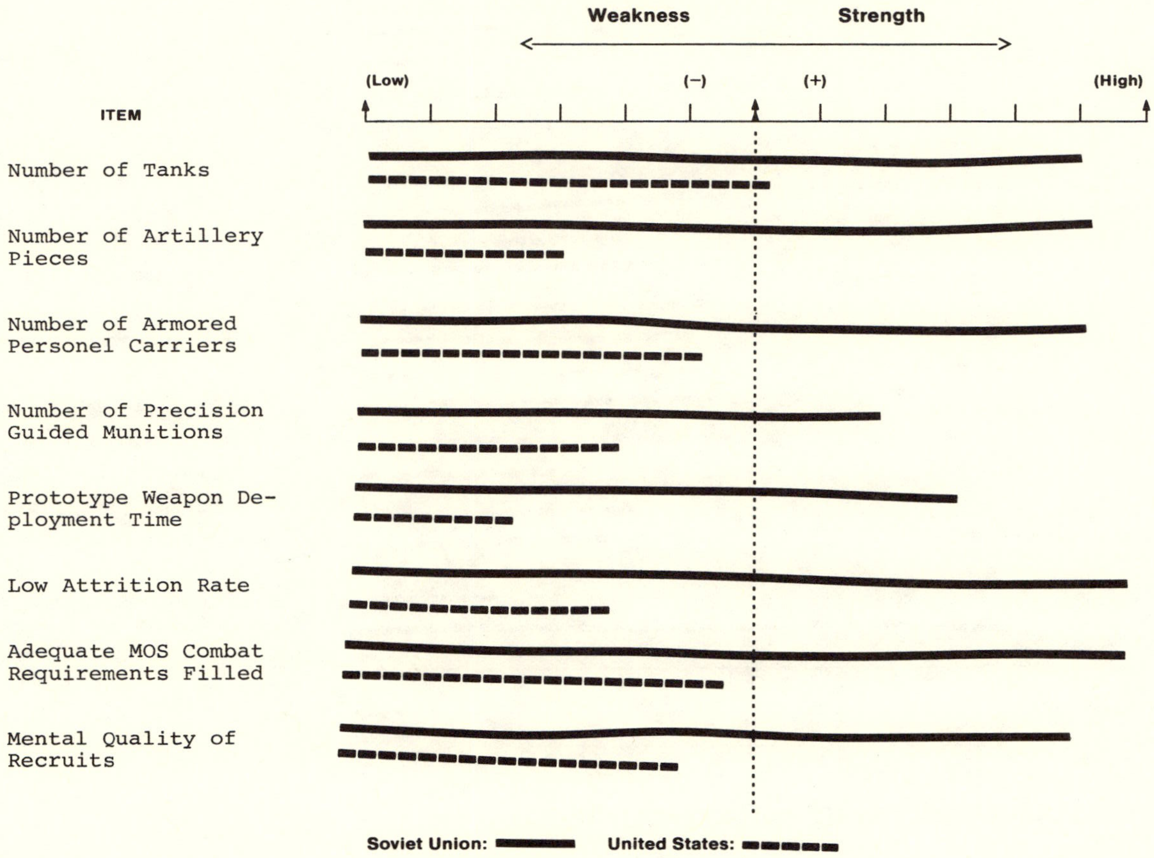

Weakness   Strength

(Low)   (−)   (+)   (High)

ITEM

Number of Tanks

Number of Artillery Pieces

Number of Armored Personel Carriers

Number of Precision Guided Munitions

Prototype Weapon De-ployment Time

Low Attrition Rate

Adequate MOS Combat Requirements Filled

Mental Quality of Recruits

Soviet Union: ▬▬▬   United States: ▬ ▬ ▬

185

Figure 3
Comparative Degree Of Advantage

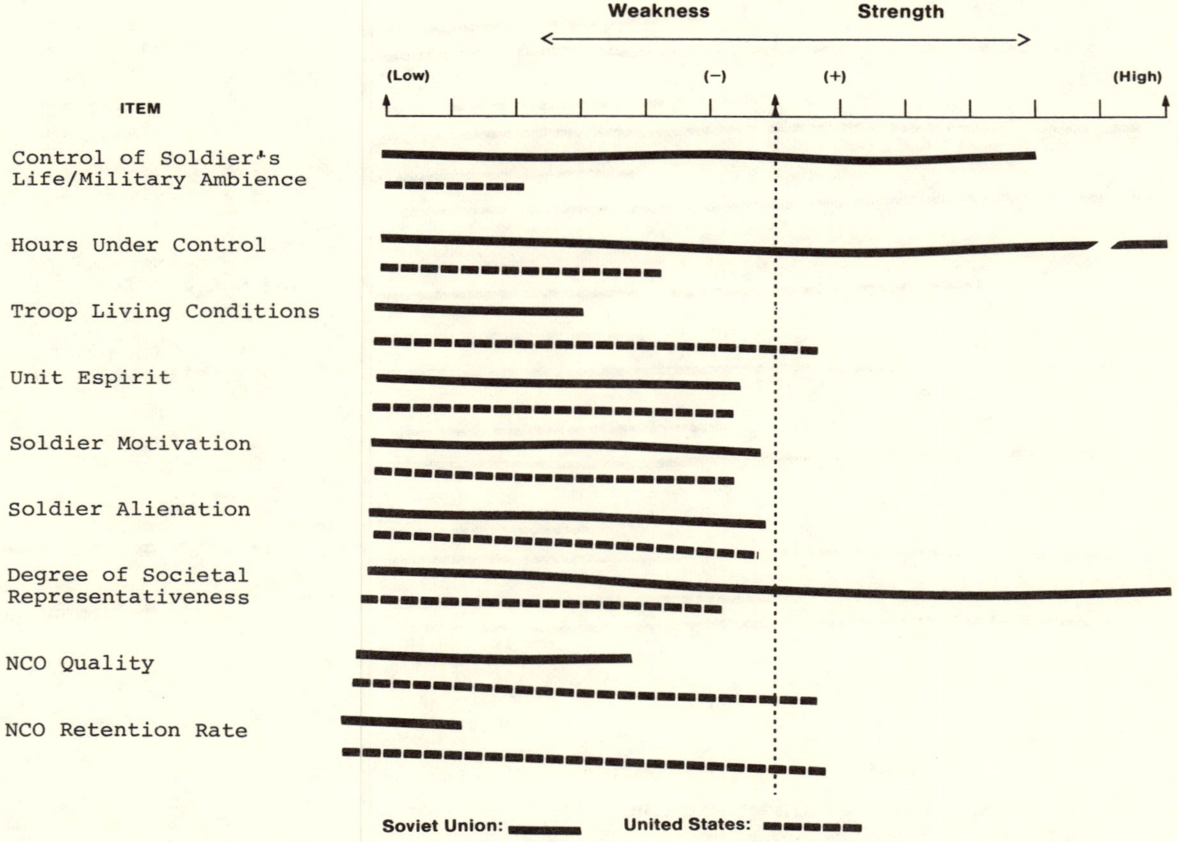

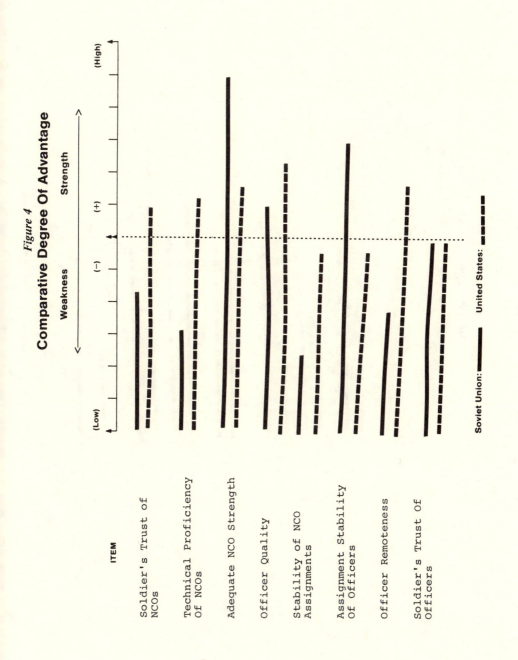

Figure 4

Comparative Degree Of Advantage

187

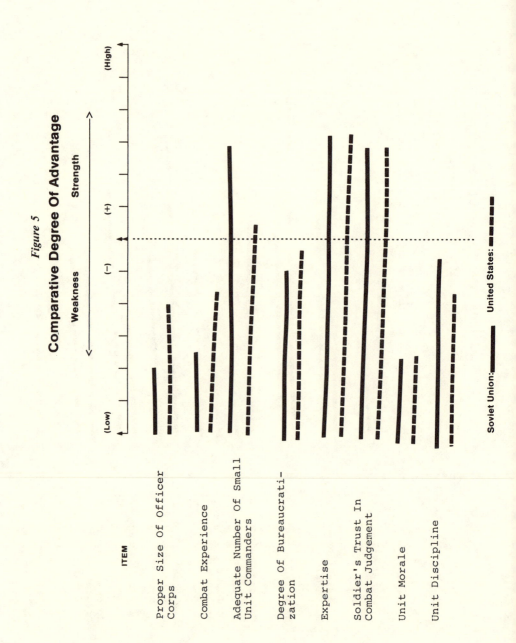

Figure 5

Comparative Degree Of Advantage

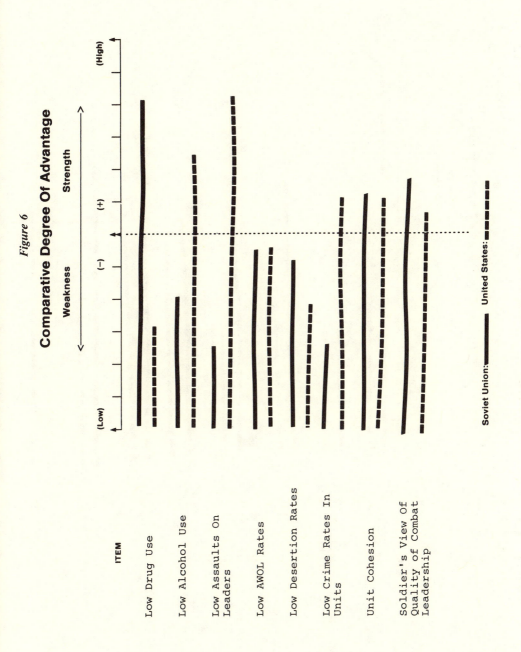

Figure 6

Comparative Degree Of Advantage

Figure 7
Comparative Degree Of Advantage

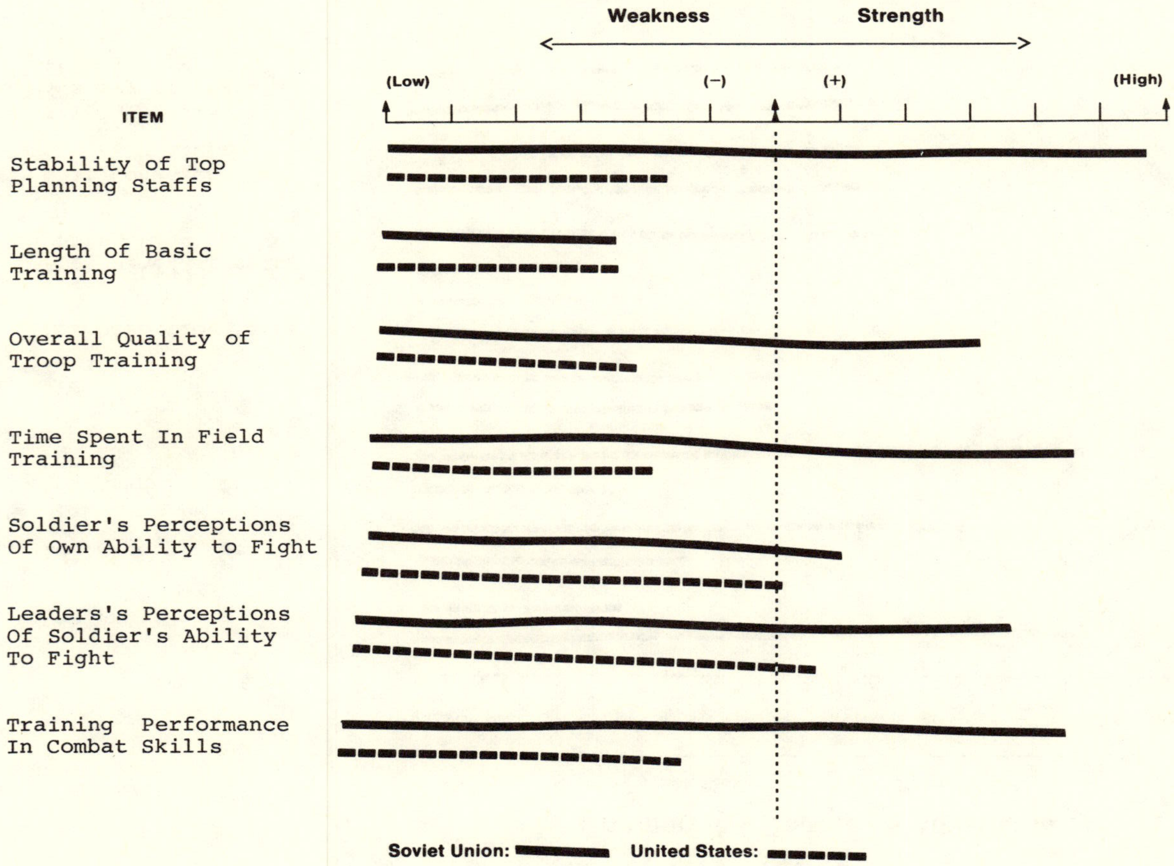

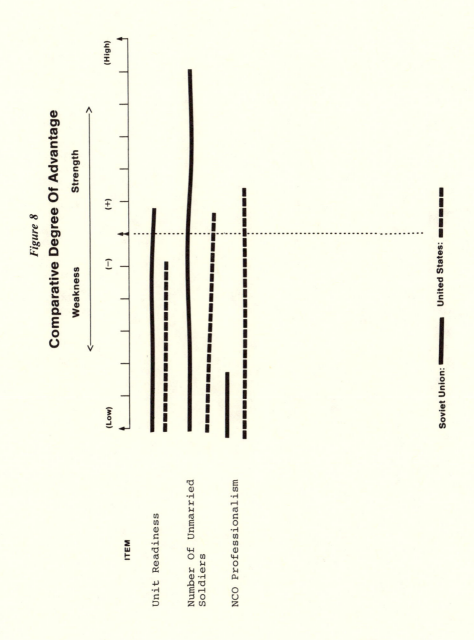

Figure 8

Comparative Degree Of Advantage

Bibliography

Soviet Army

Books

Armstrong, John A. *Ideology, Politics and Government in the Soviet Union*, Rev. ed. New York: Frederick Praeger, 1967.

Babenko, I. *Soviet Officers (Sovetskiye Komandiry)*, Moscow: Progress Publishers, 1976.

Baranov, V.I., ed. *Textbook on Educating Young Soldiers (Posobiye po pbucheniyu mododykh soldat)*. Moscow: Voyenizdat, 1972.

Borzenko, Sergey O. *Soldiers of the 1970s (Soldaty semidesyatykh godov)*. Moscow: Sovetskaya Rossiya, 1973.

Conner, Walter D. *Deviance in Soviet Society*. New York: Columbia University Press, 1972.

Danchenko, A.M., and Vydrin, I.F., eds. *Military Pedagogy: A Soviet View (Voyennaya pedagogika)*, Moscow: Voyenizdat, 1973.

Dictionary of Basic Military Terms: A Soviet View. Moscow: Voyenizdat, 1964.

Disciplinary Regulations of the U.S.S.R. Armed Forces (Distiplinarnyy ustav vooruzhennykh sil soyuza SSR). Moscow: Voyenizdat, 1971.

Dyachenko, Yevgeniy. *The Soviet Army*. Moscow: Novosti Press Agency Publishing House, 1974.

Erickson, John. *Soviet Military Performance: Some Manpower and Managerial Constraints*. New York: U.S. Army Institute for Advanced Russian Studies, 1970.

————. *Soviet Armed Forces: Capabilities and Changing Roles*. Edinburgh: Defense Studies, University of Edinburgh, 1971.

————. *Soviet Military Power*. London: Royal United Services Institute for Defense Studies, 1971.

————. *The Soviet Military, Soviet Policy, and Soviet Politics*. Washington, D.C.: U.S. Strategic Institute, 1973.

Fialatov, V.I., ed. *Profession—Political Worker. Collection of Articles (Professiya-polirabornik, Sbornik staty)*. Moscow: Voyenizdat, 1973.

General Military Regulations of the U.S.S.R. Armed Forces (Obshchevoinskiye ustavy vooruzhennykh sil SSSR). Moscow: Voyenizdat, 1972.

Gittleman, Zvi. *Assimilation, Acculturation, and National Consciousness Among Soviet Jews*. Mimeographed. Ann Arbor, Mich.: University of Michigan, December 1972.

Goldhammer, Herbert. *The Soviet Soldier: Soviet Military Management at the Troop Level*. New York: Crane, Russak, 1975.

Goure, Leon. *The Military Indoctrination of Soviet Youth*. New York: National Strategy Information Center, 1973.

Grechko, Andrey Antonovich. *Armed Forces of the Soviet States (Vooruzhennyye sily sovetskogo gosmlarstva)*. Moscow: Voyenizdat, 1974.

Gulidov, Afansiy I. *In the Combat Tradition (Na boyevykh tradisykh)*. Moscow: DOSAAF Press, 1974.

Katz, Zev, Rosemarie Rogers, and Fredric Harned. *Handbook of Major Soviet Nationalities*. New York: Free Press, 1975.

Keefe, Eugene K., et al. *Area Handbook for Soviet Union*. Washington, D.C.: U.S. Government Printing Office, 1971.

Khmel, A. Ye., *General Lieutenant*. *Education of a Soviet Soldier: Party-Political Work in the Soviet Armed Forces*. Moscow: Progress Publishers, 1972.

Kitov, Akhmed Ismaylovich, ed. *The Modern Army and Discipline (Sovremennaya armiya i distsiplina)*. Moscow: Voyenizdat, 1976.

Kochan, Lionel, ed. *The Jews of Soviet Russia 1917*. London: Oxford University Press, 1970.

Kolkowicz, Roman. *The Soviet Military and the Communist Party*. Princeton, N.J.: Princeton University Press, 1967.

Korey, William. *The Soviet Cage: Anti-Semitism in Russia*. New York: Viking Press, 1973.

Kovalev, Vladimir Nifolayvich. *Discipline Is a Factor of Victory (Distiplina-faktor pobedy)*. Moscow: Voyenizdat, 1974.

Lototskiy, V.K. *The Soviet Army*. Moscow: Progress Publishers, 1971.

Marxism-Leninism on War and the Army. Moscow: Progress Publishers, 1972.

Myagkov, Aleksei. *Inside the KGB: An Exposé by an Officer of the Third Directorate*. London: Foreign Affairs Publishing Co., 1977.

O'Ballance, Edgar. *The Red Army*. New York: Frederick Praeger, 1964.

Odom, William E. *The Soviet Volunteers*. Princeton, N.J.: Princeton University Press, 1973.

The Philosophical Heritage of V. I. Lenin and Problems of Contemporary War. Moscow: Military Publishing House, Voyenizdat, 1972.

Raygorodetsky, Yepim Yakovich. *Soldiers of the Seventies (Soldaty semidesyatykh)*. Moscow: DOSAAF Press, 1975.

Record, Jeffery. *Sizing Up the Soviet Army*. Washington, D.C.: The Brookings Institution, 1975.

Rendulic, Lothar. *Command and Control of the Troops (Upravleniye voyskami)*. Moscow: Government Printing House, 1972.

Savskin, V. Ye. *The Basic Principles of Operational Art and Tactics: A Soviet View*. Moscow: Ministry of Defense, 1972.

Seaton, Albert. *The Soviet Army*. Reading, Penn.: Osprey Publishing, Inc., 1972.

Shlyag, Y.V., Goltchkin, A.D., and Platonov, K.K. *Military Psychology: A Soviet View*. Moscow: Voyenizdat, 1973.

Shramchenko, A.F. *Psychology Problems in Command and Control of the Troops (Voprosy psikhologiiv upravleniiv voyskami).* Moscow: Voyenizdat, 1973.
Sidoreko, A.A. *The Offensive: A Soviet View.* Washington, D.C. Trans. Department of the Air Force, 1970.
Soviet Dynamics: Political, Economic Military. Pittsburgh: World Affairs Council, 1978.
Staritsyn, V.S., ed. *The Soviet Officer (A Collection of Articles. Introductory Article by Minister of Defense of the U.S.S.R. Marshal Andrey Grechko).* Moscow: Voyenizdat, 1970.
Structure of Discipline in the Soviet Army. Garmsch-Partenkirchken, West Germany: Army Institute for Advanced Russian Studies, 1975.
The U.S.S.R. In Figures for 1976. Moscow: Statisika Publishers, 1977.
Volkogonov, D.A. *Military Ethics (Voinskaya etika).* Moscow: Voyenizdat, 1976.
Yerzunov, M.M., ed. *Warrant Officers and Naval Warrant Officers. A Collection of Articles (Praporstichiki i michmani. Sbornik statey).* Moscow: Voyenizdat, 1973.

Articles

Altshuter, Mordekhai. "Mixed Marriages Amongst Soviet Jews." *Soviet Jewish Affairs*, December 1970.
Averin, A. "Improve Procedure." *Voyennyye Znaniya [Military Thought]*, February 1978.
Bedzhanyan, A., Major. "Indifference," Krasnaya Zvezda [Red Star], August 4, 1977.
Belonozhko, S. "Commander of a Regiment." *Krasnava Zvezda [Red Star]*, July 31, 1976.
Bogdanovski, V. "In the Interests of the Service?" *Krasnava Zvezda [Red Star]*, July 21, 1976.
Boleylev, S. "For the Further Raising of the Quality and Effectiveness of Party Political Work." *Vestnik PVO [PVO Herald]*, 1976.
Boroukov, A. "Promotion," *Krasnaya Zvezda [Red Star]*, April 8, 1977.
Borisov, K. "Whom Is It Necessary to Defend?" *Krasnaya Zvezda [Red Star]*, November 30, 1976.
Choron, Jacques. "Concerning Suicide in Soviet Russia." *Bulletin of Suicidology*, December 1968.
Colshko, I. "Profoundly Know and Exactly Fulfill the Requirements of the New Troop Regulations." *Tyli Snabzhenie Sovietskikh Vooryzhennykh Sil [Soviet Supply Defense]*, November 11, 1975.
Colton, T.J. "Civil-Military Relations in Soviet Politics." *Current History*, October 1974.
Druzhinin, M. "Responsibility of an Officer." *Voennii Vestnik [Military Herald]*, September 1977.
Glotov, V. and Oleinik, A. "Requirements of Discipline—A Law." *Voennii Vestnik [Military Herald]*, 3 (1977).
Golovnev, L. "An Outbreak of Anger." *Krasnaya Zvezda [Red Star]*. October 9, 1976.
Goncharov, V. "Position and Authority." *Krasnaya Zvezda [Red Star]*, August 28, 1976.
Gorny, A. "Socialist Legality and Soldierly Discipline." *Krasnaya Zvezda [Red Star]*, November 1, 1974.
———. "Observing the Requirements of Laws and Regulations. "*Krasnaya Zvezda [Red Star]*, October 24, 1976.

Grechko, [Andrey Antonovich]. "Report by Marshal of the U.S.S.R." *Krasnaya Zvezda [Red Star]*, March 28, 1973.

Gribkov. A., Colonel General. "Inculcating Demandingness." *Krasnaya Zvezda [Red Star]*, June 4, 1975.

Gudkov, V. "Transfer with Promotion." *Krasnaya Zvezda [Red Star]*, October 14, 1975.

Ishchenko, F., Lieutenant General. "Know How to Approach People." *Krasnaya Zvezda [Red Star]*, September 10, 1977.

Ivanov, N., Major General. "Socially Homogeneous Society." *Soviet Military Review*, October 1978.

Izgarshev, V., and Vikhreko, V. "On guard Over Peaceful Labor." *Krasnaya Zvezda [Red Star]*, March 17, 1977.

Jones, Christopher. "The Revolution in Military Affairs and Party Military Relations 1967-70." *Survey: A Journal of East-West Studies,* Winter 1974.

Kamalov, Yu. "Strictness and Concern." *Krasnaya Zvezda [Red Star]*, December 12, 1976.

Katz, Zev. "Sociology in the Soviet Union." *Problems of Communism*, May 1971.

Khobrostov, V. "V.I. Lenin, CPSU About Soldierly Discipline." *Military Historical Journal*, July 1977.

Klemchenko, L. "Until the Last Day of Service," *Krasnaya Zvezda [Red Star]*, November 30, 1976.

Kocherov, V. "Discipline-An Important Condition of Fulfilling Socialist Obligations." *Morskoi Sbornik [Navy Handbook]*, 7 (1977).

Kortun, V. "In Order That the Meeting Be Effective." *Krasnaya Zvezda [Red Star]*, March 26, 1977.

Kostikov, N. "Indoctrination of Cultural Behavior." *Krasnaya Zvezda [Red Star]*, December 11, 1976.

Krainin, L. "Strict Military Discipline—The Basis of High Combat Readiness of Troops, a Most Important Factor in the Achievement of Victory in Combat." *Kommunist Voorzhennykh Sil [Communist Defense Forces]*, 22 (1976).

Krivda, F. "With All the Fullness of Responsibility." *Krasnaya Zvezda [Red Star]*, October 29, 1976.

Kruzhin, Peter. "Soviet Military College." *Bulletin*, January 1971.

Kulakov, A. "After a Promotion." *Krasnaya Zvezda [Red Star]*, November 3, 1976.

Lashchenko, P. "Formation of a Military Collective." *Voennii Vestnik [Military Herald]*, 9 (1976).

L'vov, V. "Reprimand," *Krasnaya Zvezda [Red Star]*, October 17, 1976.

Lyapkalo, B. "How They Taught the Lieutenant a Lesson." *Krasnaya Zvezda [Red Star]*, January 29, 1977.

Milovidov, A. "The Growth of the Role of the Morale Factor in War." *Military Historical Journal*, 3 (1977).

Mironenko. "The Fight Against Alcoholism in the U.S.S.R." *Bulletin*, September 1967.

Nikiforov, F., Colonel. "Behind the Palisade of Exactingness. "*Krasnaya Zvezda [Red Star]*, June 11, 1976.

Odom, William E. "The Militarization of Soviet Society." *Problems of Communism*, September-October 1976.

Ovchararov, I. "Teach Them to Be Devoted, Determined, and Fearless." *Znamenosets [Standard-bearer]*, January 1978.

Pekarskii, B. "Help—Not Tutelage." *Krasnaya Zvezda [Red Star]*, November 24, 1976.

Pogrebtsov, O. "Is the Evaluation Objective?" *Krasnaya Zvezda [Red Star]*, July 1, 1976.

Prochenko. "Compulsory Treatment for Drunks, Addicts." *Sovetskaya Yustitsia [Soviet Justice]*, June 1974.

Provozin. V. "Culture and Discipline." *Krasnaya Zvezda [Red Star]*, November 1976.

Shakhuorostov, G. "And If Without Tutelage." *Krasnaya Zvezda [Red Star]*, October 19, 1976.

Shelyag, V., Rear Admiral. "The Educational Force of the Military Collective." *Kommunist Vooruzhennykh Sil [Communist Defense Forces]*, April 1975.

Shenkar, I. "Awash in a Sea of Vodka: Drunkenness in Russia." *Horizon*, Winter 1976.

Shevkun, N. "In the Center of Attention—Competition." *Krasnaya Zvezda [Red Star]*, January 29, 1977.

Shkadov, I. General. "Officer Efficiency Reports." *Krasnaya Zvezda [Red Star]*, January 7, 1978.

Shshnev, V., Major General. "The Rank of Officer Carries Obligations." *Kommunist Vooruzhennykh Sil [Communist Defense Forces]*, January 1978.

Skrylnik, A., Captain. "Ideological Indoctrination: An Overall Approach." *Krasnaya Zvezda [Red Star]*, August 3, 1977.

Smith, D. "On Maneuvers with the Red Army." *Nation*, May 20, 1978.

Studentov, V. "The Officer Grows in the Collective." *Krasnaya Zvezda [Red Star]*, October 13, 1976.

Sukhorukov, D., Colonel General. "Initiative, Self-Reliance." *Krasnaya Zvezda [Red Star]*, March 28, 1978.

Tabunov, N. "Soldiers and the Soldiers' Collective." *Kommunist Vooruzhennykh Sil [Communist Defense Forces]*, December 24, 1976.

Teplov, Yu. "The Bitter Taste of Criticism." *Krasnaya Zvezda [Red Star]*, September 21, 1977.

Tryshin, V. "Objectively and Honestly." *Krasnaya Zvezda [Red Star]*, August 11, 1976.

Vigor, P.H. "Soviet Armed Forces on Exercise." *Bulletin*, October 1971.

Volkogonox, D., Major General. "The Comprehensive Approach in Ideological Indoctrination of Soviet Fightingmen." *Voyenno-Istoricheskiy Zhurnal [Military Historical Journal]*, March 1978.

———. "Moral Conflict." *Sovietskii Voin [Soviet Forces]*, 12 (1976).

Volkov, A., Major General. "The Power of Example." *Krasnaya Zvezda [Red Star]*, October 25, 1977.

———. "Measure of Responsibility." *Krasnaya Zvezda [Red Star]*, April 15, 1976.

Yaroslavskii, M. "One for the Road for a Draftee." *Krasnaya Zvezda [Red Star]*, October 15, 1976.

Yerzunov, M. "An Important Factor in Enhancing Combat Readiness." *Krasnaya Zvezda [Red Star]*, July 16, 1976.

Zabavskaya, L. "The Whole World Studies Russian." *Soviet Military Review*, October 1978.

Zinoviev, B. "The Tact of a Commander." *Krusnaya Zvezda [Red Star]*, October 1976.

Magazines

"Be a Disciplined Soldier." *Kommunist Vooruzhennykh Sil [Communist Defense Forces]*, November 1975.

"The Company Political Worker," *Krasnaya Zvezda [Red Star]*, July 8, 1971, p. 1.

"Heighten Discipline and Organization." *Voennii Vestnik [Military Herald]*, June 1977.
"Insults," *Krasnaya Zvezda [Red Star]*, March 29, 1977.
"In the Interests of Discipline and Regulation Order." *Krasnaya Zvezda [Red Star]*, January 11, 1977.
"Know and Fulfill the Requirements of the Regulations." *Krasnaya Zvezda [Red Star]*, February 10, 1977.
"Know and Strictly Fulfill the Requirements of the Soldiers' Regulations." *Kommunist Vooruzhennykh Sil [Communist Defense Forces]*, vol. 21, 1975.
"Lack of Training Equipment." *Krasnaya Zvezda [Red Star]*, December 10, 1970, p. 2.
"Legal Indoctrination and Discipline." *Voennii Vestnik [Military Herald]*, June 1977.
"Life in the Soviet Army." *Time*, May 4, 1970, p. 46.
"Military Commissioning School—A Model of Regulation Order." *Krasnaya Zvezda [Red Star]*, October 19, 1976.
"Military Driver." *Krasnaya Zvezda [Red Star]*, September 6, 1977.
"On the Level of the Party's Requirements." *Krasnaya Zvezda [Red Star]*, July 1976.
"Organization of Military Instruction Cadres." *Krasnaya Zvezda [Red Star]*, April 28, 1971, p. 2.
"Persistent Evil." *Komolskaya Pravada [Communist Truth]*, November 30, 1967, pp. 6-7.
"75 Mutiny Cited in Soviet Journal." *Baltimore Sun*, February 5, 1977.
"Strengthening Legality and Discipline of Troops." *Krusnaya Zvezda [Red Star]*, July 9, 1971, p. 2.
"Strengthen the Authority of Sergeants and Petty Officers." *Krasnaya Zvezda [Red Star]*, May 15, 1976, p. 1.
"Teach What Is Necessary in Battle." *Krasnaya Zvezda [Red Star]*, January 24, 1978, p. 1.
Time, October 11, 1976, p. 31 (Soviet Ground Crew Drinking in Siberia to Relieve Boredom).
"Towards a New Rise in Ideological Work in the Forces." *Krasnaya Zvezda [Red Star]*, November 1, 1972.

Newspapers

"Battle Traditions Increase." *Izvestia*, January 11, 1967, p. 3.
Binder, David. "Soviet Defector Depicts Grim Life at MiG-25 Base." *The New York Times*, January 13, 1977.
"Everyday Life of a Paratrooper." *Pravda*, January 30, 1968, p. 6.
"Everyday Life of Soldiers." *Pravda*, February 20, 1967, p. 6.
Grechko. "Army of October." *Izvestia*, February 23, 1967, p. 6
"Holiday for Tank Troops." *Pravda*, September 11, 1967, p.2.
Izvestia, October 26, 1967, p. 1 (New Military Service System).
Izvestia, February 23, 1971, p. 4 (Profile of a Military Base in Siberia).
"Life in the Ground Forces (Rockets)." *Izvestia*, January 8, 1967, p. 5.
"Life of the Soviet Armed." *Izvestia*, February 22, 1967, p. 1.
"Man in a Fieldcoat," *Pravda*, February 23, 1967, p. 2.
"Our Army." *Pravda*, February 23, 1967, p.1.
"People's Armor (Volunteer Societies for Cooperation with the Armed Forces)." *Izvestia*, January 15, 1967, p.1.

Pravda, July 3, 1967, p. 3 (Soviet Military Academy Students).
Pravda, July 8, 1967, p. 6 (Soviet Army Training Camp).
"Report on Maneuvers." *Pravda*, September 25, 1967, p. 6.
"Report on Maneuvers." *Pravda*, September 26, 1967, p. 2.
Pravda, October 24, 1967, p. 2 (Ideology in Armed Forces).
Pravda, October 25, 1967, p. 1 (New Compulsory Military Service System).
Pravda, March 8, 1969, p. 6 (Military Training & Sports).
Pravda, February 22, 1971, p. 4 (Life of an Individual Soldier).
"Soldier's Leisure Time." *Izvestia*, February 24, 1971, p. 4.
"Soldier's Tea." *Pravda*, August 11, 1977.
The New York Times, October 17, 1967, p. 1 (Defection of Lt. Col. Runge).
The New York Times, October 22, 1967, p. 7 (New Compulsory Mili-service Law).
The New York Times, February 16, 1968, p. 21 (Literary Gazette Calls for Rationing of
     Liquor).
The New York Times, April 22, 1968, p. 1 (CIA & W. Ger. report on a Soviet defection).
The New York Times, October 24, 1968, p. 1 (Soviet Naval Officers Arrested).
The New York Times, January 25, 1970, p. 3 (Secret Central Committee concerning
     strange penalties for drunkenness).
The New York Times, March 29, 1973, p. 7 (Gun battle between Soviet M.P.s and
     deserters in East Germany).
The New York Times, December 3, 1973, p. 9 (Soviet military extends tour of duty).
The New York Times, September 7, 1976, p. 1 (Belenko defects).
The New York Times, September 10, 1976, p. 24 (Belenko defection).
The New York Times, January 7, 1977, p. 5 (Belenko story that Soviet pilots ordered to
     commit suicide rather than surrender or risk missing a target. Reported in West
     German Magazine *Stern*, January 6).

Miscellaneous

Kruzhin, Peter. "The Principal Features of the Latest All Service Military Regulations."
     Radio Liberty Research Reports, November 4, 1976.
Mentality of the Soviet Soldier. Ottawa: Director-General of Intelligence, 1974.
Paporshchick—A New Rank in the Soviet Army. Garmish-Partenkirchen, West Ger-
     many:Army Institute for Advanced Russian Studies, 1974.
Physical Training of the Soviet Soldier. DDB-2680-48-78, April 1978.
Review of Soviet Ground Forces. RSGF1-77, August 1977.
Segal, Boris M. "The Incidence of Suicides in the Soviet Union." *Radio Liberty Dispatch*,
     February 2, 1977.
Soviet Ground Forces Training Program. DDB-1100-200-78, July 1978.
Soviet Military Schools. DDB-2680-52-78, June 1978.

United States

Army Training Study. Washington, D.C.: U.S. Department of the Army, August 8, 1978.
Baker, John D., Lieutenant-Colonel. "Where the Soviets Are Vulnerable." *Army* (August
     1978): 23-27.
Barnard, Richard. "Problems with Army Gas Mask." *Defense Week*, July 28, 1980, p.
     2.
Baxter, William P., Lieutenant-Colonel. "The Big Guns: Is Red Army Still the 'King
     of Battle'." *Army* (September 1980): 29-31.

————. "RMD-1: A Formidable Fighting Machine." *Army* (March 1981): 41-43.

————. "A. 'Formidable' Antiaircraft Defense." *Army* (December 1980): 31-33.

————. "Logistics with a Difference." *Army* (November 1980): 30-32.

————. "River Crossing, Soviet Style." *Army* (July 1980): 39-41.

————. "The 'Scientific' Soviet Commander." *Army* (June 1980): 39-43.

————. "The Soviet Army Keeps 'Em Rolling." *Army* (January 1981): 31-34.

————. "Tenacity, Aggressiveness the Key." *Army* (February 1981): 37-39.

Beard, Robin. "GI Bodies and Brains." Office of Congressman Robin Beard, 1979.

"Beard Blasts All-Vol. Army; Cites High SQT Failure Rates." *Army Times*. Unsigned article, May 19, 1980.

Becton, Julius W., Lieutenant-General. "First Class Army . . . 4th Class Living Conditions." *Army* (November 1980): 22-26.

Boodman, Sandra G. "8-Year Term for Death of Lesbian Lover." *The Boston Globe*, reprinted from *The Washington Post*, February 4, 1981, p. 17.

The Boston Globe. "The Army Lacks Quantity and Quality." September 1, 1981, p. 1.

————. "The Army's Troubles with a Smart Tank." September 2, 1981, p. 6.

Carlisle Barracks. "Leadership for the 1970's." U.S. Army War College, 1971.

————. "Study on Military Professionalism." U.S. Army War College, 1970.

Carney, Larry. "Army Chief Cites Need for Added Support." No publisher or date.

Cincinnatus. *Self-Destruction: The Disintegration and Decay of the US Army During the Vietnam Era*, New York, W.W. Norton Co., 1981.

Collins, John M. *The US-Soviet Military Balance, 1960-1980*. New York: McGraw-Hill, 1980.

Congressional Letter to Robin Beard. Re: *The Army Training Study*, Summary by Mike Pivorotto, July 20, 1979.

Cook, John, Lieutenant-Colonel. "Commissioned Officer Retention Rates." *U.S. Army Statistical Report*, (title unknown), 1980.

Cooley, John K. "Poison Gas Weapons Stockpiling Urged on U.S." *The Christian Science Monitor*, April 25, 1980, p. 3.

Cooper, Richard V. "Military Manpower Procurement Policy in the 1980's." In Brent Scowcroft. *Military Service in the United States*. 60th American Assembly, Mount Kisco, N.Y., September 1981.

Corddry, Marion. "The Doctor Shortage." *Army* (May 1979): 18-24.

————. "War in Europe: The Enemy Is Troop Drug Use." *Army* (January 1979): 34-37.

DAPE-MPE Information Paper. "This Is Your Army, 1981." December 29, 1980, pp. 1-10.

"Defense Affirms Readiness Lag." *Army Times*, unsigned article, September 29, 1980.

Defense Manpower Data Center. "Attrition Rates." OASD (MRA and L) MPP. EPM. December 1, 1980, Mrs. Mackey, X72122.

————. "Percent Attrition Rates." OASD (MRA and L) MPP. EPM. July 1, 1980, Mrs. Mackey, X72122.

"DOD 'Cover Up' of Manpower Crisis Alleged." *Armed Forces Journal*, (April 1979): 8, 26.

Eifried, Gary, Lieutenant-Colonel. "Russian CW: Our Achilles Heel, Europe." *Army* (December 1979): 24-28.

Erickson, John. "The Soviet Union's Growing Arsenal of Chemical Warfare." *Strategic Review* (Fall 1979): 63-71.

———. *Soviet Warsaw Pact Force Levels*. Washington, D.C.: U.S. Strategic Institute, 1976.

Famiglietti, Gene. "Official View: Army Equipment 'Second Rate'." *Army Times*, March 12, 1979.

Fialka, John. "Army's Supply, Maintenance Ability Hurt by Lack of Funds General Says." *The Washington Star*, August 27, 1980.

———. "Army Views Manpower Situation As Possible Crisis." *The Washington Star*, March 31, 1980.

———. "Can the U.S. Army Fight?" *The Washington Star*, December 15, 1980.

———. "GI Proficiency at Low Level, New Study Says." *The Washington Star*, February 3, 1980.

———. "The Grim Lessons of Nifty Nugget." *Army* (April 1980): 14-18.

———. "Ill Equipped, Undermanned U.S. Army Is Decimated in 'Nifty Nugget' Exercise." First Article in a series, "The War Game." *The Washington Star*, November 2, 1979.

———. "The Officers Do More in the Volunteer Army." Last article in the series, "Can the U.S. Army Fight?" *The Washington Star*, December 19, 1980, p. 1.

———. "Pentagon Logistics Bridge Fails." From the series "The War Game." *The Washington Star*, November 3, 1979.

———. "The Pentagon's Exercise 'Proud Spirit': Little Cause for Pride." *Parameters: Journal of the U.S. Army War College*, No. 1 (March 1981): 38-41.

———. "A Question of Quality." *Army* (June 1980): 29-32.

———. "Re-Enlistments Higher Among Low IQ Recruits." *The Washington Star*, Section A, pp. 1 and 4, January 24, 1981.

———. "25% of Recruits in Low Intelligence Category." *The Washington Star*, March 11, 1980.

———. "U.S. Again Fails Test of Ability to Mobilize." *The Washington Star*, December 21, 1981.

———. "U.S. Posts Dismal Record in NATO Competitions" Second in a series, "Can the U.S. Army Fight?" *The Washington Star*, December 18, 1980, pp. 4-5. Also fourth article in the series "Social Upheaval Changes Shape of Enlisted Ranks in the Army."

Gabriel, Richard A. "About Face on the Draft." *America* (February 9, 1980): 95-97.

———. "Combat Cohesion in Soviet and American Military Units." *Parameters: Journal of the U.S. Army War College*, 8, No. 4, (December 1978): 16-27.

———. "Modernism vs. Premodernism: The Need to Rethink the Basis of Military Organizational Forms." In James Brown and Michael Collins, eds. *Military Ethics and Professionalism*. Washington, D.C.: National Defense University Press, 1981, pp. 55-74.

———. *The New Red Legions: An Attitudinal Portrait of the Soviet Soldier*. Westport, Conn., Greenwood Press, 1980.

———. *The New Red Legions: A Survey Data Sourcebook*, Westport, Conn.: Greenwood Press, 1980.

———. "The Quality of Troop Leadership in Soviet and American Armies." FII/OACSI, Washington, D.C., July 1980.

———. "The Soviet Officer: A Qualitative Assessment." (with footnotes). Article, data not printed.

————. Statement Before Senate Services Committee, delivered and written by Dr. Richard A. Gabriel, July 17, 1979.

————. "What the Army Learned from Business." *The New York Times*, April 15, 1979, p. 34.

————, and Savage, Paul L. *Crisis in Command: Mismanagement in the Army*. New York: Hill and Wang, 1978.

————, and Savage, Paul L. "The Environment of Military Leadership." *Military Review* (July 1980): 55-64.

Gart, Murray J. "Army Quantity and Quality." *The Washington Star*, June 27, 1980.

Goldrich, Robert L. "America and the Draft." Unpublished paper, Annandale, Va., May 6, 1980.

————. "Historical Continuity in the U.S. Military Reserve System." *Armed Forces and Society* 7 (Fall 1980): 88-112.

————. *Recruitment, Retention and Quality in the All Volunteer Force*. Washington, D.C.: Congressional Research Service Report, June 8, 1981.

Heymont, Irving, Colonel. "Can Reserve Units Be Ready on Time?" *Army* (March 1978): 23-26.

Hirst, Don. "Revised Criteria Cited in Readiness Reports." *Army Times*, November 1980.

HQDA Quarterly Sample Surveys of Military Personnel. "Enlisted Perceptions of Esprit in Their Present Unit by Term of Service and Geographic Area." Washington, D.C., August 1974-February 1979.

————. "Enlisted Perceptions of Unit Readiness: (D-18, 19, 21). Washington, D.C., 1979.

————. "Field Grade Perceptions of General Officer Focus." Washington, D.C., 1979. (C-14 and C-15).

————. Officer Assessment Charts. February 1974-1979.

————. Officer Perception of Hard Drug Problems in Their Units." Washington, D.C., 1979. (F-26).

————. "Prevalence of Leadership as a Problem in Army Units (Officer Assessments) Feb. 1979." Washington, D.C., 1979. (C-3).

————. "Selected Findings from Officer Interpersonal Competition Instrument Administered World-wide, November 1978." Washington, D.C., 1979. (C-18).

Human Readiness Report No. 5. Washington, D.C.: U.S. Department of the Army. (DCSPER). August 1979.

Hunter, Richard, and Nelson, Gary. "Eight Years with the All-Volunteer Armed Forces: Assessments and Prospects." In Brent Scowcroft. *Military Service in the United States*. 60th American Assembly. Mount Kisco, New York, September 1981.

Ingraham, Larry H., Major. "Anatomy of an Elephant: The Shoeleather Epidemiology of Drug Use in the US Army." Paper delivered on March 21, 1980, Counterpush Training Workshop, Ramstein AFB, Germany.

————. *The Boys in the Barracks*. Washington, D.C.: Walter Reed Army Institute of Research, 1978.

————. "Drugs, Morale, and the Facts of Barracks Living in the American Army." Summary from *The Boys in the Barracks*, unpublished manuscript. U.S. Army Medical Research Unit, Heidelberg, Germany, 1978.

Jeffer, Edward K., Lieutenant-Colonel. "The Word Is Quality, Not Quantity." *Army* (February 1981): 14-20.

Kaufmann, William W. "U.S. Defense Needs in the 1980's." In Brent Scowcroft. *Military Service in the United States*. 60th American Assembly. Mount Kisco, New York, September 1981.

Keegan, John. *The Face of Battle*, New York, Viking Press, 1976.

Kellet, Anthony. *Combat Motivation*. Ottawa: Operational Research and Analysis Establishment, Department of National Defense, 1980.

Kinnard, Douglas. *The War Managers*. Hanover, N.H.: University Press of New England, 1977.

Lacy, James L. "The Case for Conscription." In Brent Scowcroft. *Military Service in the United States*. 60th American Assembly. Mount Kisco, New York, September 1981.

Leibst, Mitzi. *Comparative US/Soviet Manpower*. (Washington, D.C.: OACSI-Study, 1980).

Marshall, S.L.A. *Men Against Fire*. New York: William Morrow, 1947.

Moskos, Charles C. "Desertion Rates." Department of Defense Statistics, January 1981 (per thousand listed personnel and FY 1979 by race and sex).

———. "Percent Attrition of FY 1976 Entrants After Three Years of Service, by Race, Education and Mental Group." Department of Defense Statistics, January 1980 and 1981. (Army, Navy, Air Force, Marine Corps)

———. "Re-enlistment Rates." (First-term, career, first-term by race). Department of Defense Statistics, January 1981.

———. "Saving the All-Volunteer Force." *The Public Interest*, No. 61 (Fall 1980): 74-89.

———. "Social Considerations of the All-Volunteer Force." In Brent Scowcroft. *Military Service in the United States*. 60th American Assembly. Mount Kisco, New York, September 1981.

———. "Surviving the War in Vietnam." Reprinted from *Strangers at Home: Vietnam Veterans Since the War*. Charles K. Figley and Seymour Leventman, eds. New York: Praeger Publishers, 1980.

———. "Unauthorized Absence Rates FY 1979, by Race and Sex." Department of Defense Statistics, January 1981.

Panzeraufklärungsbattalion 1, Orgstob Boeselager. Albert, Oberatit u Btlkdt. May 1980.

Patton, George S., Major General. Letter. *Army* (May 1981): 7.

Philpott, Tom. "U.S. Combat Capability Given Low Marks." *Army Times*, October 6, 1980.

Pirie, Robert, Jr. "Why Military Aptitude Tests Really Do Matter." *Armed Forces Journal* (July 1981): 70.

Reuven, Gal. "The Characteristics of Heroism." Paper presented at the Canadian Leadership Symposium, Royal Roads Military College, June 5, 1981.

Rolbant, Samuel. *The Israeli Soldier*. London: Thomas Yoseloff, 1970.

Rosenblum Report, 1978-1979. (Ft. Munroe, Va.: TRADOC Study, USA Army, 1980)

Savage, Paul L. "Patterns of Excellence, Patterns of Decay: The US Army in 1981." Paper presented before Annual Conference of the Militia Association of New York, October 9-11, 1981, pp. 1-21.

Scott, Harriet Fast, and Scott, William F. *The Armed Forces of the USSR*, Boulder, Colo.: Westview Press, 1979.

Scowcroft, Brent, Lieutenant-General. *Military Service in the United States*. 60th American Assembly, Mount Kisco, New York, September 1981.

Shills, Edward, and Janowitz, Morris. "Cohesion and Disintegration in the German Wehrmacht in World War II." *Public Opinion Quarterly* 12 (1948).

"6 of 10 Divisions in the U.S. Aren't Ready But That's Not Unusual, Pentagon Says." Associated Press Release, September 10, 1980.

Smith, Paul L. "Medical Units Held Unready for War." *Army Times*, June 30, 1980.

————. "Military, Civilian Rates Parallel: Survey Shows Extent of Drug, Alcohol Use." Army Times, December 15, 1980, pp. 4 and 68.

Snyder, M. Danny, Sergeant. "Opening a Window on NCO Professionalism." *Army* (December 1978): 16-18.

Sorley, Lewis. "Turbulence at the Top: Our Peripatetic Generals." *Army* (March 1981): 14-24.

"The Soviet Threat: The Shadow Lengthens." *Army Reserve Magazine* 25, No. 2 (Spring 1980): 22-29.

Toomepeau, Juri. "Ready, Willing and Able—The Fatal Assumption." Ms. from *Army*, (Winter, 1981) p. 113.

————. *Soldier Capability and Army Combat Effectiveness*, Washington, D.C.: U.S. Army Recruiting Command, 1980.

U.S. Congress Comptroller General. "Critical Manpower Problems Restrict the Use of National Guard and Reserve Forces." U.S. General Accounting Officer, Washington, D.C., July 11, 1979.

U.S. Department of Defense. "Statistical Data on Force Composition: AFQT Percentile Scores and Percent of High School Graduates." For Official Use only. FY 1971-1980.

————. Office of the Assistant Secretary of Defense. A Report to the House Committee on Armed Services. *Aptitude Testing of Recruits*. July 1980.

U.S. General Accounting Office. Report by the Comptroller General of the United States. "Active Duty Manpower Problems Must Be Solved." Classified by the Assistant Secretary of Defense, November 26, 1979.

————. Report by the Comptroller General of the United States to the Congress of the U.S. "AWOL in the Military: A Serious and Costly Problem." FPCD-79-52, March 30, 1979.

————. Report by the Comptroller General of the United States. "Overview of the Manpower Effectiveness of the All-Volunteer Force." Unclassified sections used only, April 14, 1980.

U.S. GAO Report. "Attrition in the Military." February 20, 1980, pp. 10-12.

————. "Millions Spent to Apprehend Military Deserters as Unqualified for Retention." January 31, 1977 (FPCD-77-16).

————. "Selected Job Shortages." November 1979, p. 29.

Webb, Ernest L. "NCO Corps: Is It Really Back on Top?" *Army* (July 1978): 27-29.

Westbrook, Stephen D., Major. "The Alienated Soldier: Legacy of Our Society." *Army* (December 1979): 18-23.

White, John P. "The Analysis of Military Manpower Issues." In Brent Scowcroft. *Military Service in the United States*. 60th American Assembly. Mount Kisco, New York, September 1981.

Wilson, George C. "Outlook Grim in a War for Mideast Oil." *The Washington Post*, October 28, 1980.

Index

Absent without leave (AWOL), 115-16, 120-21, 122
Air defense, 26
Alcohol abuse: and performance, 113-14, 173; rates of, 113, 117-19. *See also* Drug abuse
Alexander, Clifford, 39
All volunteer force (AVF), 22, 84, 85-86; alienation in, 44, 46-48; evaluation of, 46; failure of, 6-7; impetus for, 36, 55-56 n.7; military life in, 42-48; and NCO quality, 63-64; recruit mental ability, 38-40, 179. *See also* American Army
American Army: during colonial period, 17-18; current combat experience of, 33; as defensive force, 28; doctrine of, 27-29; and group function, 137, 143-44; as local militia, 19; manpower totals, 23; recruit mental ability, 38-40, 179; national unification role of, 19; officer tenure in, 23; organization within, 23-24; rejection rate in, 57-58 n.58; and reserve forces, 30-33; size of, 21; and socialization, 20-21; social status of, 18-19; weaponry, 24-27. *See also* All volunteer force; Attrition; Citizenship; Cohesion; Commanders; Conscription; Discipline; Drug abuse; Performance; Soldiers; Training; Vietnam War
American Soldier, The (Stouffer), 141

Armed Forces Qualification Tests (AFQTs), 39
Armies: and civilian oppression, 17-18; human dimension of, 4; institutional supports for, 92; prehistoric, 3; study of, 3. *See also* American Army; European Army; Soviet Army; Western armies
Armored personnel carriers (APCs), 24-25
Assassination. *See* Criminal violence
Attrition, 40-42, 54; among NCOs, 63, 67-68, 77

Becton, Julius W., Jr. (Lieutenant-General), 45-46
Black population, 37, 38
Boeselager combat vehicle competition, 169
Boys in the Barracks, The (Ingraham), 44

Canadian Cup tank competition, 169
Central Europe, as battlefield, 28
Citizenship, and military obligation, 17, 20, 43, 51
Cohesion, 180; collapse of, 81; and drug abuse, 108-9, 148-49; factors for, 43, 44, 74, 103, 141-42, 153-57; failure factors, 145; ideological conviction model, 131-36, 139-40, 141, 142, 151-53; importance of, 4-6; and isolation, 148-49; needs model, 136-40, 143; research on, 140-42; and social order,

Stouffer, Samuel, 5; *The American Soldier*, 141
Suicide, 125-26

Technology, from armies, 3
Training: amount of, 164-65, 175-76, 180; assessments of, 176-77; discipline during, 165; quality measures of, 167-70; rate of, 165-66; and rotation system, 166

Unit climate. *See* Cohesion
United States Army. *See* American Army
United States Army National Guard, 31
United States Army Reserve, 31-32
United States Army Training Study (1980), 168-69

United States Army War College, studies by, 89-90, 92, 100

Vietnam War, 23; cohesion collapse during, 145-46, 149; draft during, 37; drug abuse during, 108; leadership failures during, 81-84, 92; NCO losses during, 62-63
Voluntary Society for Cooperation with the Army, Aviation and Navy (DOSAAF), 49-50, 55

War in the Trenches (Lloyd), 142
Weaponry, 24-27
Westbrook, Stephen (Major), 47, 48
Western armies, 14-15
Will to fight, 8, 9

About the Author

RICHARD A. GABRIEL is Professor of Politics at St. Anselm's College in Manchester, New Hampshire, and was recently appointed a Fellow of the Inter-University Study Group at Hebrew University in Israel. A former Army intelligence officer and a Reserve Major assigned to the Directorate of Foreign Intelligence in the Pentagon, Professor Gabriel is also a consultant to the Senate and House Armed Services Committee and the Israeli Defense Force. He is the author of twelve books, including *Crisis in Command*, *The New Red Legions* (Greenwood Press, 1980), *To Serve With Honor* (Greenwood Press, 1982), and *Fighting Armies* (Greenwood Press, 1983), as well as numerous articles.